Painting in Excess

Painting in Excess

KYIV'S ART REVIVAL, 1985–1993

Olena Martynyuk

with contributions from

Asia Bazdyrieva

Alisa Lozhkina

Oleksandr Soloviov

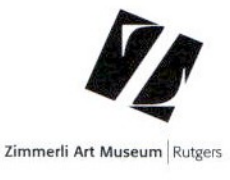

Zimmerli Art Museum | Rutgers

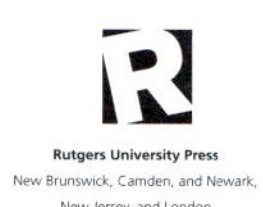

Rutgers University Press
New Brunswick, Camden, and Newark,
New Jersey, and London

This book accompanies the exhibition
Painting in Excess: Kyiv's Art Revival, 1985–1993
organized by the Zimmerli Art Museum
Rutgers, The State University of New Jersey

Jane Voorhees Zimmerli Art Museum
Rutgers, The State University of New Jersey
71 Hamilton Street
New Brunswick, NJ 08901-1248
www.zimmerlimuseum.rutgers.edu

The exhibition is organized by Olena Martynyuk, PhD, Rutgers University, Guest Research Curator, with assistance from Julia Tulovsky, PhD, Curator of Russian and Soviet Nonconformist Art at the Zimmerli Art Museum.

The project is supported by the Avenir Foundation Endowment Fund, with additional support from the Abramovych Foundation and the Dodge Charitable Trust–Nancy Ruyle Dodge, Trustee.

ABRAMOVYCHFOUNDATION

The publication received support from the Ukrainian Institute in Kyiv.

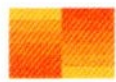

Published by the Zimmerli Art Museum and
Rutgers University Press
New Brunswick, Camden, and Newark,
New Jersey, and London

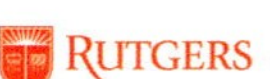

The Zimmerli's operations, exhibitions, and programs are funded in part by Rutgers, The State University of New Jersey, and income from the Avenir Foundation Endowment and the Andrew W. Mellon Foundation Endowment, among others. Additional support comes from the New Jersey State Council of the Arts and donors, members, and friends of the museum.

Library of Congress Control Number: 2021945388

ISBN: 978-1-9788-3075-2

General Editor: Olena Martynyuk
Publication Manager: Stacy Smith
Copy Editor: Carolyn Vaughan
Proofreader: Carrie Wicks
Designer: Diane Jaroch

Set in Frutiger and Bickham Script
Printed and bound in the
United States by Puritan Capital
Photographs of Kyiv on frontispiece, pp. 6–7, and p. 62 by Anna Voitenko. © Anna Voitenko.
All other photography, unless otherwise noted, by Peter Jacobs.

Front cover: Arsen Savadov, *Snake Charmer*, 1989–90, oil on canvas. Detail of cat. 30.

Contents

Foreword

Donna Gustafson, *Interim Director*

Painting in Excess: Kyiv's Art Revival, 1985–1993 joins a long list of exhibitions and publications initiated by scholars at Rutgers with the goal of increasing international awareness about the art of the former Soviet Union and the independent states that emerged after the dissolution of the Soviet federation. The Zimmerli Art Museum's Norton and Nancy Dodge Collection of Nonconformist Art from the Soviet Union is both deep and wide, affording opportunities for multiple explorations and a seemingly infinite number of new investigations. While a significant portion of the Dodge Collection is on permanent display in the galleries of the museum, there is also an enormous amount of material in storage that serves as a resource for young scholars who pass through the PhD program in art history at Rutgers as Dodge-supported Fellows. Olena Martynyuk, who completed her PhD under the supervision of Jane A. Sharp in 2018, is one of this new generation of art historians trained at Rutgers and conversant with the treasures of the Dodge Collection. With this exhibition, Olena continues her exploration of late twentieth-century Ukrainian visual culture through the lens of historical transitions. As the images and essays in this book recount, nationalism, globalism, modernism, and a sense of history's absence and presence played strategic roles in the transformation of art production by Ukrainian artists through the upheavals of glasnost and perestroika and the establishment of a modern Ukraine. Aptly described by Olena as a kaleidoscope of visual material, this multitude of styles, references, and imaginings provides evidence of a rich cultural moment ripe for examination.

The museum is grateful to the lenders to the exhibition, whose works have augmented those from the Zimmerli's Dodge Collection: Abramovych Foundation, Anatoly Kryvolap, Liudmyla and Andriy Pyshnyy, Natalia and Volodymyr Spielvogel, Stedley Art Foundation Collection, Oleg Tistol, Voronov Art Foundation, and a private collection.

Painting in Excess would not have been possible with the generosity of donors. The project is supported by the Avenir Foundation Endowment Fund, with additional support from the Abramovych Foundation and the Dodge Charitable Trust—Nancy Ruyle Dodge, Trustee. The publication was funded in part by the Ukrainian Institute in Kyiv, and a group of Ukrainian art collectors provided financial assistance for transportation of loaned artworks from Kyiv: Dmytro Averin, Stella Beniaminova, Roman Davydov, Artur Garmash, Andriy Isak, Kostiantyn Kozhemiaka, Dmytro Liakhovetskyi, Borys Lozhkin and Nadia Shalomova, Sergiy Makhno, Viacheslav Mishalov, Liudmyla and Andriy Pyshnyy, Maksym Shkil, Natalia and Volodymyr Spielvogel, Dmytro Topachevskyi, Ruslan Tymofieiev, Igor Vlasov, Igor Voronov, and Bogdan Yesipov.

Beyond acknowledging the scholarship of our guest curator, which is at the core of this project, I want also to thank the many individuals at the Zimmerli who contributed to the book and exhibition, most crucially Julia Tulovsky, curator of Russian and Soviet nonconformist art, and Jane A. Sharp, professor of art history and research curator for Soviet nonconformist art. I am grateful to the curatorial team as well as the entire Zimmerli staff for their work in bringing this exciting project to fruition.

Acknowledgments

Olena Martynyuk, *Guest Curator*

A large part of the work on the exhibition *Painting in Excess: Kyiv's Art Revival, 1985–1993* and its accompanying publication coincided with the challenging times of the global pandemic of COVID-19. Not unlike the transitional and trying period covered in the exhibition, this moment led to a reevaluation and a reminder of the things that are truly important, such as solidarity, creativity, scholarship, and invention. I am immensely grateful to everyone who shared with me this journey through uncharted territory and helped make this project happen.

First and foremost, I would like to thank my academic advisor, Jane A. Sharp, research curator for Soviet nonconformist art at the Zimmerli Art Museum and professor in the Department of Art History at Rutgers, with whom I discussed the exhibition from its earliest stages, when it existed only as an idea, to its late ones, when she helped me come up with its final title. Likewise, I am grateful to Julia Tulovsky, curator of Russian and Soviet nonconformist art, who gave me the opportunity to organize my second show of Ukrainian art at the Zimmerli and who provided invaluable advice and support along the way. Unquestionably, all my work on the Ukrainian art at the Zimmerli has been made possible by the late Norton Dodge and his wife, Nancy Ruyle Dodge, and their belief in the power of art. Their enthusiasm for the study and preservation of nonconformist art has changed many lives, including mine.

I am also immensely grateful to my Ukrainian colleagues for their belief in this project and its importance for the historicization and promotion of Ukrainian art. In particular, I would like to mention the generous and eager support of the Ukrainian Institute in Kyiv and to thank Volodymyr Sheiko, director general, and Tetyana Filevska, creative director, for their understanding of the importance of academic exhibitions and research, and Anastasiia Yevsieieva, visual art programme manager, for her organizational finesse. The Ukrainian Institute also partially funded this publication.

Heartfelt gratitude goes to my colleague and friend Igor Abramovych of the Abramovych Foundation for his support of the exhibition and his unwavering confidence in Ukrainian art and the need to promote it nationally and internationally. Not only did he engage in the interview included in this book, he provided financial support for the exhibition installation and, along with a group of Ukrainian art collectors, for transportation of the loaned artworks from Ukraine to the United States.

I would like to express my sincere appreciation to everyone who worked on the exhibition and publication. Stacy Smith, the Zimmerli's manager of publications and communications, led the project with professionalism and a considerate touch. Asia Bazdyrieva, Oleksandr Soloviov, and Alisa Lozhkina expanded the understanding of this period in Ukrainian art in their illuminating essays. The masterful copy editor Carolyn Vaughan helped make the text coherent and clear, and Carrie Wicks contributed thorough proofreading, while Bela Shayevich and Giuliano Vivaldi provided excellent translations. Diane Jaroch designed the book with sensitivity and insight. Charles Fick, art collection manager for Norton and Nancy Dodge, shared archival resources and facilitated research.

All the Zimmerli's staff have been extremely helpful. I would like to mention first the late Thomas Sokolowski (1950–2020), director, who oversaw the early stages of the show's preparation, and Donna Gustafson, interim director, who continued the support. Also invaluable were Waylen Glass, assistant registrar, Dodge Collection; Leslie Kriff, registrar; Kiki Michael, associate registrar; Rebecca Brenowitz, manager of event services; Keith Bull, exhibitions coordinator; Roberto Delgado, preparator; Amanda Potter, curator of education and interpretation; Whitney Prendergast, director of development; Ostap Kin, archivist, librarian, and research center coordinator; and Theresa Watson, communications coordinator. Irene Rybalsky, administrative assistant, gave generous help, often when it was urgently needed.

To all the Ukrainian artists who were building a new world on the ruins of the crumbling Soviet Union with passion, enthusiasm, and unrelenting love for invention and freedom in art, this exhibition is dedicated to you.

Introduction

Julia Tulovsky, *Curator of Russian and Soviet Nonconformist Art*

In our rapidly changing world, the exhibition *Painting in Excess: Kyiv's Art Revival, 1985–1993* is catching the momentum by responding to current discussions and concerns and by providing historical continuity with Ukraine's turbulent past while also shaping the future of its artistic endeavors. The core works in the exhibition are drawn from the Zimmerli Art Museum's renowned Norton and Nancy Dodge Collection of Nonconformist Art from the Soviet Union. Formed from the 1960s through the downfall of the Soviet Union, the Dodge Collection is devoted to the unofficial art of the Soviet state—art created despite official recommendations and ideological restrictions from the Communist Party. The largest of its kind in the world, the collection comprises more than twenty thousand works and represents art not only from Russian centers such as Moscow and Leningrad (now Saint Petersburg) but also from the majority of Soviet republics.

When amassing his encyclopedic collection, Norton Dodge aimed to present to the world the unique approaches and struggles for freedom of expression by artists throughout the Soviet Union. The Zimmerli Art Museum, following Norton Dodge's aspiration, makes it a point to show, through a series of exhibitions and public programs, the continuity in the development of the art that emerged in the states after the collapse of the Soviet Union. Contemporary art in Ukraine, Belarus, the Baltic states, and the Caucasian and Central Asian republics of the former Soviet Union testifies to distinct national identities that bring new perspectives to global discourse. The Zimmerli's exhibitions spotlight those national identifications within the very restrictive conditions of the Soviet Union and add new perspectives to current dialogues about diversity, equality, and cultural oppression.

Among all the Soviet republics, Ukraine's position is the most precarious in terms of identity and its preservation. Ukrainian culture, being the closest to Russia's, was not only oppressed but often absorbed by the imperial and then Soviet capitals. Russia historically relied both on Ukraine's rich land and on its cultural resources, embracing—and appropriating—many of its finest talents. This is why it is of utmost importance to showcase Ukraine's distinct artistic voice from the nonconformist era and beyond. *Painting in Excess* is the second exhibition at the Zimmerli dedicated to Ukrainian nonconformist art, following *Odessa's Second Avant-Garde: City and Myth* in 2014, also organized by Olena Martynyuk. The present exhibition outlines the painting traditions that rapidly arose in Kyiv at the dawn of perestroika and the downfall of the Soviet Union. Combining a plethora of influences from modernism to socialist realism, from the Ukrainian past to Soviet and newly formed post-Soviet myths, Kyiv's "painting in excess" emerged as one of the key identity features of new Ukrainian art.

We are delighted by the opportunity to collaborate on this exhibition with two prominent Ukrainian organizations, the Ukrainian Institute in Kyiv and the Abramovych Foundation, and we are grateful for their support. Informative contributions to this catalogue by Asia Bazdyrieva, Alisa Lozhkina, and Oleksandr Soloviov, leading Ukrainian scholars in the field, promote understanding and appreciation of contemporary Ukrainian art in the English-speaking world. Special thanks to Olena Martynyuk, the guest curator for the exhibition and an alumna of Zimmerli's Dodge Graduate Fellowship program, who conceived and realized the project. We hope that this exhibition will promote the development of new cultural ties and strengthen multicultural relationships despite the current uneasy political climate.

1 PAINTING UKRAINIAN PERESTROIKA A PARADE OF EXCESSES

Olena Martynyuk

The years following the inception of perestroika[1] policies and encompassing the collapse of the Soviet Union remarkably transformed Kyiv's art scene, successfully launching Ukrainian contemporary art as a truly global phenomenon. The calm waters of the culturally provincial capital of the Ukrainian Soviet Republic became radically stirred with new and daring art made publicly visible for the first time since the avant-garde period.[2] This explosion of styles, rediscovered histories, and newly found freedoms blossoming against the background of the collapsing Soviet empire, the Chernobyl nuclear disaster of 1986, and increasing economic scarcity created an effect of baroque excess. As if in a crooked mirror, the overabundance in art styles and the limitless production of new meanings reflected the emptiness of the hollowed-out Communist ideology and late socialist realist art. This exhibition and book trace and document the diverse artistic manifestations of these transitional and exhilarating years in Kyiv while providing some historical works of art for context.

Kyiv's artistic response to the emergent geopolitical shift was hybrid, eclectic, and heterogeneous, ranging from an organically grown version of local postmodernism to late modernist abstract painting. Both trends were compared to their Western analogues of the time. For instance, the distorted figuration of the neo-expressionist canvases by the groups Paris Commune and Resolute Edge of National Post-Eclecticism was dubbed "Ukrainian transavantgarde."[3] Such a simplistic definition was ignorant of the local implications of the artists' stylistic choices, particularly the enduring influence of the decaying socialist realist style. Similarly, the art of the Painterly Preserve group, while recalling color-field minimalism, was primarily grounded in the group's metaphysical exploration of the Ukrainian identity's relation to its landscape and a vehement rejection of socialist realist painterly storytelling.[4]

All these experiments, formally divergent yet united by the principle of innovation, gradually gained access to the public by occupying the old exhibition venues and awing unsuspecting viewers. The major art sensation of this time was the bizarre and provocative painting *Cleopatra's Sorrow* by Arsen Savadov and Georgii Senchenko (1987; fig. 1), shown at the Moscow All-Union Youth Exhibition in 1987. It was radically different from the majority of the work shown there and did not fit into either conformist or nonconformist canons. It provoked so much media interest that it impelled even the main and most conservative Soviet newspaper, *Pravda*, to react with a scathing critique that only contributed to the artwork's roaring success.[5] A handful of exhibitions subsequently transformed the Ukrainian art scene in Kyiv, among them *Kyiv-Tallinn* (1987), *The First Soviet-American Exhibition* (1988), *Crooked Caponnier* (1992), and *Kyiv-Mohyla Academy* (1993). Many of the early exhibitions were put together by artists; the first show was a project of Sergei Sviatchenko, famous for his collages, and the last two were organized by Anatoly Stepanenko, a pioneer of body art and performance art in Kyiv since the late 1970s.

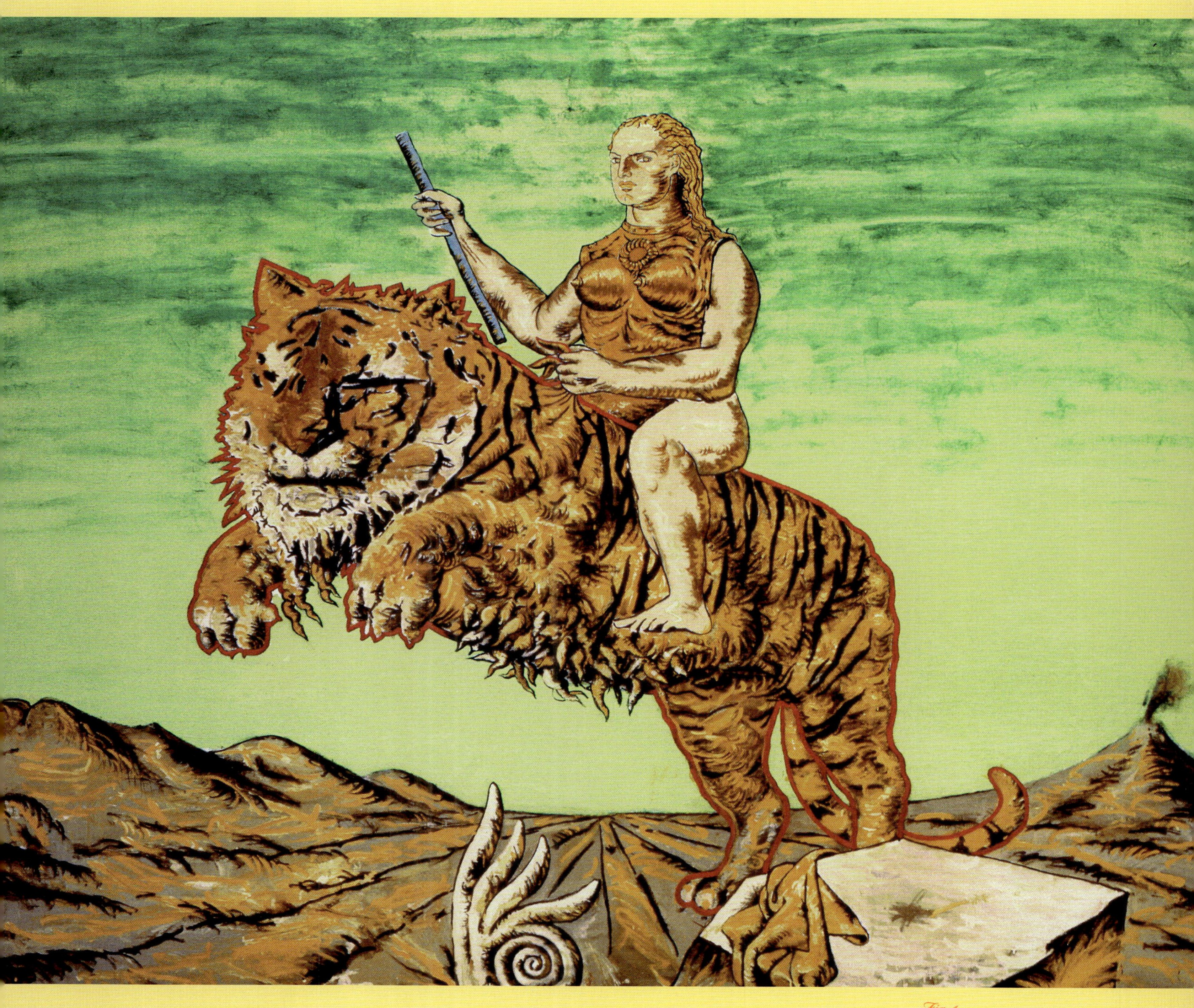

Fig. 1
ARSEN SAVADOV and GEORGII SENCHENKO
Cleopatra's Sorrow, 1987
Oil on canvas
108¼ × 129⅞ in. (275 × 330 cm)
Collection ARMAN Foundation

The kaleidoscopic multitude of new painting styles was certainly indebted to the perestroika policies of *glasnost* (openness) and *uskorenie* (acceleration), thus reflecting the need of Ukrainian late Soviet artists to catch up with history. The artists were suddenly flooded with information, about both Western art and theories (postmodernism being the most popular at the time) and their own previously forbidden and crossed-out pages of history. Another influence was the symbolic collapse of Soviet reality, when so many established notions suddenly became obsolete and hollow, prompting a major release of empty signs yearning to be filled with new meanings. Vitaly Chernetsky, the scholar of postmodern Ukrainian literature, posited that the late Soviet empire was a case of an "excess of ideological signification overwhelming and fragmenting the perceiving subjects."[6] Regarding painting, its excesses were plenty, in the size and quantity of canvases as well as in the expressivity of the painterly matter and the over-signification of the content. The surplus of meaning was generated in a postmodern manner, through citations and metaphoric appropriations. Gigantic, exuberant, and ornately decorated canvases of a new generation of artists both invoked the tradition of the Ukrainian baroque of the seventeenth and eighteenth centuries and resonated with their own tumultuous time.

Perestroika was delayed in Ukraine, since the notorious Volodymyr Shcherbytsky, first secretary of the Ukrainian Communist Party (in office from 1972 to 1989), provided the most conservative approach to governance during perestroika's defining years. The historian Serhii Plokhy described Shcherbytsky as "Brezhnev's protégé [who] crushed the national revival under way in Ukraine, turning it into an exemplary Soviet republic and a bulwark of Moscow's rule in the USSR."[7] Shcherbytsky had overseen the persecution of Ukrainian artists and dissidents in the 1960s and 1970s, with many artists and writers imprisoned and their works destroyed by the authorities.[8] His relentless vigilance contributed to the fact that before perestroika, Kyiv, as the republic's capital, did not harbor a full-fledged nonconformist movement in the vein of other Ukrainian cities such as Odessa, Lviv, or Kharkiv. Primarily, Kyivan artists enticed by styles diverging from those officially endorsed worked on them clandestinely, in their private studios, and did not seek publicity. Thus, the title "Kyivan hermits," given by the art historian Borys Lobanovsky[9] to a small group of abstract painters working in Kyiv during Shcherbytsky's rule, could be applied to many artists working in the years before Gorbachev. Set against their reclusive silence, perestroika painting was furiously loud.

This exhibition also pays tribute to the artists who, in the 1960s and 1970s, carved out creative alternative spaces at a time when Kyiv's Communist leaders aimed to solidify the city's reputation as a stronghold of Soviet official culture. These artists should not be considered direct predecessors but rather evidence of the interstitial nature of the artistic fabric of the Ukrainian capital and the lack of sound connection between generations. The limited access young Ukrainian artists in the 1980s had to Western trends and theories was far greater than their practically nonexistent knowledge of local avant-garde artists who had been physically eliminated in the 1930s[10] and their legacy hidden or destroyed.[11] In the absence of direct access to avant-garde art, the perestroika generation had only the specters summoned by their teachers, some of whom had been apprentices to the legendary first roster of professors at the Ukrainian State Academy of Arts (1917–22).[12] The avant-garde tradition, refracted through both the socialist realist style and Ukrainian folklore motifs, could be detected in most art practiced in Kyiv during the 1960s and 1970s.

Alla Horska—a steadfast member of the 1960s generation who saw her artworks destroyed by the authorities, experienced surveillance and interrogations, and was expelled from the Union of Artists—was killed in 1970 in a still-unsolved crime, allegedly by the KGB. Together with her co-members of the Kyiv Club of Creative Youth (existed 1960–64), including Opanas Zalyvakha, Horska discussed issues beyond the sphere of art, such as the politics of Russification, Stalinist purges, and the silencing of evidence of the Holocaust during the Nazi period in Kyiv.[13] Horska's *Untitled (Silence)* (1964; fig. 2, cat. 12) is a drama set in three primary colors, where blue and yellow—the colors of the Ukrainian national flag forbidden by Soviet authorities—dominate, while red accentuates the anguish of the silenced and expressively distorted naked female figure. A merging of the personification of Ukraine and a self-portrait of the persecuted artist is conveyed by the angular dynamism of the roughly outlined figure as well as by its expressive primitivism. Horska's husband, Victor Zaretsky, absorbed the Byzantine tradition by way of Fedir and Vasyl Krychevsky, founders of the Ukrainian Academy of Arts (later called the Kyiv Fine Art Institute),[14] who in turn had been influenced by the art of Gustav Klimt. Zaretsky's use of gold leaf, saturated colors, and an ornamental mosaic structure in his painting *Leda* (1980; cat. 65) appeared archaic and fantastical, symptomatic of Soviet reclusiveness, yet also resulted in a sincere and beautiful treatment of the ancient Greek myth. Although not a dissident artist like Horska, Hryhorii Havrylenko was nevertheless fired from his teaching position at the Kyiv Fine Art Institute in 1962 for his gravitation toward dangerous formalism. It was during this time that Havrylenko became preoccupied with abstraction, which he called nonobjective (*nepredmetne*) art.[15] In his series *Compositions* (1962–63; fig. 3, cat. 7; cat. 6), Havrylenko layered multiple semitransparent coatings of gouache or watercolor, building luminous architectonic structures with shifting dynamic surfaces.

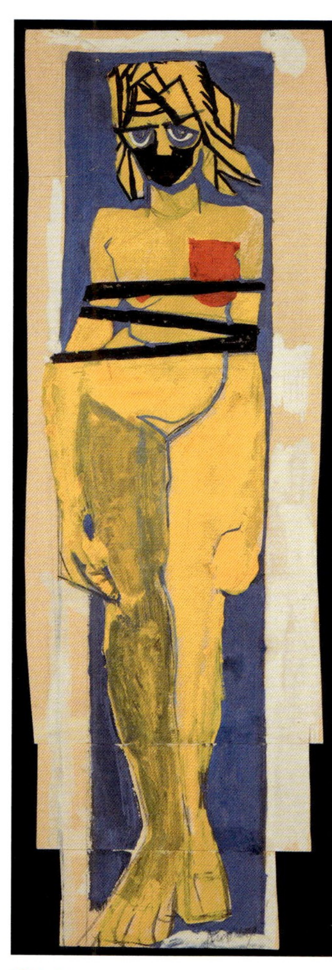

Fig. 2
ALLA HORSKA
Untitled (Silence), 1964
Gouache and graphite on paper
20⅜ × 6⅝ in. (51.8 × 16.9 cm)
Cat. 12

The heritage of Kazimir Malevich was also pertinent for the art of Florian Yuriev, the Siberian-born son of a persecuted geneticist, and Oleksandr Dubovyk, the son of a censored poet. Versatile in his creativity during his long career, Yuriev was a musician, violin maker, architect, poet, and artist striving to synthesize all arts into a *Gesamtkunstwerk* by translating poetry and music into a language of color.[16] Yuriev's works on paper *Siberian Snow* (1960; fig. 4, cat. 60) and *On Lena River* (1967; cat. 63) represent his childhood memories of a Siberian concentration camp relayed as poems and ciphers. Dubovyk combined the austere, flat geometry of Malevich with baroque ornamentation and thus could not exhibit his work from 1968 until 1989. His abstraction is logocentric and calculated, yet also symbolic, with such recurring motifs as a flower bouquet morphing into a shape suggesting a human head. In *Black Square* (1980; cat. 5), Dubovyk references the famous work by Malevich, but in place of the titular figure is the likeness of a black cube adorned with a lattice of brightly colored ornamental forms floating on top of dynamically placed squares of yellow, green, red, and blue.

Politically speaking, artists of the 1960s and 1970s illustrate a spectrum of relationships with the Communist regime, from dissident activity resulting in death and imprisonment as in the cases of Horska and Zalyvakha, to existence on the margins of

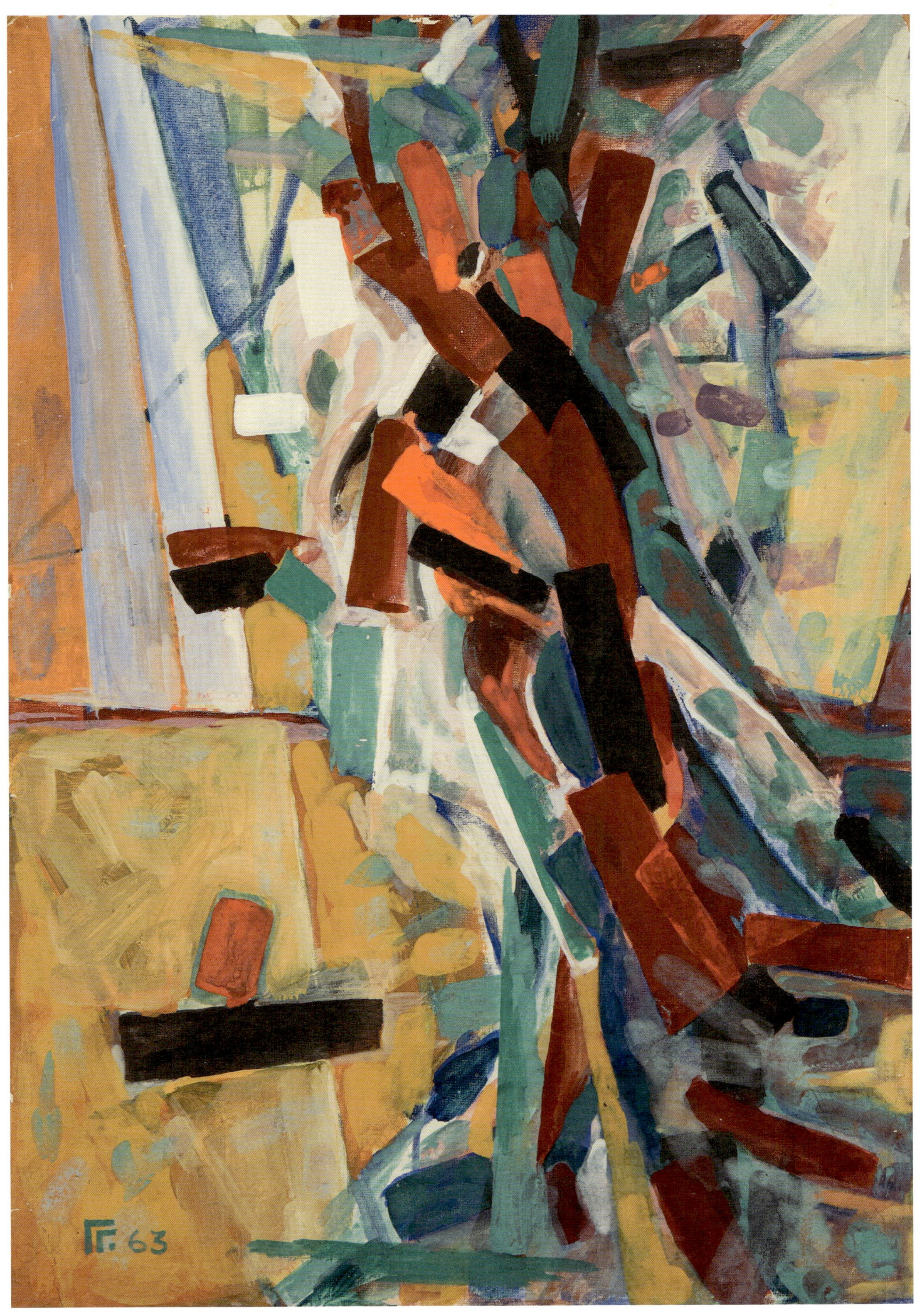

Fig. 3
HRYHORII HAVRYLENKO
Composition, 1963
Gouache on cardboard
14¾ × 10 in. (37.4 × 25.4 cm)
Cat. 7

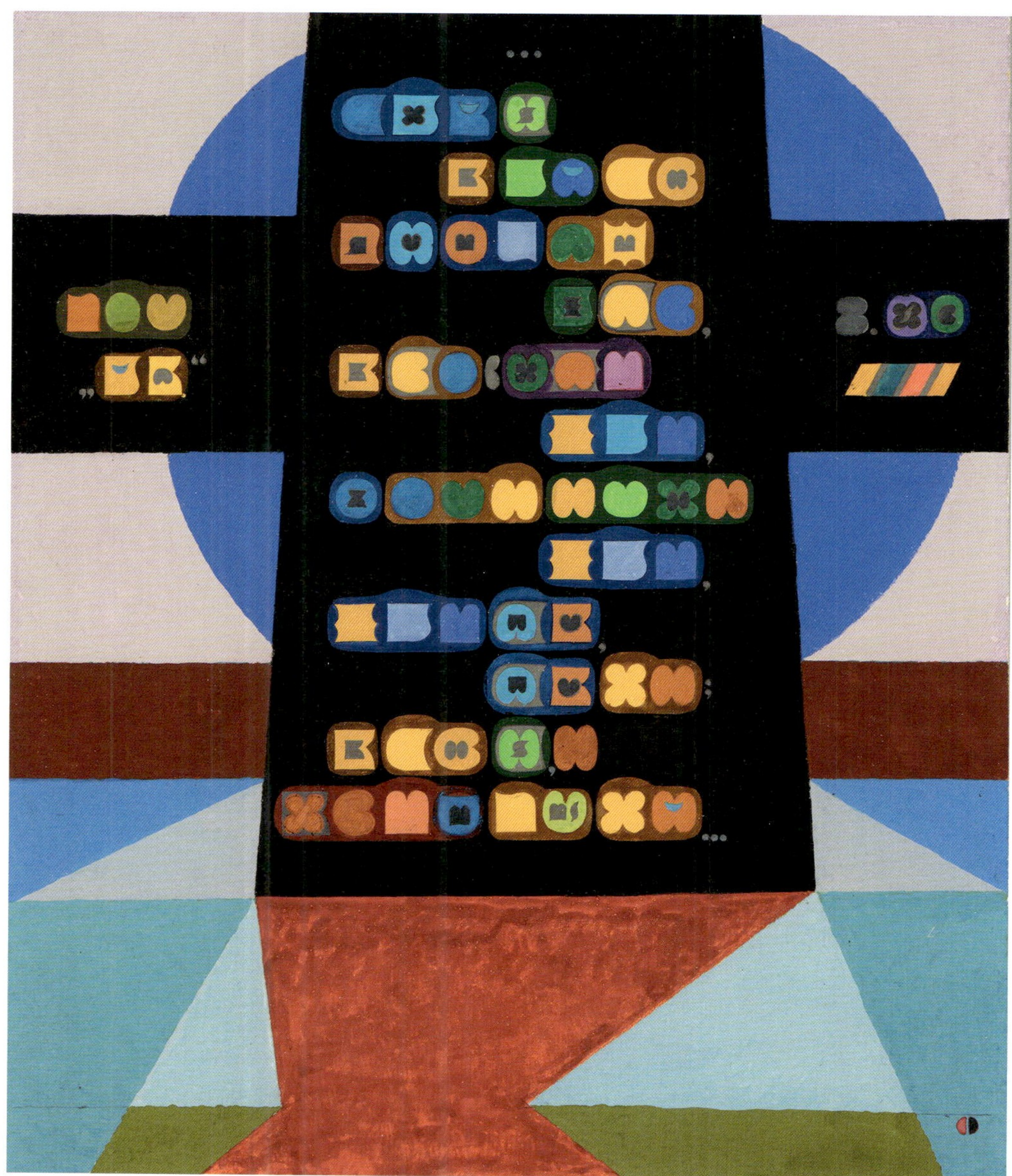

Fig. 1
FLORIAN YURIEV
Siberian Snow, 1960
Tempera on cardboard
19½ × 14¹¹⁄₁₆ in. (49.5 × 37.3 cm)
Cat. 60

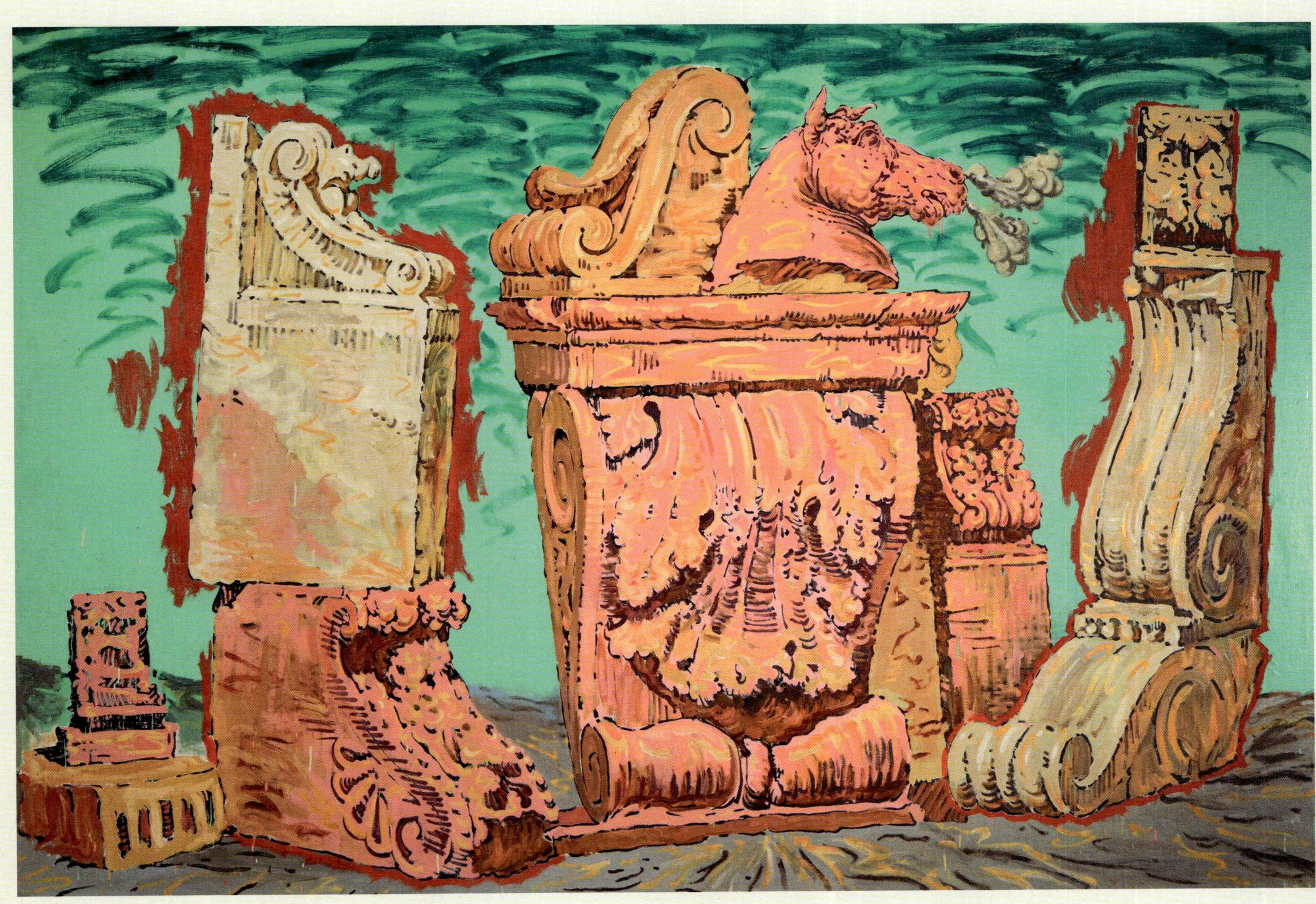

Fig. 5
ARSEN SAVADOV
***Untitled (Horse)*, 1987**
Oil on canvas
79¼ × 120 × ⅞ in. (201.3 × 304.8 × 2.2 cm)
Cat. 29

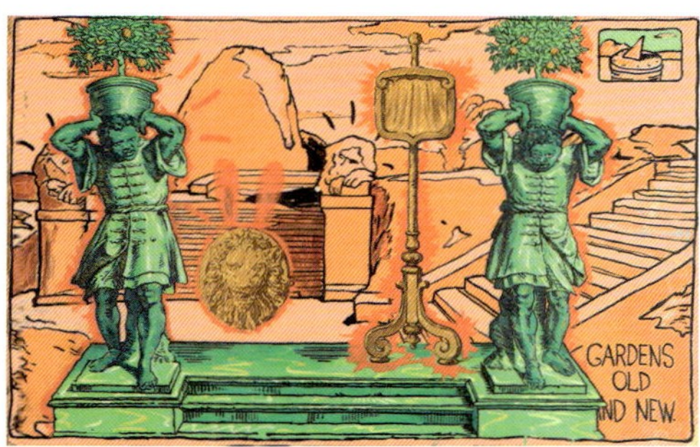

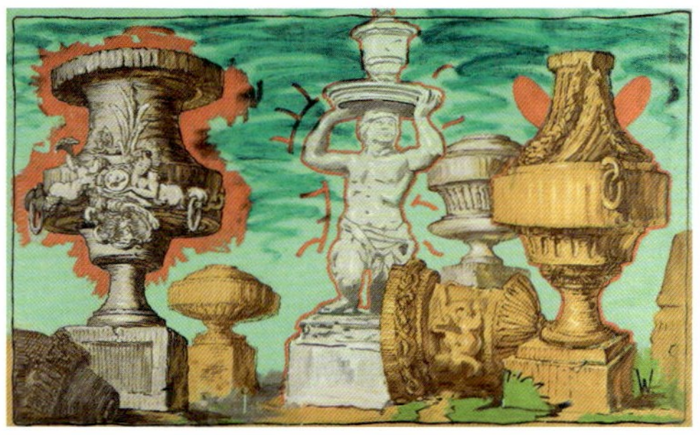

Figs. 6, 7
ARSEN SAVADOV and GEORGII SENCHENKO
Gardens Old and New, 1986–87
Oil on canvas
36 13/16 × 57½ in. (93.5 × 146 cm)
37 × 57½ in. (94 × 146 cm)
Cats. 25 and 26

the official art system as in the cases of Yuri Lutskevych and Viktor Ryzhykh, or practicing outside Soviet art institutions altogether as Valery Lamakh and Hryhorii Havrylenko did. Artists like Lutskevych, Ryzhykh, and Halyna Neledva can be grouped under the umbrella term of "permitted" (*razreshennoe*) art, suggested by the Moscow art critics Vladimir Levashov and Ekaterina Degot to describe artists suspended between their affiliation with official art institutions and their investment in unofficial aesthetics.[17] Confined to semipublic short-term shows and deprived of monumental state commissions or positions of power within institutions, these artists anticipated many features that became highly relevant for the generations of the 1980s. Intellectual, expressive, and prone to symbols, citations, and theatricality, their art was sometimes dreamlike and withdrawn. However, their interest in mythology and historical styles, including the Ukrainian baroque, greatly contributed to the boisterous freedom of perestroika art.

Still, the continuity between generations was not completely organic during this time. After *Cleopatra's Sorrow* by Savadov and Senchenko became synonymous with scandal, Savadov brought a reproduction of it to Zaretsky, only to discover that the teacher who had endorsed many of his earlier experiments did not approve of this one. Thus, perhaps for the first time, the rupture between generations of Ukrainian artists did not happen due to some violent historical event like war or purges but because of the rapid change of scenery and vertigo brought about by the geopolitical shift of perestroika.

Inconceivable yet inevitable,[18] the shattering collapse of the Soviet Union was perceived by many as the perfect "end of history" event.[19] The deserted landscape of *Cleopatra* is apocalyptically hedonistic, while the painting *Untitled (Horse)* (1987; fig. 5, cat. 29), made by Savadov shortly afterward, follows suit by featuring an assemblage of scattered and forlorn ruins. To diminish the eschatological mood, though, in both paintings the artists outlined many objects with a garish red contour, ironically reminding their viewers that they are only looking at a picture, an artifice. While both paintings seem to present the same cartoonish noir universe, *Untitled* is unpopulated. Yet, among the oversized decorative architectural fragments, there is a stone bust of a horse bizarrely animated and snorting fumes out of its angry nostrils. The canvas is also connected to two paintings from the series *Gardens Old and New* (1986–87; figs. 6, 7; cats. 25, 26), again made in tandem by Savadov and Senchenko. Bright in color but exuding the same derelict and phantasmagoric ambience, they reflect the moment of grandiose collapse of empire, its reverberations resonating even in the provinces.

While Russia was going through the trauma of empire loss,[20] Ukraine was painfully discovering its own provinciality and exclusion from the world's library of art. Thus, allusions to antique ruins and other spoils of Western culture abound in Ukrainian neo-expressionist painting, as seen in the monumental canvas *Sacred Landscape of Pieter Bruegel* (1988; fig. 10, p. 25; cat. 33) by Senchenko, an oil rendering of Bruegel's ink drawing *The Beekeepers and the Birdnester* of 1568 (fig. 11, p. 25), shown in the 1988 Moscow Youth exhibition. The reevaluation of history connects such art to the Western postmodern tradition; Ukrainian artists additionally questioned and analyzed the forbidden avant-garde along with officially sanctioned socialist realism. However, unlike Western postmodernists, they were not trying to undermine the canon, since they had not yet discovered it. After peeling off the layers of socialist realism, they saw the porous nature of Ukrainian art history, with gaping voids in the place of the crossed-out names, purged artists, and destroyed artworks. As a result, Ukrainian postmodernism was not as uncompromising toward older authorities as its Western counterpart was. With such definitions as *novye nezhnye* ("new tender") applied to it, the new art did not favor ironic distance as a device.[21] Oleksandr Roitburd and Mikhail Rashkovetsky, in their article "On the Intimate in Art" (1989; see p. 50), declared that the Ukrainian transavantgarde possessed a human face, alluding, tongue in cheek, to the famous slogan of the Prague Spring.[22] Senchenko, speaking about his now-famous *Sacred Landscape*, announced that its primary goals were neither citation nor deconstruction but rather the "permanently lasting moment of transgressive transition into *the other.*"[23] Discovering their own difference, Ukrainian artists were reinventing their lost canon in postmodernist terms.

Nowhere else was excess in painting more evident during perestroika than in Kyiv art squats, buildings emptied out for reconstruction and temporarily occupied by artists, first on Lenin Street (1989–90) and then on Paris Commune Street, the latter lending its name to the group of artists who worked there from 1990 until 1994. Kilometers of canvas were covered with oil painting in those squats, bristling with the creative energy of young artist-residents affected and challenged by the immense success of *Cleopatra's Sorrow* and the imminent collapse of the Soviet Union. Students of the Kyiv Fine Art Institute (now National Academy of Fine Arts and Architecture) such as Oleksander Hnylytskyj, Valeria Troubina, and Oleg Holosiy witnessed the absurd incongruity of the rigorous socialist realist method of their education to the world in flux around them. Still, as Alisa Lozhkina's essay in this catalogue demonstrates, their training was easier to disavow than completely dismiss. The outcome of their protest against the official method was a carnival of freedom erupting on large-scale canvases filled with expressive and ornate figuration. The accelerated pace of time was echoed in the speed with which the paintings appeared in squats; the special term *nonfinitism* was invented by the artists who refused to endow their creations with academic finish but could pronounce them ready at any moment.

Rapidly executed, emotional, and dynamic, the paintings produced by Paris Commune artists often assumed a shape of phantasmagorical pseudo-narration, presenting shallow carcasses of dreamlike stories with no beginning and no end. Situated in flat or decorative spaces, their characters appeared to be trapped in some mysterious unpronounced dramas or partaking in esoteric rituals. Holosiy's *The Angel Has Come* (1992; cat. 11) and Troubina's *Bowing* (1985; cat. 55) reverberate with religious resonance but contain no direct allusions to any particular religion. The same quality is present in the untitled canvas by the Odessa artist Oleksandr Roitburd (1985; cat. 23), who frequented the

Paris Commune squat. Suspended in some indefinite space and surrounding the totem on a pedestal are floating fragments of figures, one bearing a likeness to the artist and the other gesturing to viewers to keep their silence regarding the mystery they have had a chance to witness but not comprehend. Far from being ironic, their paintings were solemn and enigmatic, with such subjects as angelic visitation retaining on Holosiy's canvas the pathos of a sacred event while the paint exploded in expressive materiality. The appeal to the unconscious and the thrill of mystery and myth are qualities of the neobaroque pertinent to the Paris Commune artists as well as globally in the late 1980s. For Ukrainian artists, it was an opportunity to explore the heritage of the "Cossack baroque" of the seventeenth- and eighteenth-century Hetmanate era.[24] Hnylytskyj's *Yearning* (1988; fig. 13, p. 27; cat. 8) is a formally baroque Paris Commune canvas, with its pronounced corporeality and staged drama set in motion by the undulating texture of the canvas surface.

Even more immersed in the exploration of the national tradition was the group called the Resolute Edge of National Post-Eclecticism, founded by Oleg Tistol and Kostiantyn Reunov in 1987 and joined by Marina Skugareva (see fig. 8), Yana Bystrova, and Aleksandr Kharchenko. In 1991 Tistol and Mykola Matsenko developed a parallel artistic program under the name NATSPROM.[25] The group was connected to late Moscow conceptualism by their residence in the Furmanny Lane art squat in Moscow during the late 1980s. There they were called *nats-artists*—on the model of *sots-art*—because of their exploration of national stereotypes in their post-conceptual painting.[26] These artists indiscriminately combined modernist aesthetics with Soviet clichés, audaciously borrowing from the languages of the avant-garde, Soviet propaganda, and Western advertisement to invent national symbols for a country that had yet to attain statehood. For Tistol, the controversial Pereyaslav Treaty of 1654, which sealed Russia's protectorate of Ukraine, merited inclusion among those symbols, together with a pestilent pop-song visual, an allusion to an Old Master painting, or a Soviet cigarette pack design.[27] His prominent perestroika canvas *Reunification* (1988; fig. 9, p. 21) appropriates the Soviet historical cliché of brotherhood between the Ukrainian and Russian nations. Two embracing figures are shadowed by their nonidentical embracing doubles, all four engulfed by multilayered riotous painterly matter erasing the borders between figures and surroundings. Tistol assembles not only fragmented particles of Ukraine's distant past but also the ideological and pop culture debris quickly accumulating on the ruins of a not yet fully disintegrated Soviet Union.

This excess in the production of meaning through staggering chains of signification was complemented on the canvases of the Resolute Edge by a cornucopia of formal devices. Combining the bright lattice of gestural brushwork with stenciled patterns and letters as well as dripping paint, Reunov's painting *Only There* (1990; cat. 21) also features a virtuoso academic painting of a monumental female nude in a complex contortion. The woman is running toward the viewer while simultaneously pointing backward beyond the horizon line. The ambiguity of running away from the desired direction harks back to the urgency of the civilizational choice for Ukraine, eternally suspended between East and West yet forced to choose a direction during each transitional historical moment. The subject of the faceted multipanel oil-on-paper work *Piłsudski* by Tistol and Matsenko (1993; cat. 18) is the ill-fated 1920 Treaty of Warsaw, signed by the Polish Józef Piłsudski and the Ukrainian

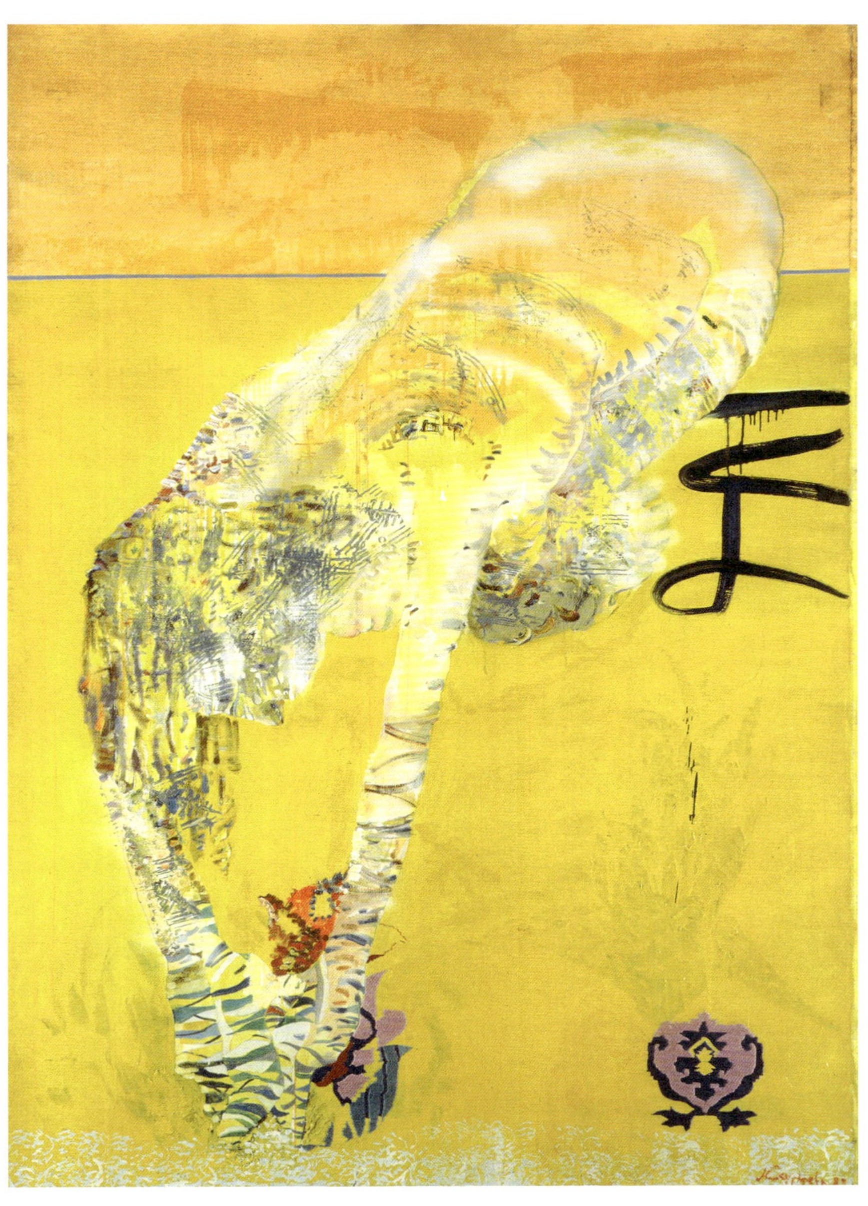

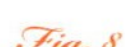

Fig. 8
MARINA SKUGAREVA
Harvest Holiday, 1989
Oil on canvas, embroidery
78¾ × 59$^{1}/_{16}$ in. (200 × 150 cm)
Private collection

Fig. 9
OLEG TISTOL
Reunification, 1988
Oil on canvas
106½ × 94½ in. (270 × 240 cm)
PinchukArtCentre, Kyiv

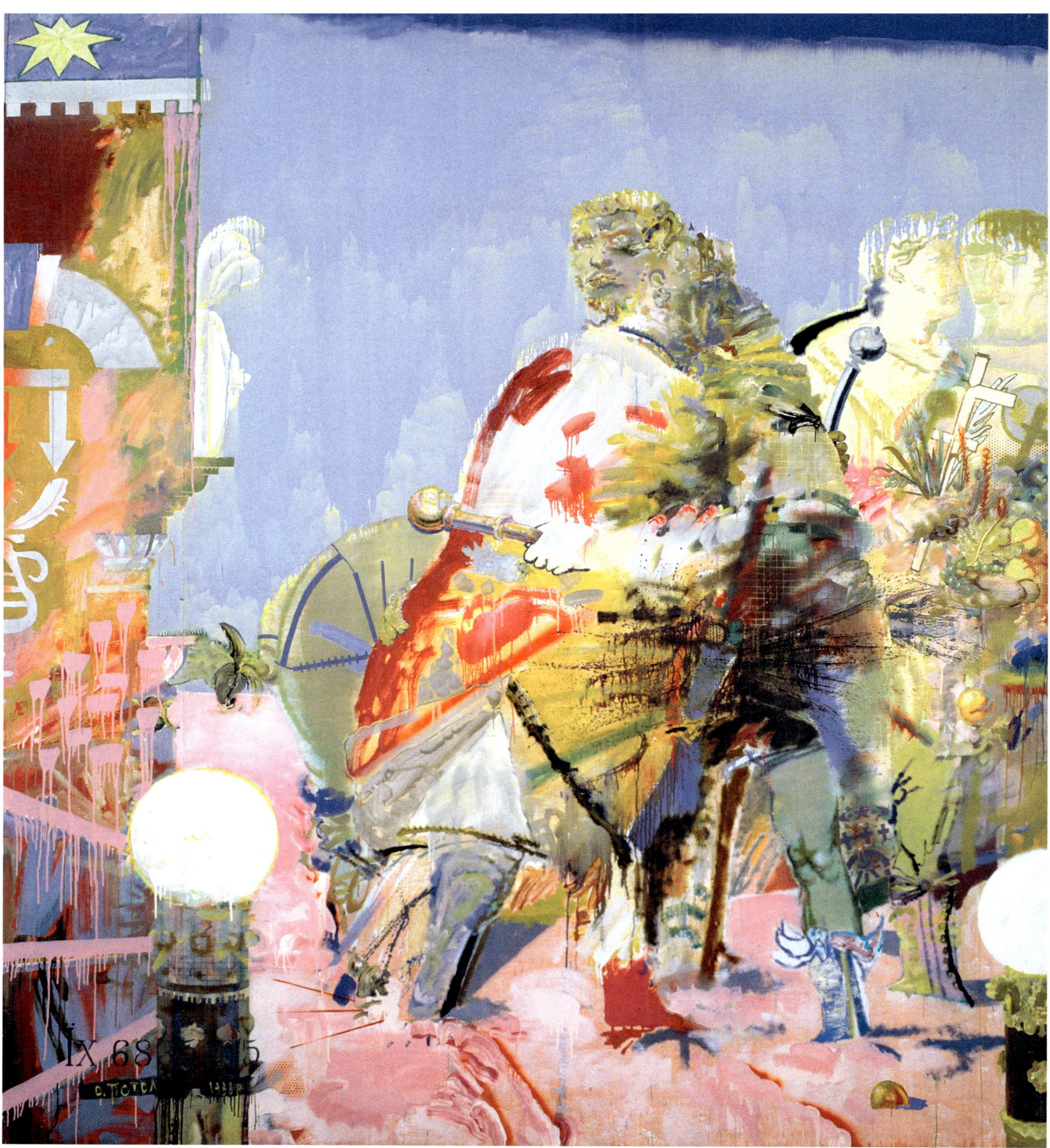
IX 68

Symon Petliura against Bolshevik Russia. The ornamental repetitiveness of the two equestrian figures puts history in perspective, as viewers recognize in one of the figures the features of Bohdan Khmelnytsky, responsible for signing the Pereyaslav Treaty in 1654. This whimsical constellation of symbols relates the Resolute Edge's output to the neobaroque, where the surplus of meaning signals both overabundance and catastrophic decay in accordance with the baroque's predilection for contrast.

The neobaroque was also invoked through the image of Ukraine's natural bounty, with its beautiful landscapes and fertile terrain juxtaposed against the invisible threat of the Chernobyl nuclear catastrophe. Dangerously beautiful and alluring, the Ukrainian land was a fata morgana[28] for generations of Ukrainians deprived of the ability to rule their own territory. The concept of the Ukrainian landscape was explored by the collective the Painterly Preserve, founded in 1992 by artists gravitating toward abstraction. Even though the group's name was formulated after the perestroika years, one of its most socially active members, Tiberiy Silvashi, had been on the forefront of change since the late 1980s and had organized plein-air painting expeditions in Sedniv (in 1988, 1989, and 1991), where figurative and abstract painters worked together, cross-fertilizing one another's art with new ideas.

The Painterly Preserve group foraged the Ukrainian countryside in search of pure pictorial sensations, discovering the Greenbergian idea of medium specificity[29] simultaneously with the realization of its historicity. Their formal experiments were timely in the late Soviet context, since the socialist realist method had been formally blind for decades, with didactic content prevailing over formal explorations. Nevertheless, their intention of protecting the painterly medium by its own means and saving it from the dictates of a text, as Asia Bazdyrieva establishes in this catalogue, did not stem primarily from the group's strict adherence to modernist aesthetics. Their painterly reductionism was informed to a greater extent by subjects outside of pure painting, such as Christian spirituality for Alexander Zhyvotkov, the transcendent energy of color for Silvashi, or the mythology of the Ukrainian landscape for Oleksandr Babak and Anatoly Kryvolap. As the Ukrainian critic Oleksiy Tytarenko said about Kryvolap, "His famous stripes condense the Ukrainian sensation of landscape, its density and austerity."[30] Silvashi's *Midnight* (1981; fig. 22, p. 44; cat. 34) and *Guest* (1982; fig. 23, p. 44; cat. 35) demonstrate the gradual erosion of subject matter on his canvases and the prevalence of the materiality of color that would soon overcome his rudimentary storytelling, transitioning into pure abstraction.

Whether excessive in painterly matter and colors or in signification, Kyivan painting of the 1980s and 1990s was multifaceted and prodigious. Oozing radioactive and symbolic meaning, the large-scale canvases reflected a postmodern hopelessness in the face of an overabundance of the past and at the same time a great euphoria in a historic transitional moment anticipating and defining the future.

Notes

1 Perestroika (1985–91) (from Russian "restructuring") was a policy implemented by the last Soviet leader, Mikhail Gorbachev, to rejuvenate the Soviet economy and to democratize Soviet society. In the social sphere, open discussion of the Soviet regime's crimes galvanized society. The economic reforms could not save the situation, however, and eventually brought the country to dire shortages of everyday goods.

2 "Russian avant-garde" is an umbrella term used to refer to the experimental art produced in the early twentieth century by artists from the Russian Empire and then the Soviet Union, including suprematism and constructivism. Many artists born in Ukraine and exploring traditional Ukrainian art themes were part of the movement and suffered the consequences of the curtailing of such art in the 1930s during the rule of Stalin.

3 The Moscow art critic Leonid Bazhanov, in his review of the 1988 all-USSR exhibition, had defined the new art trend as "Ukrainian transavantgarde of the neobaroque type," both in publications and in conversation with Ukrainian art critics like Oleksandr Soloviov and Valery Turchin. "Ritorika Totalnogo Somnenia" [The rhetoric of total hesitation], *Tvorchestvo*, no. 2 (1989). Oksana Barshynova, "From an Interview with a Well-known Curator and Art Critic, Oleksandr Solovyov, One of the Ideologists of the New Ukrainian Art of the Second Half of the 1980s to the Beginning of the 1990s," in *New Ukrainian Wave*, ed. Oksana Barshynova (Kyiv: National Art Museum of Ukraine, 2009), 30–35. It was later defined as New Wave, a title confirmed by the eponymous exhibition at the National Art Museum of Ukraine in 2009.

4 See Alisa Lozhkina's essay in this catalogue.

5 D. Gorbuntsov, "Glubokie Korni" [Deep roots], *Pravda*, May 18, 1987; E. Gorchakova, "Davaite Sporit" [Let's argue], *Moskovskiy Komsomolets*, April 15, 1987; L. Nekrasova, "Skvoz prizmu romantizma" [Through a lens of romanticism], *Moskovskaia Pravda,* March 1, 1987; Oleksandr Sidorov, "Ravnenie na…?" [Should we take them for a model…?], *Tvorchestvo* no. 8 (1987): 16–17; Olga Kholmogorova, "Deistvo, Mirazh?" [Action, mirage?], *Tvorchestvo*, no. 8 (1987): 12; Vladimir Levashov, "Molodost Strany: Zametki s vystavki" [Youth of the country: Notes from the exhibition], *Dekorativnoe Iskusstvo SSSR*, no. 9 (1987): 2, 22. Oleksandr Soloviov, "Po Tu Storony Ochevidnosti: Predvaritelnye Razmyshlenia po Povodu Odnogo Iavlenia [Beyond that side of the obviousness: Preliminary reflections concerning a certain phenomenon], *Iskusstvo*, no. 10 (1988): 35–36.

6 Vitaly Chernetsky, *Mapping Postcommunist Cultures: Russia and Ukraine in the Context of Globalization* (Montreal: McGill-Queen's University Press, 2007), 30.

7 Serhii Plokhy, *The Last Empire: The Final Days of the Soviet Union* (New York: Basic Books, 2014), 53.

8 For example, the imprisonment of the poets Vasyl Stus and Ivan Drach and the interpreters Ivan Svitlychny and Valeriy Marchenko and the destruction of the monument *Memory Wall* by Ada Rybachuk and Volodymyr Melnychenko in Baikove cemetery in Kyiv in 1982.

9 Borys Lobanovsky, "Kievskie anakhorety. Obrashchenie k bstraktnym formam v tvorchestve riada kievskikh khudozhnikov 50-kh-60-kh godov" [Kyiv hermits: Turning to abstract forms in art by several Kyiv artists of 1950s–1960s], *Vizantiiskii Angel*, 1997, no. 3: 31–40.

10 "Executed Renaissance" (*Rozstrilyane vidrodzhennya*) was a term referring to a generation of Ukrainian poets, artists, and writers who were either eliminated or forced to commit suicide by the authorities during the Stalinist terror. The term was coined by the Polish publicist Jerzy Giedroyc while he was working on an anthology of Ukrainian literature in 1958. For further information on the phenomenon of Executed Renaissance, see Yury Lavrinenko, *Rozstrilyane Vidrodzhennia: Antolohiia, 1917–1933* [Executed Renaissance: An Anthology] (Kyiv: Smoloskyp, 2004).

11 *Special Fund,* an exhibition of the forbidden Ukrainian avant-garde at the National Art Museum of Ukraine in 2015, showcased many artworks seen for the first time since they were forbidden by the authorities in the 1930s.

12 The Ukrainian art academy was founded in 1917 by the short-lived Ukrainian republic Tsentralna Rada (1917–18).

13 In 1964, a monumental stained glass window dedicated to the Ukrainian poet Taras Shevchenko by Horska, Zalyvakha, and other artists was destroyed the night before its opening. Zalyvakha was imprisoned for anti-Soviet propaganda from 1965 to 1970, and she was among the signers of Letter of 139 demanding a stop to political repression in the USSR in 1968.

14 The Ukrainian Academy of Arts was renamed Kyiv Fine Art Institute in 1922. Today it is known as the National Academy of Fine Arts and Architecture.

15 Mykola Kryvenko, *Khudozhnyk Hryhorii Havrylenko* [An artist Hryhorii Havrylenko], October 3, 2018, https://kyivdaily.com.ua/grigoriy-gavrilenko/.

16 According to this theory, each sound has its own color, facilitating the translation between the languages of music and visual arts. Thus, the artist aimed to reconcile time (music and poetry) and space (painting and color). Halyna Skliarenko's entry on Florian Yuriev in Olga Balashova and Lizaveta German, eds. *Iskusstvo Ukrainskikh Shestidesiatnikov* [Art of the Ukrainian 1960s generation] (Kiev: Osnovy, 2015), 266.

17 Ekatarina Degot and Vladimir Levashov, "Razreshennoie Iskusstvo" [Permitted art], *Iskusstvo,* no. 1 (1990): 58–61.

18 Alexei Yurchak, *Everything Was Forever, Until It Was No More: The Last Soviet Generation* (Princeton, NJ: Princeton University Press, 2006).

19 The idea was introduced in Francis Fukuyama, *The End of History and the Last Man* (London: Penguin, 2012). On the relevance of the concept for the Ukrainian art scene of the early1990s, see Kateryna Stukalova, "(Ne)vtrachene desiatylittia: Mystetstvo v sotsialno-politychnomy konteksti 90-x rokiv" [(Not)Lost decade: Art in the social-economic context of the 1990s], http://www.korydor.in.ua/ua/context/nevtrachene-desiatylittia-mystetstvo-devianostyh-rokiv.html, published October 12, 2016.

20 "Russia is going through a trauma of losing empire." Myroslav Shkandrij, *Russia and Ukraine: Literature and the Discourse of Empire from Napoleonic to Postcolonial Times* (2001; Montreal: McGill-Queen's University Press, 2009), 264.

21 Oleksandr Roitburd and Mikhail Rashkovetsky, "O dushevnom v iskusstve" [On the intimate in art], in *Dekorativnoe iskusstvo* 12, no. 386 (1989): 24–26.

22 "Socialism with a human face" was a slogan of the Slovak politician Alexander Dubček in 1968.

23 Oleksandr Soloviov's interview with artists of the Paris Commune Art Squat of 1989, published December 1, 2016, http://www.korydor.in.ua/ua/context/solovyov-ukrainskaya-zhenshenevaya.html.

24 A period of national revival and blossoming of the arts in Ukraine, accompanied by wars and political turmoil giving birth to a Ukrainian identity.

25 Tistol and Matsenko met at the Lviv Art Academy in 1979. They began collaborating in 1991, exploring similar subjects as the Resolute Edge. The title *NATSPROM*, from "National Crafts or National Production," appeared in the mid-1990s.

26 Konstantin Akinsha, "Poetika surzhika ili kotleta po-kievski" [Poetics of Surzhyk or a Chicken-Kiev], *Dekorativnoe Iskusstvo SSSR* 12, no. 385 (1989): 27.

27 Tistol's series *Kazbek* is referred to here.

28 Mykhailo Kotsyubynsky, *Fata Morgana* (Kharkiv: Folio, 2017). The first version was published in the magazine *Kievskaia Starina* in 1904. It was rewritten in 1910 to include the events of the 1905–7 revolution in the Russian Empire. It depicted the tragic and futile quest of a peasant family to attain a plot of land.

29 "In turning his attention away from subject matter of common experience, the poet or artist turns it in upon the medium of his own craft." Clement Greenberg, "Avant-garde and Kitsch" (1939) in *Art in Theory, 1900–2000: An Anthology of Changing Ideas*, ed. Charles Harrison and Paul Wood (Malden, MA: Blackwell, 2003), 541.

30 Oleksiy Tytarenko, Introduction to *Landschaft of the "Painterly Preserve,"* exh. cat. (Kyiv: National Art Museum of Ukraine, 2002), 5.

2 THE **POINT** OF NO RETURN
THE ART OF KYIV AT A HISTORICAL **CROSSROADS**

Oleksandr Soloviov

The key feature of the art of Kyiv from the second half of the 1980s—which had already openly portrayed itself as modern—was that it emerged at the same time that the Soviet empire was in its death throes. The real impetus for that collapse had come from perestroika. It was perestroika that opened up all those floodgates previously off-limits, and now there was no longer any need for Kyiv artists to look to the underground for salvation. Instead, they could follow in the wake of generally accepted trends of their time.

Yet the birth of the new had to pass through a stage of overcoming the inertia of "*Homo sovieticus*," both in the cultural sphere and in public life. Perestroika was not a smooth process. Rather, it constituted a juncture between a highly regulated past and an emancipatory modernity. A similar situation could be designated as a kind of "match point" moment, where one was a "heartbeat away from a new life," at a threshold, a turning point, where a choice is made between two paths, when everything is still touch-and-go. It was still unclear where things were heading. With each day, there was greater and greater freedom. The Iron Curtain had fallen; the number of public discussions snowballed; literature exposing Communism flooded in; dissidents who had sat in jail for their anti-Soviet beliefs returned; human rights activists no longer needed to speak in whispered tones. It got to the point that the popular mood against the injustice and pointlessness of the Afghanistan campaign was so strong that the withdrawal of troops began. On the other hand, there were the Chernobyl catastrophe, market "shock therapy" and growing social inequality, rising crime, national and ethnic conflicts, and the attempted coup d'état of August 1991.[1] All this caused severe turbulence. Yet few could have imagined that very soon a huge country would disintegrate literally overnight—that would happen in December 1991 at Belovezhskaya Pushcha.[2] These events were clearly reflected in the art world—in its organization and, most important, its aesthetics. Seismic developments became inevitable.

The upheaval in Soviet art began with the new generation of artists. A series of exhibitions by young artists, taking place between 1987 and 1989 in Kyiv and Moscow and youth residencies in the House of Creativity in Sedniv facilitated this. One of the starting points of the period was the 1987 exhibition of Arsen Savadov and Georgii Senchenko's celebrated work *Cleopatra's Sorrow* (1987; fig. 1, p. 11) at the All-Union Youth Exhibition in Moscow. Rumors about it spread rapidly, and soon the authors of the canvas became the linchpin of a nascent Ukrainian "New Wave." By the time of the next Youth Exhibition in 1988 in Moscow's Manezh, where the exhibition was for the first time divided into apartment-like zones for different national republics, the Ukrainians had acquired such a degree of spatial and aesthetic autonomy that now one could speak of them as a prominent and original creative phenomenon. In addition to works by Savadov and Senchenko, this time working on their own (rather than as a duo), other names attracting attention were

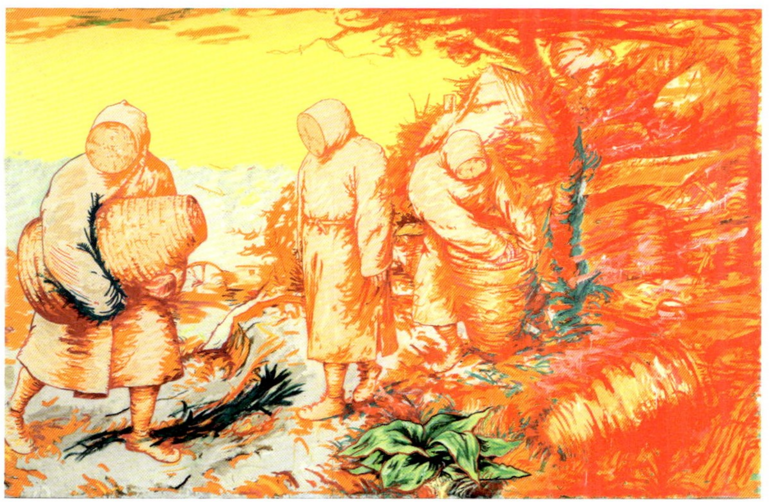

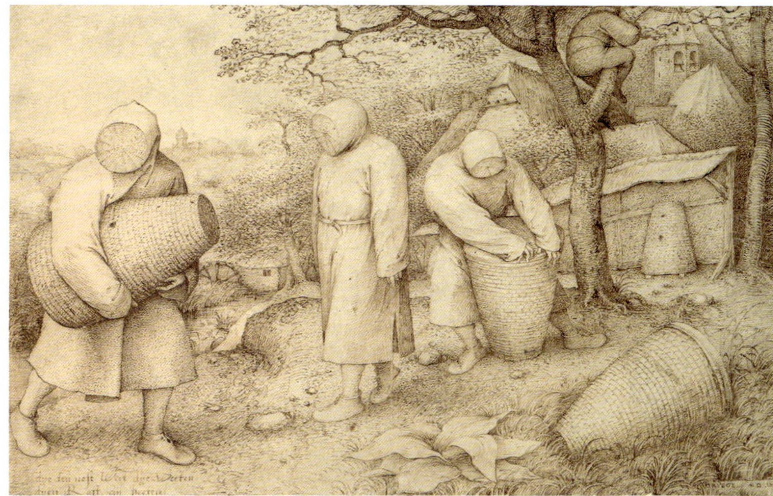

Fig. 10
GEORGII SENCHENKO
Sacred Landscape of Pieter Bruegel, 1988
Oil on canvas
110 × 166 in. (279.4 × 421.6 cm)
Cat. 33

Fig. 11
PIETER BREUGEL THE ELDER (Netherlandish, ca. 1525–1569)
The Beekeepers and the Birdnester, 1568
Pen and india ink
8 × 12⅛ in. (20.3 × 30.9 cm)
Staatchliche Museen zu Berlin, Kupferstichkabinett

Oleg Holosiy, Kostiantyn Reunov, Oleksander Hnylytskyj, Oleksandr Roitburd, Valeria Troubina, Valentin Rayevsky, Sergei Panich, Pavlo Kerestey, Yuri Solomko, and Dmytro Kavsan. It was after that exhibition that critics began to write about a Ukrainian revival, as Ukraine had previously been associated above all with the factory of "applauding socialist realism" or reproducing the national colors of the "Malorossiya look."[3] It was after this exhibition that critics formulated a definition of new Ukrainian art as a "transavantgarde of the neobaroque type."[4]

Large-format figurative painting, laced with allusions but with shifting deconstructed, mythological, radically eclectic meanings, became the cornerstone that united a generation. Indicative is Georgii Senchenko's *Sacred Landscape of Pieter Breugel* (1988; fig. 10, cat. 33), which appeared in the exhibition mentioned above. The Ukrainian artist transformed a small-scale drawing by the Flemish artist Pieter Bruegel (1568; fig. 11) into a large-scale and very expressive figurative space, endowing it with a different conceptual aura without tearing it from the umbilical cord of the original. Its spontaneous composition and *nonfinito* technique evinced a feigned disregard for high quality. For all its outward showiness and theatricality, the painting nonetheless possesses hidden meanings with ramified undertones and connotations. The surface is just a disguise. A hallmark of paintings like this one was that they didn't carry a directly political or socially critical charge. They reveled in the freedom, in the very possibility—after many years of ideological directives—of simply being paintings, beyond politics.

In Kyiv, the consolidation of the new movement was also actively taking place in art squats. For young artists, besides the pressing need for studios, there was a further motive for settling in empty buildings awaiting major repairs—the desire to mark out the borders of their communities from what were still predominantly conservative surroundings, the desire to create an autonomous territory for contemporary art. The first squat was located on Lenin Street (now Bohdan Khmelnytsky Street), and it proved to be very fertile ground for artists, though it lasted only from the fall of 1989 to the summer of

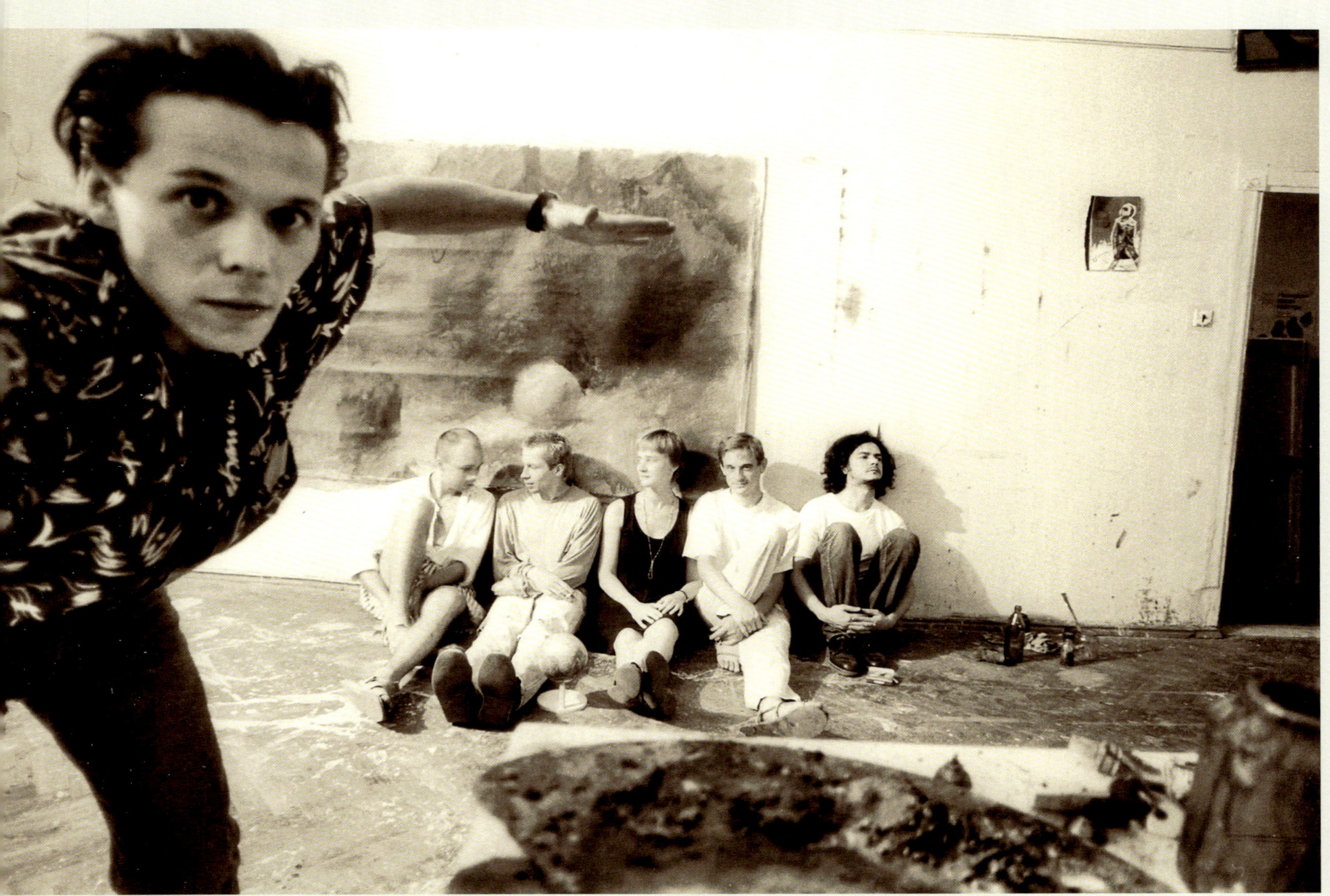

Fig. 12
OLEKSANDR DRUHANOV (b. 1961)
Paris Commune art squat, studio of Oleg Holosiy, Kyiv, 1992
Photograph. Oleksandr Soloviov Archive

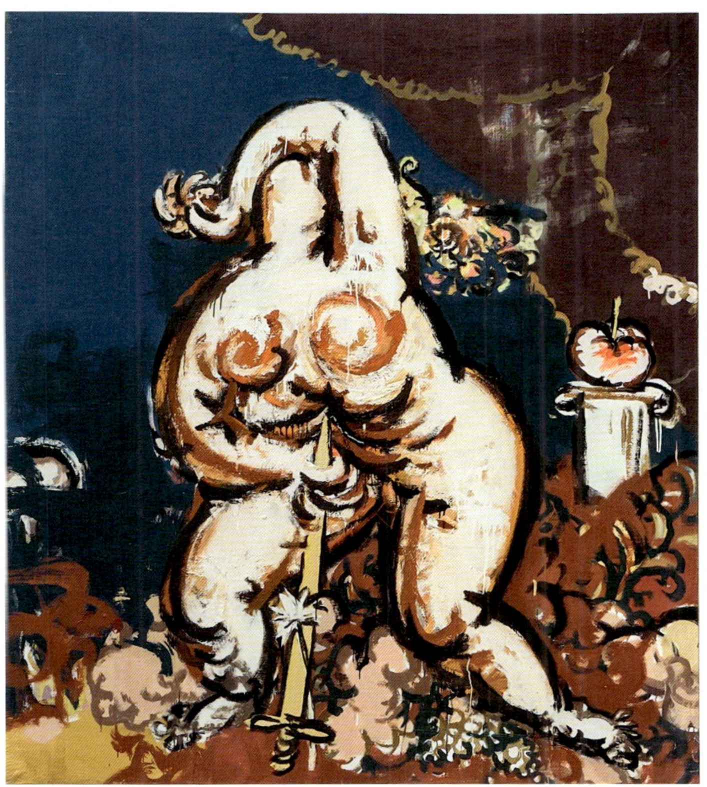

Fig. 13
OLEKSANDER HNYLYTSKYJ
Yearning, 1988
Oil on canvas
77 15/16 × 66 15/16 in. (198 × 170 cm)
Cat. 8

1990. In a new squat (fall 1990 to summer 1994) on Paris Commune Street (now Mykhailivska Street) (see fig. 12) and in two other houses adjacent to it, work was in full swing; at the same time this was very much the center of bohemian life. The location also performed the function of an alternative institution. In November 1991 in an exhibition hall on Volodymyrska Street, the defining exhibition *The Artists of the Paris Commune* portrayed the group as a specific entity. Yet it was not the typical art group with a declarative manifesto but rather an ad hoc alliance between a circle of close-knit artists and a broader one that was much more diverse.

The paintings of Savadov and Senchenko from the end of the 1980s are notable for their characteristic style: a dematerialized brightness of background, a two-dimensional "comics-like" shading, and the curly intaglio stroke, with a red outline bringing a sense of unreality to the picture space. All these features and techniques were graphically displayed in Savadov's panoramic canvas *Vital Season* (1987, Museum of Contemporary Art of Bordeaux). At the beginning of the 1990s, the works in their large exhibition at the Moscow Central House of Artists[5] were presented not so much as self-sufficient objects but as parts of an identifiable installation structure. The intriguing design was built on a dialogue of deliberate contradictions: the previously uncharacteristic minimization of visual signs, on the one hand, and the flamboyant monumentalism on the other. The first feature, for example, was exemplified by monochromatic canvases with columbaria painted on them, and the second by a huge installation of illuminated paintings-turned-objects adorned with images of monkeys. The exhibition also bore witness to an expansion of the arsenal of technical means. In addition to painting on canvas, the artists also actively used screenprinting on canvas cloth, drawing on bronzed paper, photography on canvas, intaglio printing on metal, and computer graphics.

Oleksander Hnylytskyj's "curly style" began with the paintings *A Debate About Mystery (Adam and Eve)* (1988, State Russian Museum, Saint Petersburg) and *Ausonia—Abode of Paradise* (1989, location unknown). In the painting *Yearning* (1988; fig. 13, cat. 8), from the same series, the characteristic traits of the style, inspired by early works of Savadov and Senchenko, are apparent, among them fabricated myths and a specific painterly style based on the combination of flat color fields with expressive outlines around objects and figures, often resembling drawing swirls. Subsequent series created in the workshops of the squats unexpectedly announced an almost total figurative austerity in the paintings *Lisa Is Crying* (1991, location unknown) and *Hark!* (1990, PinchukArtCentre). The grisaille

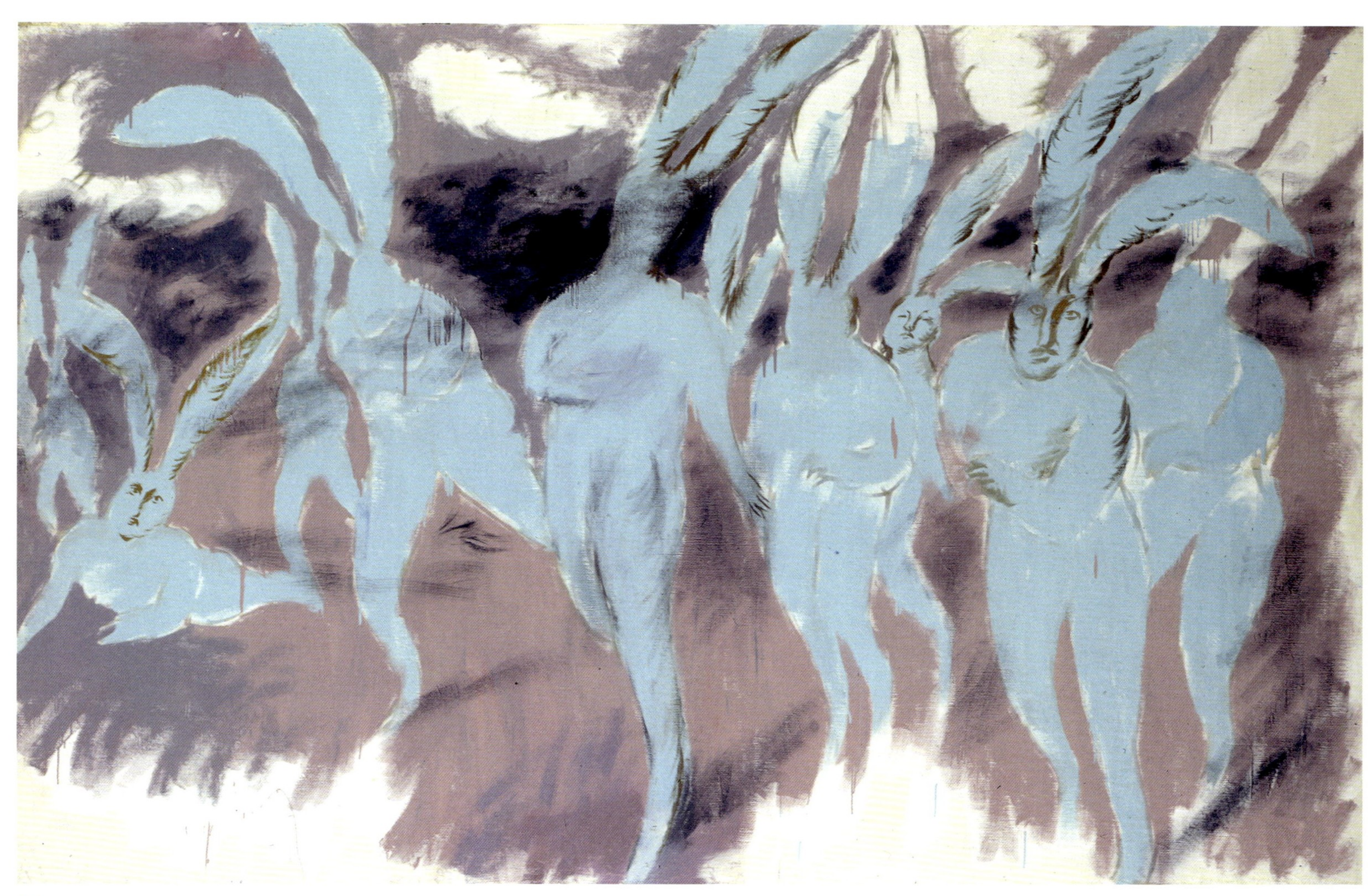

Fig. 14
OLEG HOLOSIY
Psychedelic Attack of the Blue Rabbits, 1990
Oil on canvas
78¾ × 118⅛ in. (200 × 300 cm)

of an aesthetically "annihilated" composition, the white primer of the canvas acting as a trap for the viewer, allusions from the history of art: these are the distinctive features of these paintings. Hnylytskyj was among the first Ukrainian artists to turn to video. In the early 1990s, while living in the Paris Commune art squat, he adapted his poem "The Sleeping Beauty in a Glass Coffin" (1992) for a movie. In his film *Crooked Mirrors—Living Pictures* (1993), shot at the squat working alongside Nataliya Filonenko and Maksim Mamsikov, a stream of video improvisations, sexual hallucinations provoked by distorting optics, unfolds before the eye of the viewer.

Yet another dweller of the squats was Oleg Holosiy, who tragically passed away in 1993. His rare artistic talent was embodied in a stream of images, as if raised from the depths of the subconscious, from his "inner cinema." Many of his paintings are a kind of broadcast from a dreamland. *Psychedelic Attack of the Blue Rabbits* (1990; fig. 14) seems refracted through the prism of altered consciousness and a frenzied color citation of the 1916 painting *In the Line of Fire* by Kuzma Petrov-Vodkin (1878–1939).[6] Holosiy's exhibition at the Central House of Artists in October 1991[7] became one of the most striking projects of the period. The installation, devised by Oleg Kulik, rejected the traditional layout of exhibitions in favor of a kinetic pictorial action. All the impressively sized paintings were put on special carts to which bells were attached; children in simple black-and-white clothes hauled the constructions around the room. The accompaniment of the chimes induced the audience into a state of near-trance.

The paintings from Vasiliy Tsagolov's *Rubber of Feelings* series (1992) were executed in a sketchy, pseudo-realistic manner and included textual inscriptions, often directly on the top of the image. At the same time, working with the Paris Commune, Tsagolov began to use photography and created a specific "pavilion" series, using an old aquarium as a set. In it, he posted magazine clippings framed by real pieces of meat as micro pinups, with other absurd additions, as in the image *I Like My Job Very Much* (1992; fig. 15, cat. 56). Shot later on film, these "puppet-show" mise-en-scène compositions looked like real "life-size" footage. He also invented the concept of "solid television," which he developed through the framework of a number of projects, in particular, performances.

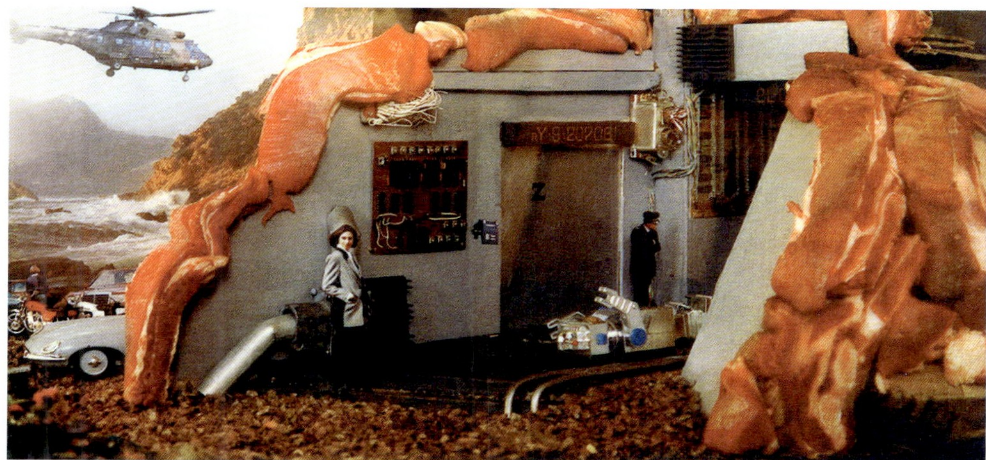

Fig. 15
VASILY TSAGOLOV
***I Like My Job Very Much*, 1992**
Color photograph on paper
27⁹⁄₁₆ × 49¼ in. (70 × 125 cm)
Cat. 56

In the action *Karl Marx–Père Lachaise* (1993), a script based on a criminal plot (a simulated execution of the Paris Communards in broad daylight in the heart of Kyiv) was only the outward form of the idea pronounced in the text. The essence of it lies in the perception of reality as fiction and as a three-dimensional television broadcast.[8]

A significant branch of art in Kyiv at the turn of the 1980s and 1990s was a group of artists who became known as the Resolute Edge of National Post-Eclecticism. They first actively announced their presence in 1987 at the Ukrainian-Estonian exhibition at the Kyiv Polytechnic Institute, for which Sergei Sviatchenko acted as curator.[9] The leaders of the group were Oleg Tistol and Kostiantyn Reunov. In contrast to the cosmopolitan mythologies of the majority of Kyiv and Odessa transavangardists, the Resolute Edge artists were drawn to the national myth. Their unified creative credo was the "struggle for the beauty of a stereotype." The group developed the idea of national art (*nats-art*) as a kind of response to the late sots-art then popular in the Moscow milieu. "The Ukrainian mindset," we read in Tistol and Matsenko's text, "suggests a principally different method of achieving victory, in contrast to the one practiced by the general Suvorov and the like." "Born and formed as a nation with active help from Genghis Khan and raised among the Sobeskys and the Osmans, the Piłsudskis and the Atatürks, we have mastered the great 'lore of defeat.'"[10] The paintings of the group, composed in a contemporary style—at that time "contemporary" was defined by neo-expressionist–pictorial language, but with conscious references to the techniques of pop art, in particular, the use of the stencil—were dominated by the theme of rethinking entrenched national ideas or familiar historical models. Tistol, for example, in his paintings *Reunification* (1988; fig. 9, p. 21), *Bohdan Khmelnytsky* (1988, location unknown), and *Exercise with Maces* (1989, location unknown) merged the Ukrainian baroque, the colors of the *parsuna*,[11] subjects and heroes of national or ancient history, Soviet symbols or banknotes, and samples of industrial graphic art, leading to a convoluted postmodernist, ironic playfulness. In the neobaroque project *Museum of Ukraine*,[12] created by Tistol and Matsenko, which includes *Piłsudski* (1993; cat. 18), a superficial vitalism is blended with the gloomy experience of the transience of existence, the fragility and the variability of the cultural archive. This project consisted of separate modules with gaps between them, inevitably revealing the dematerialization of the painting and its transformation into a kind of wall object.

The Resolute Edge had several rooms in the art squat on Lenin Street, where the artists of the group lived and worked, but only during short visits, because in 1989 they moved to Moscow, where they became involved in the Moscow art life in the well-known squats there—first in Furmanny and then Trekhprudny Lanes. In the fall of 1989 at the Kashirka Gallery in Moscow, a separate exhibition of the association also took place.[13]

At the start of the 1990s, the Ukrainian New Wave's interest in postmodernism began to fall away; its complex metaphors and ornate baroque style were considered anachronistic. There was a noticeable interest in works based on genre and plot (especially among artists like Holosiy, Hnylytskyj, Tsagolov, Mamsikov, Ilya Chichkan, and Kyrylo Protsenko). The artists increasingly borrowed their aesthetics from film and magazines. Under the influence of the then-widespread tendency of moving away from painting, artists began to actively introduce elements of installation into their works.

The exhibition *Calm at Sea,* held in March 1992 in Kyiv, documented the abandonment of the previous course: art progressed from the frenzied transavantgarde to a calmer, cooler harbor. This exhibition, among other things, served as an impetus for the Paris Commune's move to a substantial artists' residence in Munich and to two exhibitions of Ukrainian artistic groups there, *Dialogue with Kyiv* and *Post-anesthesia,* which took place in the fall of 1992.

The 1993 international exhibitions *Angels Over Ukraine* in Edinburgh and *European Steppes* in Warsaw, along with the 1994 project *The Space of Cultural Revolution* exhibited at the Ukrainian House (the former Lenin Museum) in Kyiv, were to represent the symbolic closure of this period of the fall of the Soviet Union and to mark the transition in Ukrainian art to a new cultural identity alongside the country's newfound sovereignty. According to the Kyiv exhibition's plan, everything on view was to be transformed into a collective installation whose ideology was elaborated by Savadov and Senchenko. A long orange fence was erected along the perimeter of the exhibition; the artworks were placed as though sacrificed behind this barricade-like construction. Arriving at the exhibition, the viewer was faced with an inability to see the work immediately; the only way to see it was a kind of "voyeuristic" glancing beyond the fence with binoculars with reverse optics, definitively flummoxing the viewer. This barrier, in the context of the then-ubiquitous crisis of representation, became a symbol for both the predicament and the new frontier beyond it. It became, to a great degree, the metaphor for the end of the epoch of figurative thought in Ukrainian art and the transition to a new way of seeing and representation. Exactly ten years later, Ukrainian House became one of the arenas for the real Orange Revolution, giving rise to, among other things, a new art generation. But that is another story for another time.

Notes

1 The State Committee for the State of Emergency was a self-proclaimed committee made up of members of the Soviet government who were opposed to Mikhail Gorbachev's perestroika policies and who seized power in the USSR between August 18 and 21, 1991.

2 The Belovezhskaya Pushcha Agreement was signed between the Belorussian Republic, the Russian Federation, and Ukraine on December 8, 1991. It declared the creation of the Commonwealth of Independent States and effectively confirmed the breakup of the USSR.

3 Malorossiya (Little Russia) is the historical name for the major part of the territory of contemporary Ukraine, referring ideologically to the time of the Russian Empire and Ukraine's loss of autonomy.

4 The Moscow critic Leonid Bazhanov was the first to give this definition during a discussion in November 1988 at the All-Union Youth Exhibition at the Manezh. *Parkomuna. Mistse. Spilnota. Yavyshche* [Paris Commune. Place. Community. phenomenon], exh. cat. (Kyiv: Publish Pro, 2018), 173.

5 The exhibition *Arsen Savadov and Georgii Senchenko* took place at the Central House of Artists in November 1991.

6 Kuzma Petrov-Vodkin (1878–1939) was a Russian and Soviet artist.

7 *Autonomous Art,* solo exhibition.

8 Tsagolov's concept of solid television reflected the impact of the media on the perception of reality, when anything broadcast on television appeared more real than real life observed with the naked eye, thus making television's existence exclusively solid, while ordinary life became dematerialized.

9 The exhibition was held under the title *Kyiv–Tallinn*.

10 *Kyiv Art Meeting*, exh. cat. (Kyiv: Ukrainian House, 1995), 56. See also "The National Culture" in this catalogue, p. 54.

11 The early Ukrainian portraiture tradition. Initially, during the baroque period, it incorporated some traits of icon painting, but it later transformed into a specific secular genre of portraiture common in the Russian Empire in the seventeenth and eighteenth centuries.

12 The artists worked on this project in the first half of the 1990s. The key images were *Suvorov* (1992), *Piłsudski* (1993), and *Atatürk* (1994).

13 The exhibition was held under the name of the group, *The Resolute Edge of National Post-Eclecticism*.

3 BACK AND DOWN TO **EMPTY** LANDSCAPES: NOTES ON **UKRAINE'S** REVERSE **MODERNISM**

Asia Bazdyrieva

I wanted to paint only the sky and earth, but in a way that this contained everything.

HRYHORII HAVRYLENKO

Landscape Resistance

It was the end of the 1960s. A massive exhibition pavilion near the October Palace in Kyiv was hosting an over-the-top show of Soviet art. The halls were ordered by importance: hundreds of gigantic images of revolutionary heroes and leaders of socialist labor in the first, followed by works by the most decorated artists in the second, closing with a dead end where one could find all the rest—those considered the least important. Here hung a tiny painting in whose humble brushstrokes—almost abstract horizontal touches of muddy green and yellow—one could clearly recognize a familiar landscape: the banks of the Dnipro River in Kyiv. After all the ideologically correct paintings that shouted the party line, it was this understated landscape that would suddenly stop time and its immense narrative of Soviet history and, instead, speak intimately on a very human scale.

This landscape was called *The Beach*, and it was not a political statement; its creator, the artist and teacher Hryhorii Havrylenko, did not have the intention of disrupting the exhibition's pompous agenda. Yet as Tiberiy Silvashi, then a student, later remembered, this work was "a flash, a new language": this landscape resisted the socialist realist canon that had been emptied of its supposed revolutionary agenda after many decades of repetitive and almost automatic gestures of glorification.[1] Twenty years later Silvashi, by that time a well-established Soviet artist, would take his peers to the Ukrainian countryside in search of landscapes suitable for such visual expression (see fig. 16). These seasonal trips, known as Sedniv-88, -89, and -91, were the first laboratories that heralded a group of abstract painters—Painterly Preserve—that would be founded in 1992.[2] For Silvashi, the marginalized abstraction of the 1960s linked the Soviet avant-garde of the 1920s to its resurfacing in the 1980s, a continuity that had been interrupted by socialist realism; abstraction's emergence now also coincided with the dissolution of the USSR. However, abstract painting had a marginal history, growing inside and throughout the Soviet system. And it was emerging out of the Ukrainian soil.

Black Earth

While Silvashi contextualized Soviet history as a radical deviation from the lineage of modernity, the history of the USSR—a gigantic geopolitical construct of the twentieth century—is precisely a modernist project that evolved out of the Western idea of the rationalization of nature.[3] Soviet ideology was grounded in the modernist ideal of human supremacy over nature, whose only value was found in its vast resources, which could be used for the economic development of the country. Complementing this vision, the

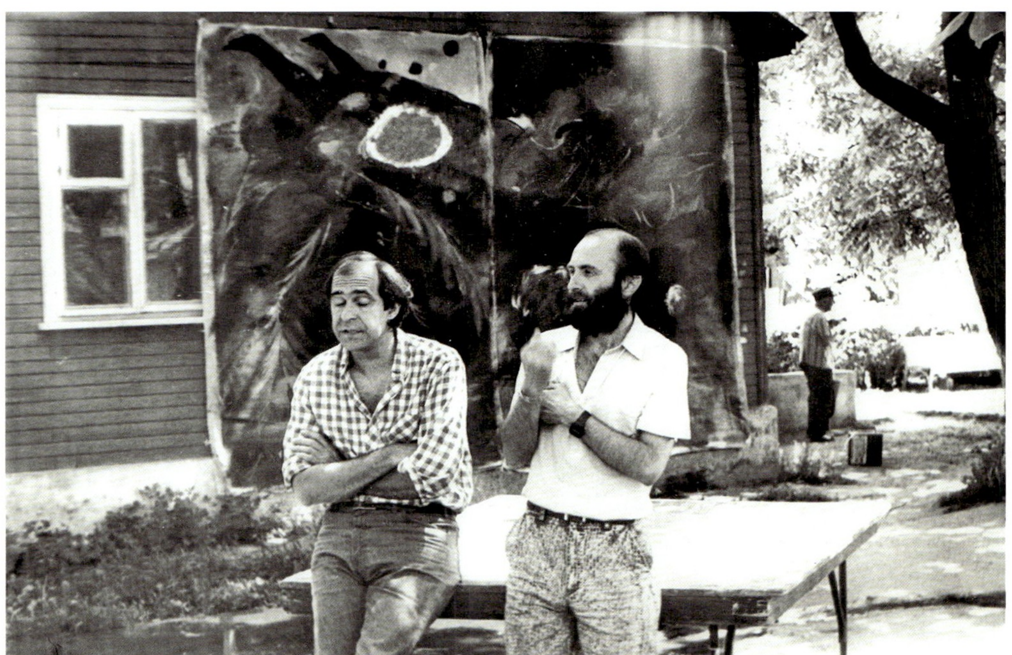

Fig. 16
PHOTOGRAPHER UNKNOWN
Artist Tiberiy Silvashi and art critic Oleksandr Soloviov with the painting *Attis* by Oleg Holosiy in the background.
House of Creativity in Sedniv
Photograph, 1989
Oleksandr Soloviov Archive

early Soviet avant-garde manifested the need to design a new state and a new citizen by disrupting links with nature.[4] Stalin, the master artist behind this creation, took the idea to an extreme: within only a few decades, the Soviet project redrew maps and rewrote lives, dried out seas and reversed rivers, launched off the ground and into space, accelerated with atomic speed and exploded with Chernobyl.

Ironically enough, the largest anthropogenic disaster in history occurred in Ukraine, whose postcolonial identity preceding and following the dissolution of the USSR was articulated through its link with nature.[5] Whereas the Western vision saw post-Soviet states as destined to catch up with the interrupted, future-oriented progress of modernity, here, time went backward. Turning its back on the bright socialist future promised by the Soviet era, Ukraine undertook a gigantic leap toward the past and its premodern cosmologies of land. Instead of going up toward cosmic exploration and the supremacy of man, there was an intuitive need to go down toward the black soil and empty landscapes, a need to feel them as if for the first time, to start from zero, to redefine—yet again—humans' relationship with land.

Against this background, abstract painting emerged as a tiny footnote on the margins of the totalized Soviet art industry.[6] Still, as an unspoken opposition to the strongly political early avant-garde's ambitions to supersede nature, it was both a spiritual source and a means to escape from the politicization of visual language amid a growing ideological vacuum. Artists such as Havrylenko and his peers made up for their professional compromises by seeking refuge in artistic residencies in Kaniv or Sedniv or by spending their free time in the countryside. From the 1960s onward, many would go to the Carpathian Mountains, the region the artistic community discovered when Sergei Parajanov invited some of them to work on *Shadows of Forgotten Ancestors*—the classic 1965 film based on a novel by Mykhailo Kotsiubynsky, whose writings explored Ukrainian ethnography. This rediscovery of authenticity recorded in literature and remembered through generations of families prompted an interest in local cosmological ideas and in forms of human mediation of the land. Following the example of the early Ukrainian intelligentsia of the nineteenth century, the artists took to the Ukrainian roads and again collected folk ontologies. Here, the land had been a constant throughout the centuries, reflected in the people's growing need for existential self-identification and echoed in relation to reality. The land, muted by industrial regimes and the narratives that drove them, attracted artists as a primary matter—a starting point for silent contemplation.

These practices were a loner's exercise. This time period is marked by individual cosmologies meticulously developed in home studios or indirectly woven into the mundane production of mosaics, book illustrations, and bas-reliefs commissioned by the Union of Artists, which left little record in written history.[7] This was the case with Valery Lamakh's *Books of Scheme*s, Florian Yuriev's theory of color-sound painting, or Fedir Tetianych's "biotechnospheres," all of which remained marginalized or unpublished. At the time of perestroika, when stagnating systems became more turbulent, individual artistic searches reflected the political situation almost unconsciously, with a gradation of tones: from playful appropriation of classic themes, as in the case of Arsen Savadov and Georgii Senchenko's meditations on the new and the old, to apocalyptic, as in Yevhen Petrenko's technogenic mutating landscapes, or in Serhii Yakutovych's dreamlike, dark graphic arts that echoed the Leipzig school of Neo Rauch (which occurred during a similar time of the dissolution of the German Democratic Republic). But there was no artistic scene where individual attempts to inject experimental techniques into the official agenda could unfold into a fruitful exchange of ideas. The urgency to establish such a scene had crystalized by 1987, when Silvashi was appointed secretary of the youth section of the Ukrainian Union of Artists. There he held a regular review to select works for republic exhibitions. The distinctive presence in the works of art of what he called a "new language" urged him to mobilize administrative resources and create a secure space for painting that was free of sociopolitical conventions.

Painterly Preserve

This attempt for autonomy in art echoed the nineteenth-century European claim of "art for art's sake." Even the title of a newly formed group—Painterly Preserve—bore the notion of a cordoned-off and protected area where painting could be safe. Silvashi would later argue that the history of painting as a vehicle for transcendence—where matter and color embody a nondescriptive manifestation of spirit—was already too much affected by the Soviet past and post-Soviet present.[8] He imagined a place where art could find refuge when the "exhausted and outdated language of cultural codes becomes empty and one needs to come back to their origins."[9] The Preserve was a metaphor of antecedence—the place where nature remained untouched by culture. Initially, the artists within the group were Oleksandr Babak, Marko Heiko, Pavlo Kerestey, Mykola Kryvenko, Anatoly Kryvolap, Serhii Semernin, Tiberiy Silvashi, and Alexander Zhyvotkov, who united for three exhibitions. (By the second show, the group had already receded, each of them ultimately taking solo paths in 1995.)

Following the first Painterly Preserve exhibition in 1992 and onward, Silvashi was keen to articulate Painterly Preserve's philosophy through the lens of early twentieth-century modernism, and he would make many attempts to shape the program of the group, while mixing Havrylenko's legacy with Clement Greenberg's texts and bits of philosophical thought retrieved from art journals smuggled through the Iron Curtain. The Painterly Preserve's early works were indeed sometimes inspired by episodic encounters with works of Western artists, such as Heiko's discovery of Giorgio Morandi, or the impression Willem de Kooning made on Kryvenko, or by the shared longing for an ongoing dialogue with the forefathers Malevich or Kandinsky. The latter's concept of "verticality"—the idea that transcendence cannot be represented and thus can only be embodied in an abstract painting—later evolved into Silvashi's version of Ukrainian art history, in which the "matrix of Ukrainian visuality" comprised a "transcendental" vertical scale of the sacred and a "descriptive" scale of the mundane. According to this theory, the magical and the sacred coexisted in the territory of Ukraine until the eighteenth century and were embodied in the tradition of icon painting that was interrupted by the representational tradition of the baroque movement. Malevich's *Black Square* in turn disavowed descriptivism in art, but that development was soon interrupted by socialist realism, which lasted until its abrupt political end in the 1980s. It was in Kyiv during that period, according to Silvashi, that two principal directions were taken: the one of the Paris Commune group, which continued the baroque "descriptive" tradition, and the other of Painterly Preserve, which sought to depart from the linguistic toward the "transcendental"—space and time embodied in color, the picture plane, and the act of painting.

Yet, the crucial point was that the circles of Kandinsky and Mondrian—whose thinking would become formative for Silvashi's artistic articulation—denounced nature and religion to further argue that painting (both as a gesture and as an end product) stood for an absolute of art as such, a total disruption with mimetic connection to reality as well as with the spiritual aspect of it.[10] On the contrary, abstract painting of the late Soviet and early independent Ukraine periods would not fit such an agenda, emerging primarily as a synthesis of sorts: a rediscovery of land in its rather archaic sense multiplied by a search for transcendence in an orthodox way.

Silvashi himself started with figurative painting, and his early works—such as *Guest* (1982; fig. 23, p. 44; cat. 35), *Time for the Reception of Guests* (1983), as well as a number of portraits—demonstrate the artist's interest in his immediate material surroundings. When gravitating toward abstraction, he further developed the materiality of color and light—with the attention to these aspects inherited from Havrylenko. In 1988, while on an exchange visit to the United States, he encountered the works of Mark Rothko, which inspired a series of abstract paintings called *Fields*. This was an easy choice of subject matter, as he would say later, since fields are conveniently geometrical. Yet, quite in the opposition to postwar American abstract expressionism as well as to their early twentieth-century antecedents, these paintings were mimetic, as in the case of *Field III* (1991; fig. 17), in which the yellow paint immediately invokes familiar Ukrainian fields. Intentionally or not, the artist tapped into the essence of what had long been a key point for Ukraine's cultural identity—the landscape.

Even in the most "radical" of the group's abstractions—be it Silvashi's *Rainfalls* or Kryvolap's entire body of work—there is a horizon line that organizes the pictorial world according to the familiar, earthbound sense of space (see fig. 18). Here, the presence

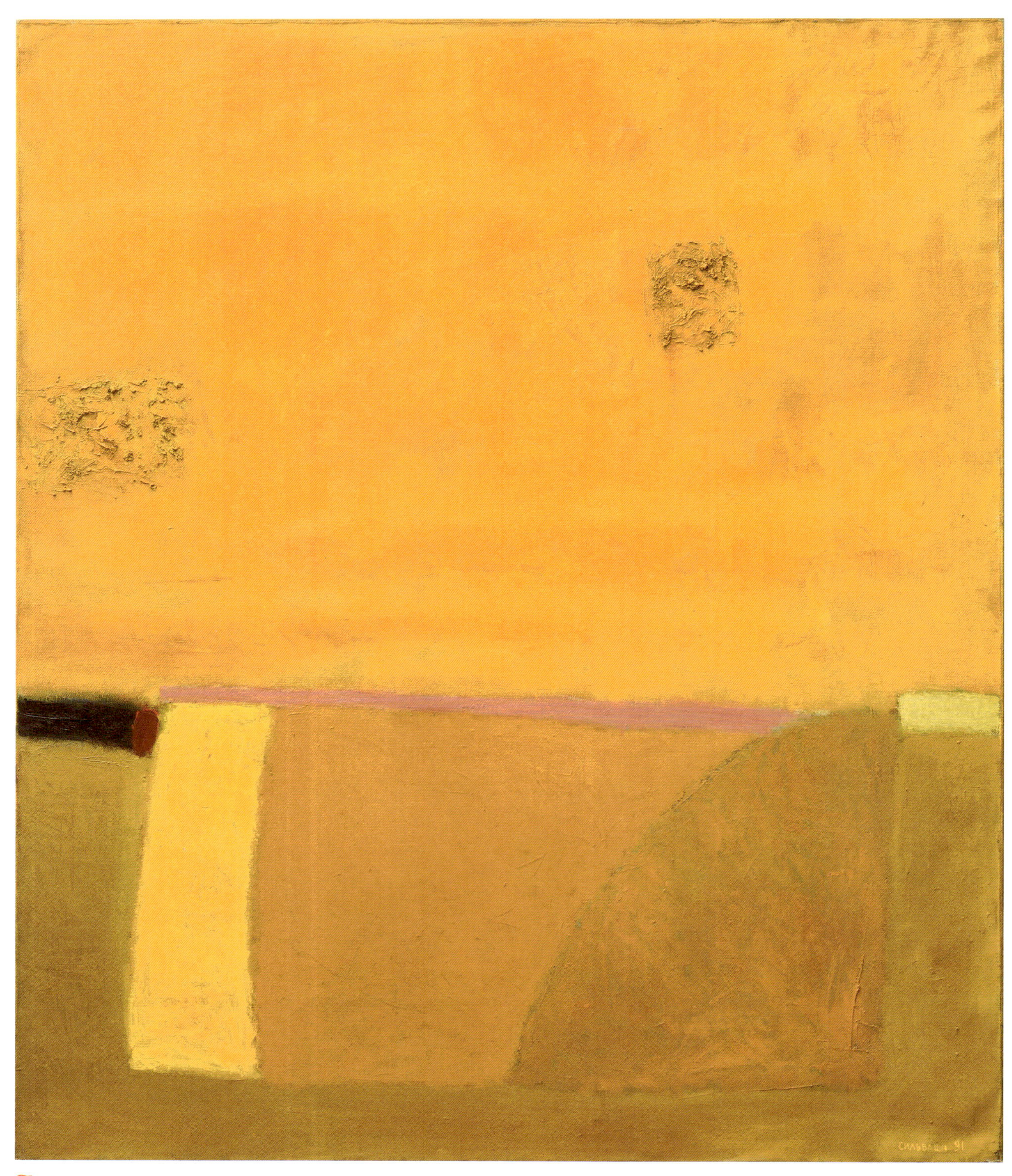

Fig. 17
TIBERIY SILVASHI
***Field III*, 1991**
Oil on canvas
70⅞ × 59⅛ in. (180 × 150 cm)
Collection of the artist

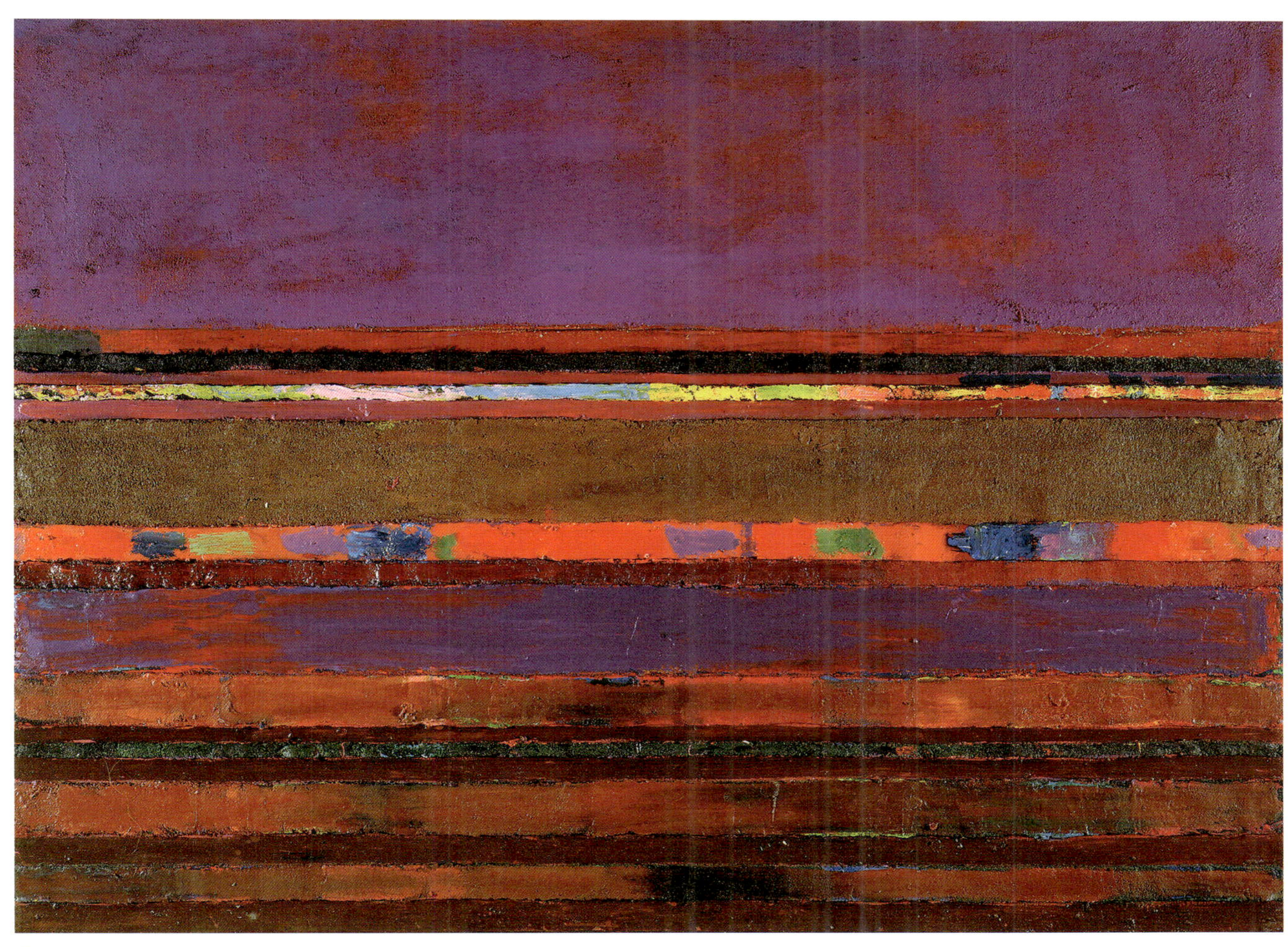

Fig. 18
ANATOLY KRYVOLAP
Untitled, 1994
Oil on canvas
47¼ × 62⅝ in. (120 × 159 cm)
Collection of the artist

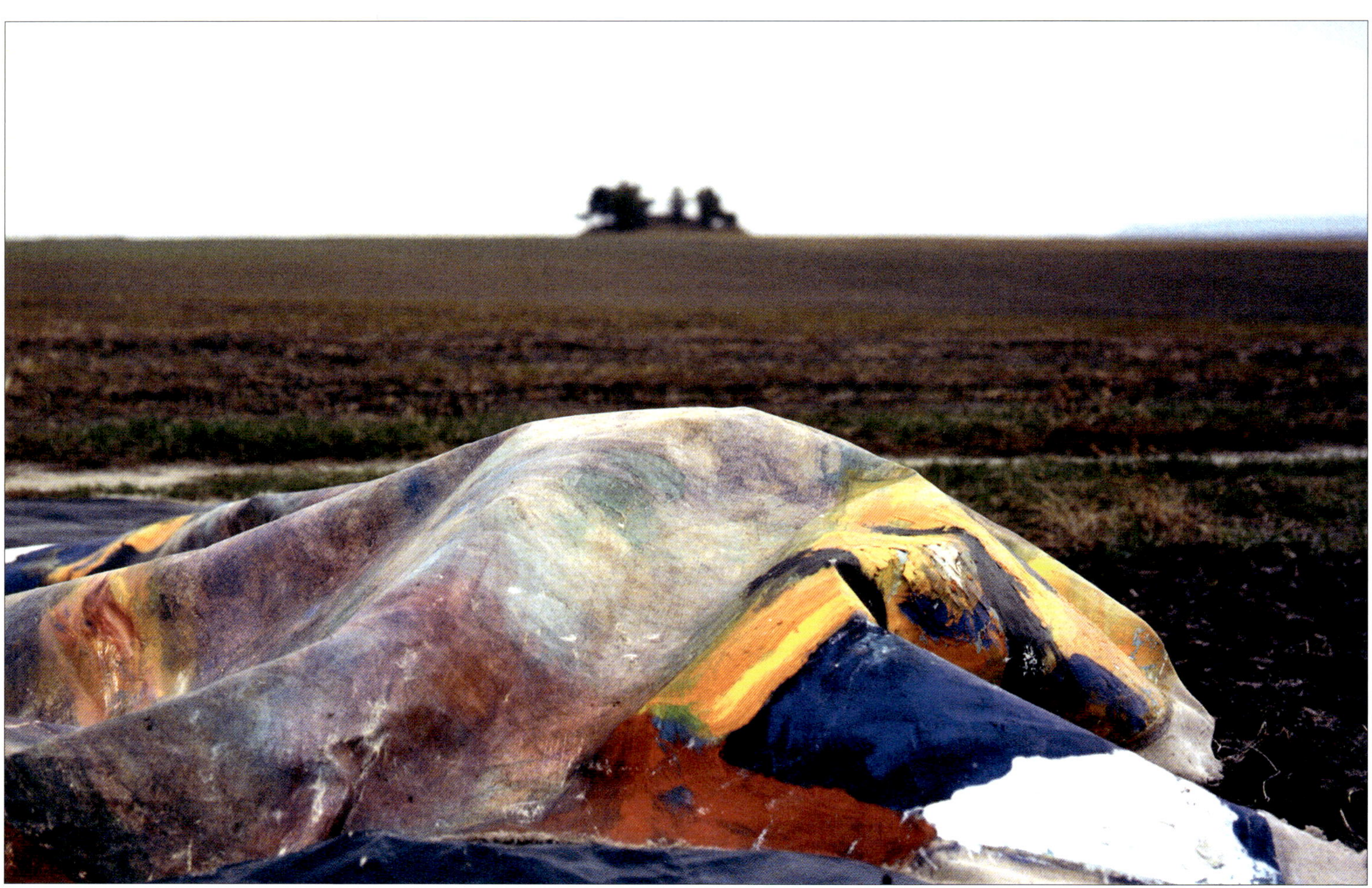

Fig. 19
OLEKSANDR BABAK
Barrow. Trench, Stack, June 22, 2003
with the assistance of T. Babak and E. Mukhoyid
Mixed media, dimensions variable, photo documentation
Collection of the artist

of landscapes or land as subject matter or as a structuring element had a distinct treatment for every participant of the group, while still remaining in close connection to particular geographies. Kryvolap, who eventually settled in a village near Yahotyn, established himself as the most recognized landscape abstractionist of his time. Yahotyn, where "nature materializes as cosmos while human beings are temporary," inspired a plethora of distinctively phenomenological works, based on the artist's spatiotemporal perception.[11] His bright and jazzy dynamic series *Pulsating Coordinates* (close in tone to Mondrian's boogie-woogies) represents visualized flashes and evening sounds, glimpses of the Ukrainian night.

Finally, a less obvious connection to the land reveals itself through the reinvention of Christian motifs, as seen in Zhyvotkov's work, including *Annunciation* (1991; cat. 66), his best-known piece from the period. As the vacant space of Soviet ideology was replaced with attempts to build Ukraine's national myth, a significant part of which was rooted in religion and departed from the Christianization of Kievan Rus, a rediscovery of spiritual devotion was inextricably intertwined with the search for national identity, which was, again, linked to soil and land. Essentially, for the artists of Painterly Preserve, these were only formative years, ones that would later be remembered for attempts to find an absolute, to structure the chaos with the help of what they believed was the sacred capacity of raw paint. Perhaps the most representative image for this movement was Babak's tender gesture of covering haystacks with massive canvases of abstract painting (fig. 19). His escape to the countryside in the aftermath of Chernobyl became a sobering encounter with the abandoned and gradually disappearing village of Leikiv. It is there that he embarked on a lifelong journey of rediscovering the sense of the human and their bond with the land—clays, woods, and soils that he incorporated into his quasi-archaeological abstract sculptures and paintings, including the Christian imagery from his untitled series (cats. 1, 2). The group was lost between modernist vocabularies, yet it grasped the zeitgeist of late Soviet stagnation and its narrative of the land, while smoothly turning to the need for healing, not breaking. Reinforced by the disaster of Chernobyl and the geopolitical collapse of the opposition between East and West, Ukrainian abstract painting was a "reverse modernism" that drifted dramatically away from future-oriented progress back to the earthly narratives of the past. Thus, the Painterly Preserve evolved into an antithesis of its supposed agenda: not using the landscape to protect abstract painting but using abstract painting to protect the landscape. Unsurprisingly, a reunion initiated by Babak a decade after the birth of Painterly Preserve took place in a village and was called "Landscape." It was an exercise in peaceful contemplation of abstracted lines of horizons, rivers, and rains without any of the urgency of narratives of modernity.

Notes

1 Tiberiy Silvashi, interview with author, February 9, 2019, in his studio in Kyiv.

2 Sedniv is a small town in the Chernihiv region of Ukraine. During the Soviet period, it hosted so-called houses of artistic creativity that provided residencies and stipends for seasonal plein airs under the aegis of the Union of Artists.

3 Boris Groys, "Beyond Diversity: Cultural Studies and Its Post-Communist Other" in *Art Power* (Cambridge, MA: MIT Press, 2008), 147–62.

4 Boris Groys, *Gesamtkunstwerk Stalin* (Moscow: Ad Marginem Press, 2013), 6. [*The Total Art of Stalinism,* trans. Charles Rougle (Princeton, NJ: Princeton University Press, 1992).]

5 I refer to Orest Subtelny's *Ukraine: A History,* first published in English in 1988 (Toronto: Toronto University Press) and then in Ukrainian in 1992. The vision of Ukraine's formation here is centered on the fertility of its lands nourished by the generosity of rivers and the sun, and on the fragility of these territories in the face of colonial invasions. Starting with the first known agricultural settlements, it is the richness of these lands that, throughout centuries, has been a defining factor for the social organization of peoples and their cosmological beliefs, while a profound connection with the land gave a legacy of folklore that mixed rhapsodies over idyllic village life with laments over those taking advantage of it. Subtelny also emphasizes how the early local intelligentsia of the nineteenth century—a handful of a highly educated people who were committed to the improvement of the social, cultural, and political situation of peasants—was foundational in the concept of Ukraine as a nation-state. Under the influence of the German philosopher Johann Gottfried Herder, who emphasized the need to study rural life and language for the formation of a nation, they turned to ethnographic expeditions of Ukrainian villages. Over the long duration of Ukrainian history, the country's picturesque landscapes have been a canvas for the construction of its cultural and political identity.

6 On April 23, 1932, the Central Committee of the Communist Party of the Soviet Union issued a decree banning all kinds of artistic activity outside of the newly established "artists' unions," with the goal of controlling the working process of artists as well as monitoring their communication with one another. By 1934, socialist realism was declared the mandatory method for all artists, while art was reorganized, along with industries, according to the planned economy, where industrial complexes were operating within five-year plans to produce artworks commissioned by the Ministry of Culture.

7 Borys Lobanovsky, "Kievskie anakhorety. Obrashchenie k abstraktnym formam v tvorchestve riada kievskikh khudozhnikov [Kyiv hermits: Turning to abstract forms in art by several Kyiv artists], in Olga Balashova and Lizaveta German, eds., *Iskusstvo ukrainskikh shestidesiatnikov* (*Art of the Ukrainian 1960s generation*) (Kyiv: Osnovy, 2015), 42–53.

8 Silvashi recalls a visit to Paris in 1991, where the name of a soon-to-be-formed group was coined in a conversation with Aleksandr Akerman, who suggested that "such painting," "such priming of canvas no longer exists here." Silvashi exclaimed, "This, rather, is an oasis, painting is dying." "The Painterly Preserve!" Akerman responded. See Oleh Sidor-Gibelinda, "Encyclopedia of the Preserve" in *Aleksandr Zhyvotkov. Kholst. Derevo. Karton. Rabota s materialami, 1984–2014* [Alexander Zhyvotkov. Canvas. Wood. Cardboard. Work with Materials, 1984–2014] (Kyiv: Stedley Art Foundation, 2014), 207.

9 Tiberiy Silvashi, "A Description of the Sky Above the Preserve," in *Picturesque Sanctuary: Golden Period,* exh. cat. (Kyiv: Zolotoe sechenie, 2018).

10 In his "Reflections on Abstract Art" (1931) Kandinsky postulates that abstract art enables man to touch the essence of nature: "Abstract art does not exclude an association with nature, but that on the contrary, this liaison is greater and more intimate than in recent times." This point of view changes drastically in 1936, when in "Abstract Painting" he asserts that "the abstract painter does not use nature, and aims to manage without it." Thus, over time Kandinsky's path to abstraction gradually changed from the idea of nature as an integral part of abstraction to the idea of abstraction independent of nature. See Wassily Kandinsky, *Kandinsky: Complete Writings on Art,* Kenneth C. Lindsay and Peter Vergo, eds. (Boston: Da Capo Press, 1994).

11 Heorhii-Hryhorii Pylypenko, "Khudozhnyk Anatolii Kryvolap: 'Ia zmalechku bachyv po-inshomu, tomu mii shliakh takyi skladnyi i nerivnyi,'" *Uriadovyi kur"ier,* April 30, 2016, accessed March 19, 2019, https://ukurier.gov.ua/uk/articles/hudozhnik-anatolij-krivolap-ya-zmalechku-bachiv-po/.

4 PRODIGAL CHILDREN OF **SOCIALIST** REALISM
NEW UKRAINIAN **ART** AND THE **SOVIET** ART SCHOOL

Alisa Lozhkina

The latest Ukrainian art is the result of a historical rupture. Modern artistic practices were conceived in the late Soviet Union in opposition to the socialist realism that had outlived itself. However, the Soviet art system proved to be rather more tenacious than the Soviet Union itself. Even to this day in independent Ukraine, the infrastructure of modern art still exists side by side with the remnants of the old system. The Union of Artists, created in the Soviet era, still operates, and a spirit of aggressive conservativism is dominant in Ukraine's main artistic university, namely the National Academy of Fine Arts and Architecture. Many of the old masters of socialist realism adapted rather well to the new historical conditions. After the fall of the USSR, they depicted Orthodox churches and portrayed bandits, businessmen, and new Ukrainian bureaucrats instead of Lenin and collective farmers. Lacking any ideological bedrock, that art rapidly deteriorated, but those artists did not entirely surrender their artistic talent. New art, arising amid the ruins of utopia, announced a clean break with the art of the previous generation of senile "fathers," declaring its intention to keep pace with current global trends.

The fact that there was such a fundamental break with Soviet tradition and that this break was proclaimed so relentlessly, accompanied by a hostility lasting for many years to any Soviet remnants, meant that any objective analysis of the continuum between the first post-perestroika generation and previous generations has been severely hampered. And yet, the connections between the new art and the Soviet art system are rather obvious. This is particularly the case with the Kyiv school of figurative postmodernist painting of the late 1980s and early 1990s.

Unlike Odessan conceptualism and the Kharkiv school of photography, formed in those deeply rich local traditions of nonconformism, art in Kyiv in the middle and late 1980s had little to do with the local nonconformist scene. In fact, in the mid- to late 1980s, any such scene in Kyiv was practically nonexistent. Persecution of all forms of dissidence in the capital of Soviet Ukraine had been far more severe than at the periphery, and even more so than in Moscow. Kyiv painting of the late 1980s was closer to the so-called permitted art.[1] Aware that it was no longer able to fully suppress nonconformist trends, the Soviet system permitted an easing of ideological pressure after the 1970s. So, from the deepest recesses of official Soviet art, there emerged artistic phenomena linked to young artists, giving them some space for limited experiments with form. This is the context of the late 1980s in which the Ukrainian New Wave[2] was born, following on from the euphoric wave of perestroika. To a certain extent, their art found kindred spirits in the "left" wing of the Kyiv Union of Artists,[3] comprising figures such as Viktor Ryzhykh, Halyna Neledva, Akim Levych, and others.

The generation belonging to the Ukrainian New Wave found itself in propitious circumstances. It was shaped in an era of radical change. Whereas their forerunners, gingerly and faltering in their approach, would become reticent, these artists had the chance to shout at the top of their voices. Their rebellious desires resonated with contemporary reality. A critical mass of artists suddenly formed. With their interest in contemporary philosophy and current trends in international art, and united by a vital energy, they seemed to embrace the spirit of an era of hope and rebirth.

Students of the Kyiv Fine Art Institute[4] formed the backbone of the Ukrainian New Wave. Many had previously studied at a republic art school. In the USSR, it was deemed that complex technical nuances of fine art had to be grasped at an early age. With this in mind, a whole network of specialized boarding schools was established, and their most talented graduates would go on to enroll at the art institutes. Arsen Savadov, Georgii Senchenko, Oleg Holosiy, Oleksander Hnylytskyj, Valeria Troubina, Vasiliy Tsagolov, Oleg Tistol, and Mykola Matsenko were all alumni of the Soviet art system. From an early age, they studied academic drawing and painting with teachers who had themselves been students of the leading masters of Soviet art, many of whom had been awarded Stalin Prizes in the 1940s and 1950s and who had defined the agenda of socialist realism at the peak of its development. Mykhailo Khmel'ko, Viktor Puzyrkov, Tetiana Yablonska, Oleksandr Lopukhov, Viktor Shatalin—these teachers were living legends and the bearers of the artistic tradition that had made Kyiv in the late 1940s and early 1950s one of the main centers of the conveyor-belt-like production of socialist realist canvases.

The artists of the New Wave were shaped in a system in which there reigned a deference to painting as the highest form of artistic expression. Multifigure canvases; bright colors; an impulse for narrative; sweeping, confident brushwork; huge formats—all these features of postmodern Ukrainian painting were inherited from their closest of kin, socialist realism.

Young artists of the first post-perestroika generation transmuted traditional form, breathing a radically new content and energy into it. And so, dying out, Ukrainian socialist realism paradoxically breathed life into a new art. No matter how the generation of the Ukrainian New Wave revolted, experimented with new media, or tried to suppress the centrality of painting, large-scale figurative painting still haunts it to this day, like a witch's spell from a fairy tale. Postmodernism in Ukrainian visual arts is, first and foremost, post–socialist realism.[5]

Ukrainian postmodernism engages dynamically with local art history. For example, in the works of Oleg Tistol, who belonged to the association Resolute Edge of National Post-Eclecticism, there are tangible parallels with the work of Soviet Ukraine's main "romantic," Mykhailo Derehus, and with many other artists who addressed the topic of Ukraine's distant past. Unlike other representatives of the New Wave who embraced a cosmopolitan mythology, the artists of Resolute Edge gravitated toward exploring national myth. The "beauty of the national stereotype" was the formula for their main source of inspiration. For Tistol, the primary stereotype of Ukrainian culture and the object of a deep ironic exploration was the sugarcoated, glossy Soviet propaganda of the history of Ukrainian Cossacks. Once the USSR collapsed, the narrative of the heroic pre-Soviet past became the leading myth deployed by the adherents of independent Ukraine. The artists of Resolute Edge scrutinized how, having barely slipped from the grasp of one historical myth, Ukraine did its utmost to start building another.

Piłsudski, by Tistol and Matsenko (1993; cat. 18), also plays with the national myths of Ukraine's closest neighbor. It portrays Józef Klemens Piłsudski, the distinguished statesman of Polish interwar history, with Symon Petliura, the key figure in Ukraine's struggle for independence following the fall of the Russian Empire—both depicted in a pompous way. The scene refers to the 1920 Treaty of Warsaw signed by the two men in an attempt to fight together against the pro-Soviet Russian troops—a seemingly impossible union between age-old enemies.

Fig. 20 (top)
OLEG HOLOSIY
Yellow Room, 1989
Oil on canvas
78¾ × 165⅜ in. (200 × 420 cm)
PinchukArtCentre, Kyiv

Fig. 21 (bottom)
MYKHAILO KHMEL'KO
Toast to the Great Russian People, 1947
Oil on canvas
118⅛ × 196⅞ in. (300 × 500 cm)
Collection National Art Museum of Ukraine

In *Yellow Room* (1989; fig. 20), a showpiece work by Oleg Holosiy, the leading representative of the New Wave, there seems at first glance to be little alluding to socialist realist classics. However, in Ukrainian art there was already one famous "yellow room." That is St. George's Hall of the Kremlin Palace in Moscow, depicted on an enormous classical canvas by the socialist realist Mykhailo Khmel'ko (1947; fig. 21). The solemn reception of May 24, 1945, in honor of the victory in the Second World War culminated in the famous toast by Joseph Stalin "to the Great Russian People." Khmel'ko's painting is the apotheosis of Stalinist grand style, with its characteristic megalomania, its passion for multifigure art, and the cult of personality for the leader of the USSR. Holosiy's *Yellow Room* was part of the revolt against the stuffy ideological spell under which Soviet painting found itself. Like Khmel'ko's painting, it combines a colossal format, strident color, and a closed space in which the action takes place. It is a psychedelic irruption into pretentious grand style, its dissection and elimination, with the aid of boorish expression and a new mythology.

Committing a Freudian "parricide," the artists of the New Wave repeatedly emphasized their radical aversion to Soviet art, rejecting any suggestion that it was "part of their DNA." In the late 1980s, they directed their gaze toward the Italian transavantgarde and the German Neue Wilde ("New Savages"). At the same time, interested in postmodernist painting, the artists discovered its methodological resemblance with the formal language of socialist realism. This correspondence offered them an opportunity to use those skills acquired at Soviet art schools. Later on, by the early 2000s, after years of experiments with new media, this group returned to painting and now quite consciously began to emulate Soviet academic painting. But in the late 1980s and early 1990s, the connection with socialist realism was more unconscious in character.

Another branch of art developed in Kyiv in parallel with postmodernism. Here a group was taking shape whose main focus was attention to plastic abstraction, metaphysics, and the alchemy of the artist's engagement with the painterly surface of the canvas. Artists slightly older than those of the New Wave were the backbone of this school. Tiberiy Silvashi, Mykola Kryvenko, and Anatoly Kryvolap were all over forty at the time of the breakdown of

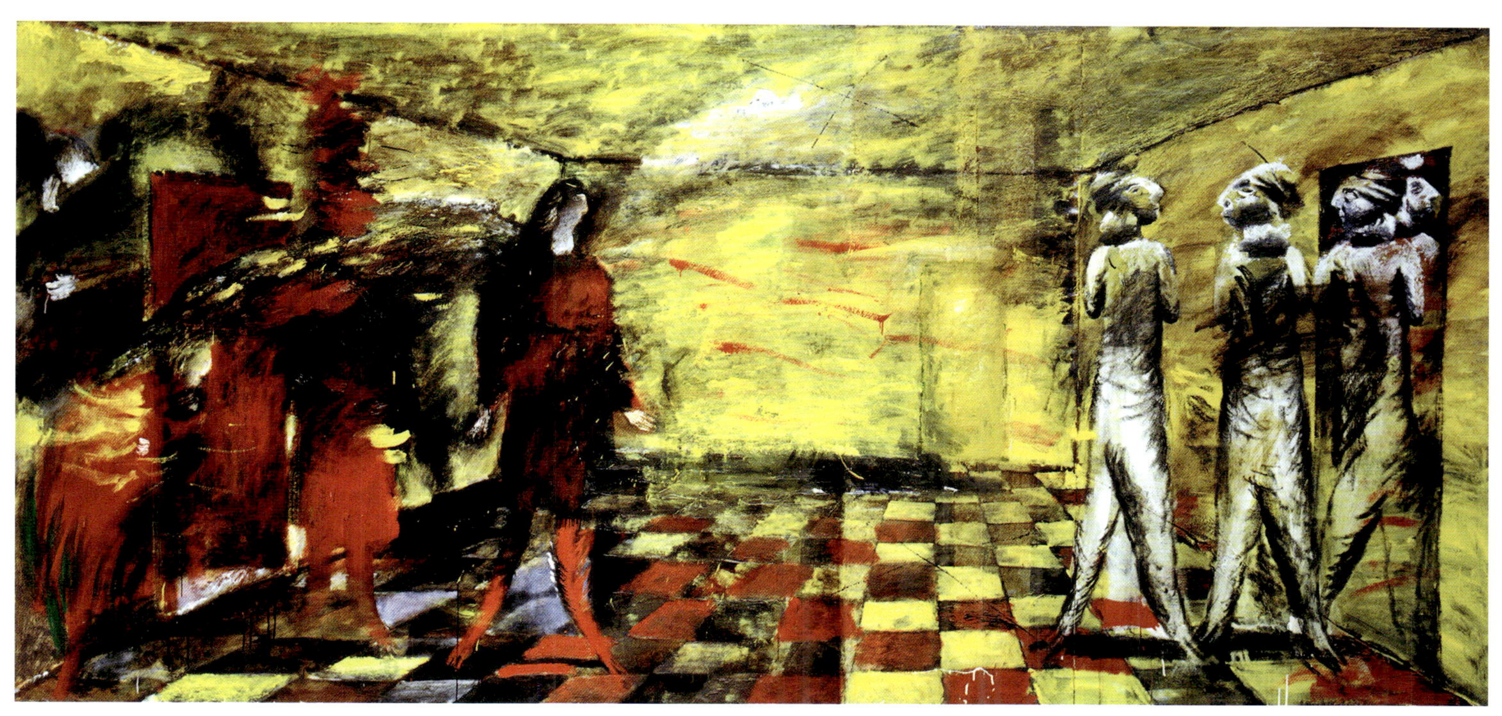

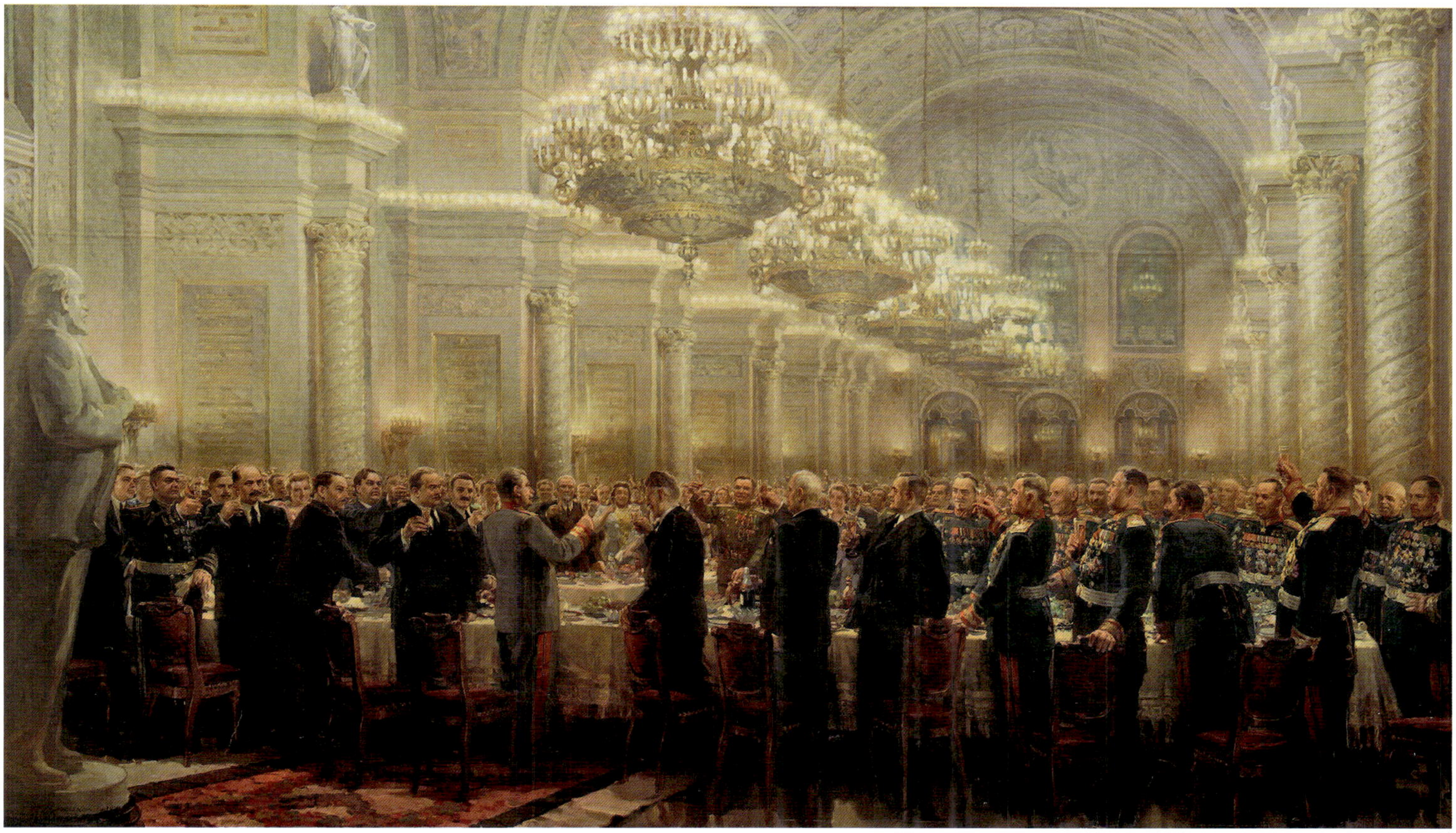

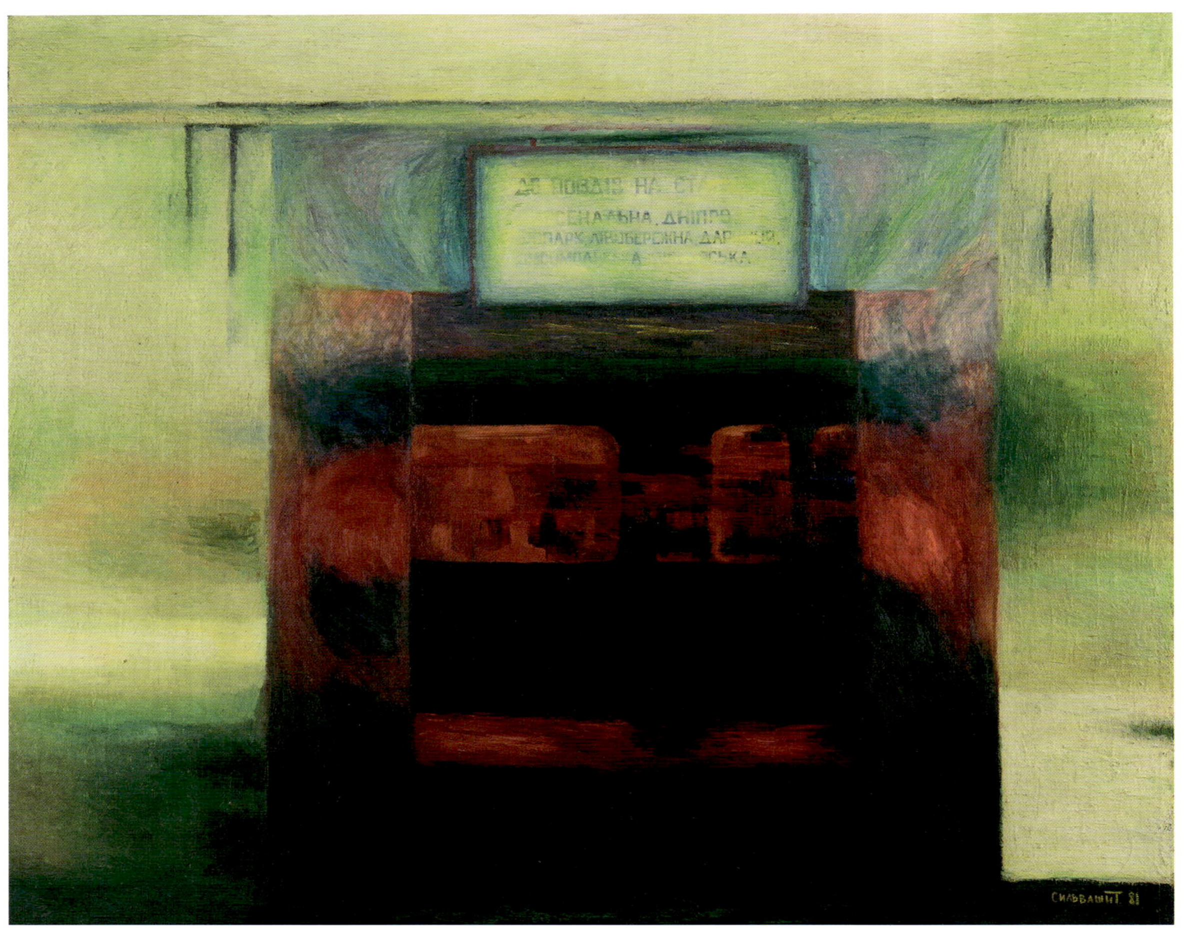

Fig. 22
TIBERIY SILVASHI
***Midnight*, 1981**
Oil on canvas
39$\frac{3}{8}$ × 47$\frac{1}{4}$ in. (100 × 120 cm)
Cat. 34

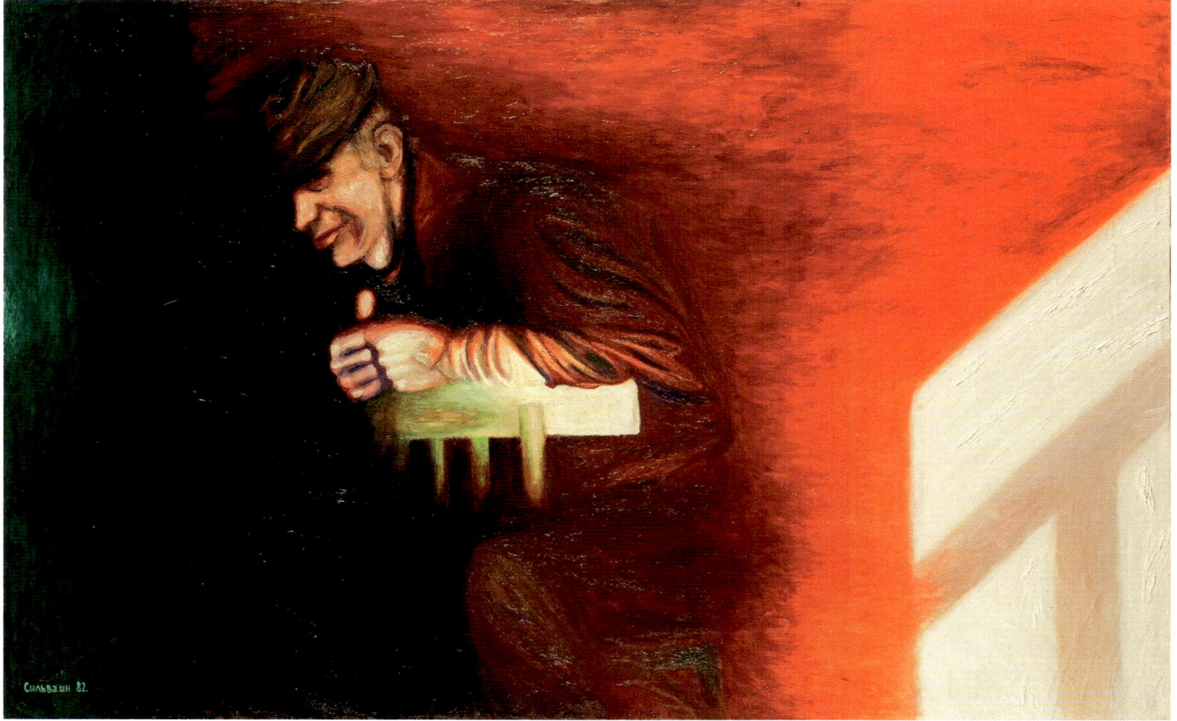

Fig. 23
TIBERIY SILVASHI
***Guest*, 1982**
Oil on canvas
39$\frac{3}{16}$ × 59$\frac{13}{16}$ in. (99.5 × 152 cm)
Cat. 35

the USSR and were already recognized artists. Painterly Preserve, as the members of this circle called themselves, did not create collective works or manifestos. Rather, they constituted a sphere of communication, a laboratory to generate new meanings. The artists tried to find and formulate their answer to the question of what kind of art should arise after the collapse of ideology. In an era in which a spirit of experimenting with new media reigned, Painterly Preserve remained loyal to painting, limiting their formal experiments to it. The group's title reflected its declared conservatism, or more accurately, its chivalrous loyalty to the medium and its Stockholm Syndrome–like allegiance to it. Painterly Preserve represents the self-perception of artists in a world where painting was rapidly going out of fashion.

The art scholar Oleksandr Soloviov placed this group on an imaginary equator between the radicalism of the New Wave and the retrograde work of tired late Soviet academism.[6] In a certain sense, Painterly Preserve did have a stance of reclaiming modernism in Ukrainian art where its tradition had been interrupted. Mykola Kryvenko, one of the participants of the group, in his youth had studied under the legendary Hryhorii Havrylenko, a subtle master and a member of Kyiv's unofficial artistic and intellectual circle of the 1960s generation, which had experimented with nonfigurative art during Soviet times. The artists of Painterly Preserve restored a continuity between the avant-garde, the unofficial tradition, and the art of the new independent Ukraine.

The biography of the chief proponent of Painterly Preserve, Tiberiy Silvashi, is emblematic in terms of the transformation of late Soviet art. In the Soviet era, he was one of the most successful young artists of Soviet Ukraine. In the late 1970s, he became interested in the limits of realist painting, and in the early 1980s, he created a series of poetic realistic paintings where the figurative aspect gradually diminished, as seen in the paintings *Midnight* (1981; fig. 22, cat. 34) and *Guest* (1982; fig. 23, cat. 35). After turning to an abstract style in the late 1980s, he started experimenting with pure color. The evolution of the artist from the soft realism of the beginning of the 1980s to the monochrome of his later career stemmed from his careful fumbling for new meanings in an epoch in which the old meanings had lost any currency. On the one hand, this development somewhat exemplifies the complex of one who had always excelled in whatever he did. An effective Soviet functionary famed for his liberalism would naturally wish to say his piece in the new art of independent Ukraine. Abstraction, from the perspective of the late Soviet period, was one of the most radical violations of taboos. And yet, works by Silvashi and other painters of the group, with their surfaces covered by pure color, were not just paying tribute to global modernism but consciously departing from the excessive narrative drive of Soviet art, taking a stance of artistic austerity and creative seclusion.

By the time the Soviet Union collapsed, Soviet art found itself in a deep inner crisis and on a quest. Effectively, both the New Wave and the Painterly Preserve were timely and exhaustive answers within the system to this crisis. The evolution of both schools toward a westernized "contemporary art" spared them the crisis and stagnation that befell the most conservative wing of Soviet art and which, amid the ruins of the USSR, had degenerated into pure kitsch. Opting for modernity opened up new horizons and gave an impetus to the birth of an artistic tradition, whose equal in force and integrity had, arguably, not been known since the era of the avant-garde.

Notes

1 The term "permitted art" was introduced by the Russian art critics and scholars Ekaterina Degot and Vladimir Levashov in their article "Razreshennoie iskusstvo" [Permitted art], *Iskusstvo* no. 1 (1990): 58–61.

2 The umbrella term "New Wave" for a number of phenomena in Ukrainian art of the late 1980s and early 1990s was introduced in 2009 by the curator Oksana Barshynova as the name of an exhibition dedicated to the art of the late 1980s held at the National Art Museum of Ukraine.

3 Mikhail Grobman wrote about an analogous and far more expressive movement which was to be found in the Moscow "left" wing of the Union of Artists: "Apart from avant-gardists and the 'neo-officialists,' there existed a 'Left MOSKh,' that is, the left edge of official art. The artists of the 'left MOSKh' came out of the 'Itinerant Socialist Realism' to a socialist realism of a new type, built on impressionism, expressionism and cubism. Apart from this, they found their inspiration in the reanimated Association of Artists of Revolutionary Russia, the OST and other various post-avant-garde trends of the 1930s. The 'Left MOSKh' was an eclectic and very ostentatious phenomenon and led a very sharp struggle with their socially proximate official retrograde artists who were fighting for a place in the large Soviet feeding trough." "Vtoroi russkii avantgard" [The second Russian avant-garde], *Zerkalo* 29–30 (2007).

4 The current National Academy of Fine Arts and Architecture.

5 On this subject, see also Konstantin Akinsha, "Ukraine: Art on the Ruins of the Empire" in *Permanent Revolution: Ukrainian Art Today*, exh. cat. (Budapest: Ludwig Museum, 2018), 99–103.

6 "V kontekste kartiny" [In the context of the picture] in *Turbulentnyie shliuzy* [Turbulent sluices] (Kyiv: Modern Art Research Institute, 2006), 24–31.

5 COLLECTING ERAS
A CONVERSATION

Igor Abramovych
Ukrainian curator, collector, and art consultant, Abramovych Foundation

Olena Martynyuk

Olena Martynyuk (OM):
Tell us how you started to become interested in Ukrainian art.

Igor Abramovych (IA): In the 1990s, I had a transport company in Kyiv, and because of that business and a fortuitous turn of events, I got to know the art critic Oleksandr Soloviov in 1998–1999. Since he opened up a whole new world to me, I still call him my art "godfather." Before long, I would meet artists like Oleg Tistol, Vasiliy Tsagolov, Mykola Matsenko, Oleksander Hnylytskyj, and Anatoly Kryvolap. I began to socialize with them and later became friends with many of them. Through these contacts and this dialogue, which was very valuable and fascinating, I gradually gained entry into the contemporary art world. I became incredibly passionate about this art, not even thinking that it would later be my profession. At first, I wanted to have a collection of my own. Art really inspired me, and I simply wished to see these works decorating the walls of my home. So, I started collecting smaller works but chose only what I liked.

When you start to get to know artists, you understand that they are quite different, unique people. But even if you feel closer in spirit to some than to others, you need a certain balance and consistency regarding the historical epoch and the generation of artists when you are collecting. Learning how to build a collection is something that comes gradually; at first, it was simply a question of buying the paintings I liked by certain artists. I then started traveling around the world and visiting museums, including those based on personal collections. Through this, I learned how one's love of art takes shape. It is fascinating to observe a phenomenon in its development, so I think that, in a good collection, it is possible to trace the evolution of artists, to discover the different periods of their art. I have begun to understand that assembling a collection is akin to collecting an era. After all, an artist's works are a kind of reflection of the nature of the times when they are created. And if we are talking about a time of transition, an era of transformation, like the time of perestroika, then this is twice as fascinating.

OM: **Was the information about Ukrainian art easy to come by?**

IA: From the very beginning, my main source of information was conversations with the artists themselves. Anton Solomukha and Oleksander Hnylytskyj are no longer among the living, but I remember our discussions, and as a result, I discovered a lot. I also spoke a great deal with Ukrainian art specialists, from whom I learned much of the history that had passed me by, for example Oleg Holosiy, who died so young.

Quite recently, I had the great fortune of getting to know Sergei Sviatchenko, a Ukrainian artist who has lived for many years in Denmark and is famous for his collages. But when he began his career in Ukraine at the end of the 1980s, he was simply an artist who also

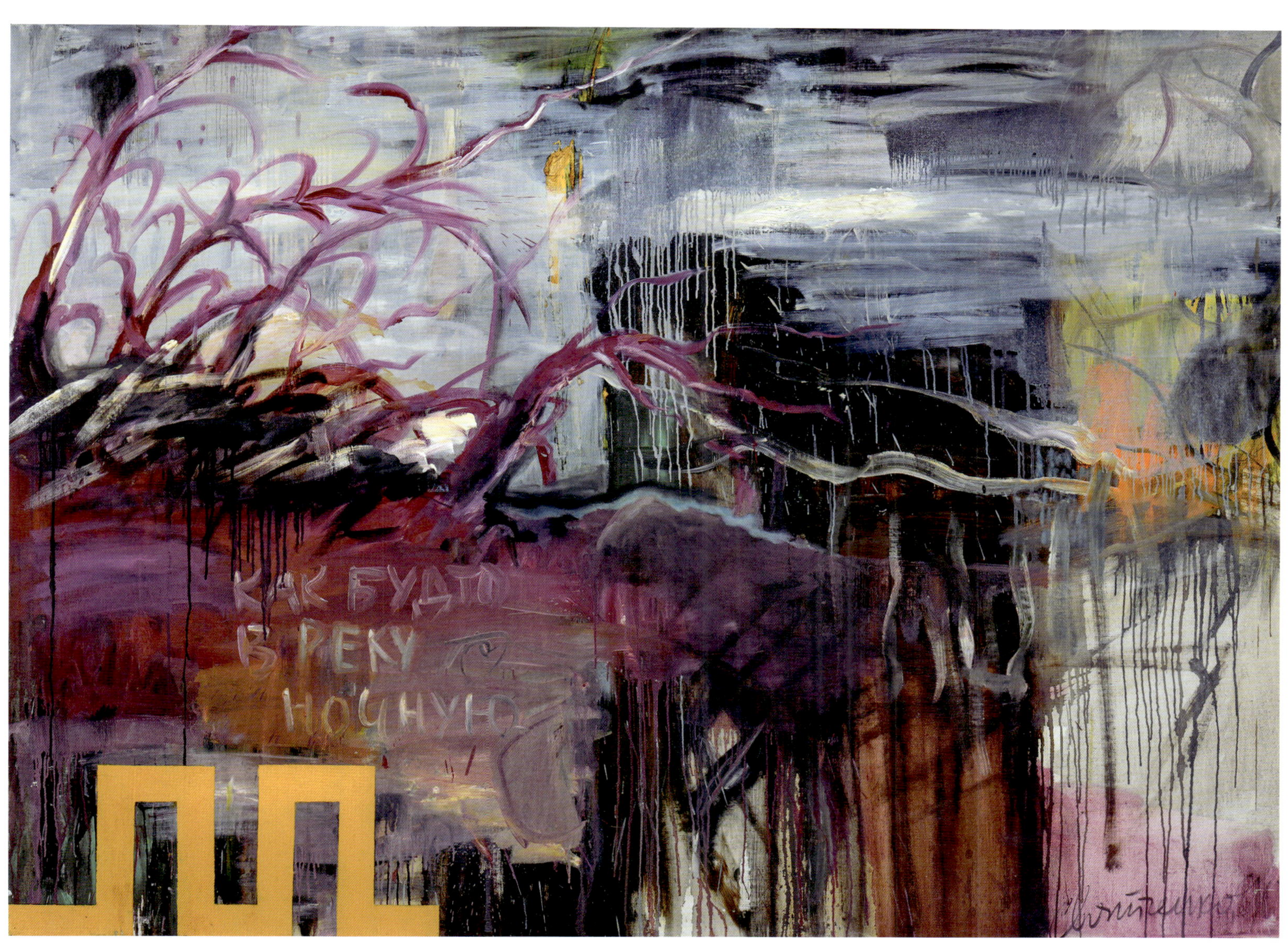

Fig. 24
SERGEI SVIATCHENKO
Like in the Night River, 1990
Oil on canvas
59⅛ × 70⅞ in. (150 × 180 cm)
Abramovych Foundation

published magazines, organized exhibitions. He has told me a lot about those momentous times and has shown me materials from his very rich archive of journals and catalogues of that period. That's how we get to fill in the jigsaw puzzle, by assembling all these pieces.

An oral history was, of course, my personal choice, but in general, the more I was professionally involved in Ukrainian art and its promotion, the more I saw that there was catastrophically little available in print, and how few historical exhibitions were held. Therefore, alongside helping to shape people's collections, I also became involved in printing, preparing major catalogues for exhibitions as well as collections of essays by art scholars such as Halyna Skliarenko. There is no museum of contemporary art in Ukraine, and there has been no systematic attempt to bring together knowledge of Ukrainian art of the independence era. Therefore, I am actively working on preserving the history of Ukrainian art, and I am very happy to learn of yet another project of the Zimmerli Art Museum, which is dedicating its second exhibition to Ukrainian art.* Thanks to such projects, this history is now being recorded and analyzed, and a foundation for future research is being created. The global cultural community has only episodic and sporadic knowledge of Ukrainian art, yet we have much to show and much to talk about.

* The exhibition *Odessa's Second Avant-Garde: City and Myth*, organized by Olena Martynyuk, was held at the Zimmerli Art Museum in 2014. —Ed.

OM: **What do you think about the generation of Ukrainian artists of the 1980s and 1990s?**

IA: I was born in 1975, so I still remember the Soviet Union well; I was among those children instructed to carry banners in the May Day parades. I was fortunate to live through an era of changes, to catch that momentous period when a new country is being built. The art of that time was involved in all those processes, reflecting this period of rupture. At that time, Western curators and collectors were phenomenally interested in Ukrainian art, as if confirming the importance of what was happening. The emergence of Ukrainian contemporary art, which bears almost the same age as our country, was such a heady, turbulent affair. We are now only about thirty years old and have managed to achieve a lot but still have much to do. It is important that Kyiv has suddenly come to life, has begun to try on its new role as the capital of the country as well as its art capital. Now it is important to continue down this path of development. I am sure that our work should go in two directions. First, it is important to support the dynamism of the current artistic process, to facilitate the participation of Ukrainian artists in more global cultural processes. And second, we must gain a thorough understanding of our heritage; after all, we still have many blind spots in our knowledge.

OM: **What do people abroad know about Ukrainian art? What kind of opinions have you come across in this regard?**

IA: I travel a lot throughout the world and come across the fact that Ukrainian art is better known for its personalities than as an integral phenomenon. That is to say, people may know individual names, for example, Oleg Tistol or Arsen Savadov, but they are not acquainted with Ukraine's cultural context. I am interested in American art and its development, that moment when America became the world art center after the Second World War. The role of people like Peggy Guggenheim is important in this respect. I believe it is strategically vital for each country to promote its art in the world, and I am honored to play a role in introducing the Kyiv New Wave period to the American audience.

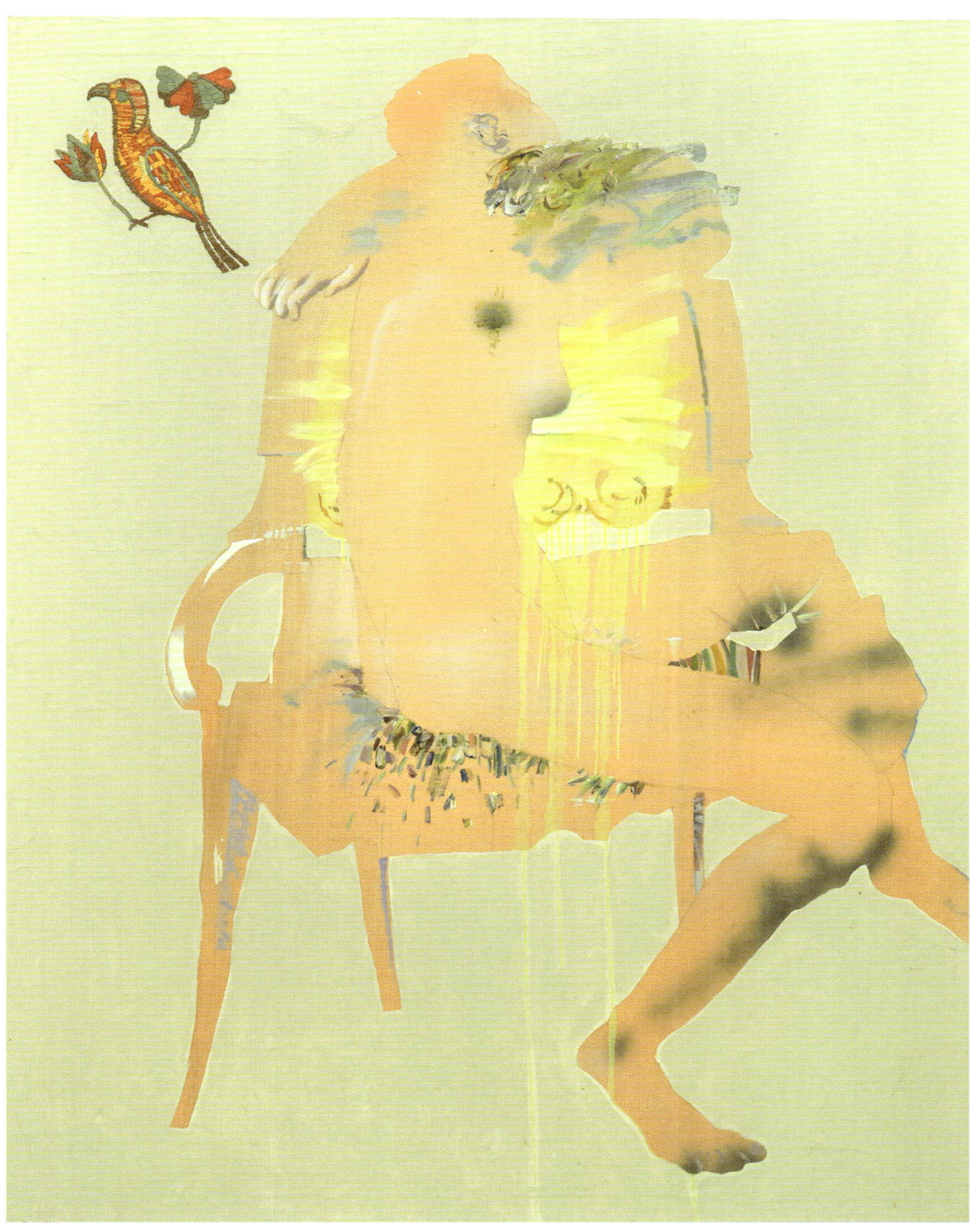

Fig. 25
MARINA SKUGAREVA
Parrot, 1992
Oil on canvas, goldwork, and embroidery
70⅞ × 55⅛ in. (180 × 140 cm)
Abramovych Foundation

Fig 27 (opposite)
OLEKSANDR HNYLYTSKYJ
Mother's Bra, 1994
Manuscript
Courtesy of the artist's family

Excerpts from a manuscript in the artist's family's collection (fig. 27). The original text is in Russian, but Hnylytskyj used the Ukrainian word for *bankruptcy*, with a difference of one letter: *bankrotstvo* and *banrkutstvo*.
—OM

Mother's Bra

Oleksander Hnylytskyj

a) Confucius and the Paris Commune

b) Collectivism and Capitalism

c) Strangulation of capitalism by the collective idea of happiness

d) The Collective Unconscious and radical individualism

e) Ketamine and Ecstasy (the individual and the collective)

f) Forward into history

g) The drowning man clutches at a guillotine

h) Better shame in plain daylight, than a solitary death

i) Interactive sex and collective masturbation

j) Children's asthenic syndrome at their parent's wedding

k) Jizzing graves

l) Aesthetic bankruptcy

m) Collective death through individual salvation

n) Individual salvation through collective death

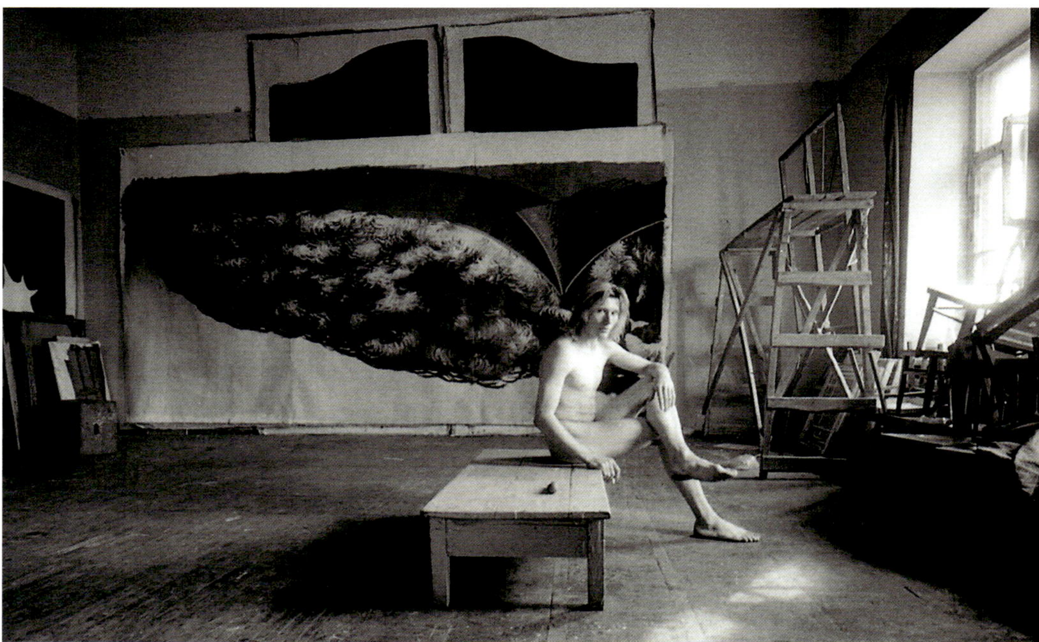

Fig. 26
VASYL RIABCHENKO (b. 1954)
Artist Oleksandr Hnylytskyj in front of his painting *Ausonia in the Abode of Paradise* in the art studio of the National Academy of Fine Art and Architecture, Kyiv, 1989. © Vasyl Riabchenko

Бюстгальтер матери.

а). Конфуций и Парижская Коммуна.
б). Коллективизм и Капитализм.
в). Удушение Капитализмом коллективной идеи счастья.
г). Коллективное бессознательное и радикальный индивидуализм.
д). Калипсол и Экстези (индивидуальное и коллективное).
е). Вперед в историю.
ж). Утопающий хватается за шлепанцы.
з). Лучше позор на виду, чем смерть водиночку.
и). Интерактивный секс и коллективная мастурбация.
к). Астенический синдром детей на свадьбе родителей.
л). Вафление могил.
м). Эстетическое банкротство.
н). Коллективная смерть через индивидуальное спасение.
о). Индивидуальное спасение через коллективную смерть.

Живое существо с коллективным сознанием (человек, муравей, пчела, рыба, лошадь и др.) всегда смотрит на свой долг перед коллективом через вуаль некоторого противопоставления и даже презрения к себе подобным, иногда доходящего до ненависти. Немного поразмыслив над этим феноменом, нельзя не понять, что это всего лишь часть программы, заложенной в индивидуум тем же ненавидимым им коллективом, из которого последний (т.е. коллектив) всего лишь хладнокровно извлекает свою пользу (Вспомним таких отъявленных индивидуалистов, как лорд Байрон, Элвис Пресли, Иван Грозный или последние тираны). Коллектив просто использует их энергию, провоцируя безудержный индивидуализм. По этому поводу очень интересно наблюдать феномены взаимоотношений коллектива творческих индивидуальностей на примере группы художников, объединенных адресом „Парижская коммуна. 18 а".

① Наблюдаемые индивидуумы объединены возрастом, сферой деятельности, средой обитания, поиском рынка для продуктов своей деятельности, экономически сходного „уровня" жизни, сексуальным партнерством, некогда существовавшим и мало чем отличавшимся

② от других групп одной возрастной категории и имевшим традиционный характер (молодецкие „блядования" с последующими женитьбами без смешения полов и прочих содомий, столь модных в современных субкультурах).

Мы не говорим сейчас об искусстве (как вы и заметили), мы пытаемся на фоне разрушения общей социальной структуры, условно именуемой „социализмом", наблюдать и анализировать существование, а, может быть, и распад небольшой группы людей, искусственно создавших себе нишу в уходящем мире коллективного счастья или коллективного безумия. Люди, которые периодически сходились и расходились во времени, как атомы, и все же продолжающие иметь какие-то общие точки соприкосновения, заставляющие их отталкиваться друг от друга, и подсознательно ищущие сходства, которое заставляет их искать какие-то новые, но все же общие сферы обитания. Или, наоборот, подсознательно отталкивающиеся и сознательно ищущие частную выгоду от общего существования, что в общем-то тоже заставляет искать и находить внутреннее родство. Ломая голову в самоидентификации и бросаясь вновь в кошмар коллективного безумия поиска и ненахождения истины и вновь скрываясь в несладкое одиночество внутричерепья, в котором нет спасения от коллективного одиночества, я надеюсь в который раз выйти из водоворота раскрытых черепов и слившихся мозговых масс светлым, и радостным, и осознающим неповторимость своей резьбы винтиком, тающим от радости в мощи и блеске энергии творящей неведомый маразм машины. Так страшно противостоять ржавчине на обочине жизни. Так же, как таять терминатором в общей стали. О, Путь, дай увидеть себя, чтобы познать Великое Между. Именно там, — „между", я смогу балансировать, извлекая радость из иллюзии, любуясь прекрасной голограммой перекрещивающихся и сплетающихся энергий и индивидуальных представлений о неуловимом „нечто", представляя которое каждый отдельный блистает своим фамильным перстнем, осознавая недостижимость иллюстрирования себя несущими печать тщеты инструментами общего соития. Боль, радость и пустота сопутствуют каждой новой попытке объяснить свою непостижимость другим, делающим в тот же момент то же самое, и все же роднящим души тем, которые подозревают в другом то же количество

③ Невысказанного и похороненного навсегда за крепкими мясными оболочками. Тихое мясное братство. Гулкое эхо грудных клеток, звенящих в унисон на одной частоте, печально звенит в закатном эфире, созывая рожденных настроенными на одну частоту и электризуя пространство гнетущим томлением. Так рождаются революции. Революции, которые, свершаясь, разрушают иллюзии, разрушают надежды на существование идеи в реальности. Мы знаем это на себе, мы — жертвы последней реализованной иллюзии. Как скоро человечество создаст новую иллюзию о счастье, оправясь от горечи невозможности существования последней. Дети Парижской Коммуны, ваша сперма отравлена безверием, ваша сперма бесплодна. Дети Парижской Коммуны, вы не знаете счастья тела, ибо ваш дух устремлен в пустоту. Вы — честные азиаты, исполнившие светскую шутку европейцев, воплотившие галантный флирт Просвещения в кровавые роды Революции, принявшие из своего чрева и пережившие смердящее разложение переноска, смрад от гниения которого физически разит ноздри мозга. Как и куда двигаться, если ноги увязли в гниющем теле прекрасной идеи? Солнце капитализма, иссуши труп своего ребенка — Великой Революции. Коридоры времени, похожие на колбасы желудка, перекачивающие дерьмо вчерашнего пира. Время, выдави из себя сладкий кал на грядки новых идей в раю цветов и танцующих кришнаитов. А?

5. 5. 94.
Гнилицкий А.

It's fascinating to observe how a collective of creative individuals interact, for example, the group of artists gathered at the address "Paris Commune 18A." . . .

Now, as you have noticed, we are not talking about art; we are attempting to observe and analyze existence against the background of the collapse of the general social structure conventionally referred to as "socialism," and maybe the collapse of a small group of people, who artificially created their niche in the retreating world of collective happiness or collective madness. . . .

Racking one's brains over self-identification and rushing back once more to the nightmare of collective madness in a futile search for the truth, once again hidden in bitter solitude within a skull in which there is no salvation from collective solitude, I hope yet again to emerge bright and joyful from the maelstrom of skulls laid bare amalgamated into a brainy mass, to emerge as a cog aware of the uniqueness of my thread, melting with joy from the power and brilliance of the machine's energy creating that uncharted insanity. . . .

Pain, joy, and the void accompany each new attempt to explain one's inscrutability to another, who in turn is doing so to another, and so bringing together souls suspecting in the other that same quantity of the unexpressed which is buried forever behind their robust meaty casing. A quiet brotherhood of the flesh. The reverberant echo of the chest, ringing in unison on a single frequency, ruefully ringing in the sunset ether, convokes those born tuned in to a single frequency and electrifying the space with an oppressive weariness. This is how revolutions are born.

Revolutions that come into being destroy illusions, destroy hopes of the existence of ideas in reality. We know this in our experience, we, the victims of the last realized illusions. But soon humankind will create a new illusion about happiness, recovering from the bitterness of the impossibility of the existence of the latter. Children of the Paris Commune, your sperm is poisoned by disbelief, your sperm is sterile. You do not know the joy of the body for your spirit is drawn toward the void. You, honest Asians, enacting the secular joke of the Europeans, materializing embodying the gallant flirt of the Enlightenment in the bloody birth pangs of the Revolution, delivering from its womb and living through the stinking birth of the overdue child, reeking of its rotting stench in the nostrils of the brain.

How and where to move, if the legs were stuck in the rotting body of a fine idea? Let the sun of capitalism dry the corpse of its child—the Great Revolution. Corridors of time, like a stomach's sausages, pumping the shit out of last night's feast. Time, squeeze from yourself the sweet feces onto the flowerbeds of new ideas in that paradise in bloom with its dancing Hare Krishnas. Huh?

Translated from *Dekorativnoe Iskusstvo SSSR* 385, no. 12 (1989), p. 26.

Oliva Seed[1]

Oleksander Hnylytskyj

Left undisturbed, O lovely lamp, you still adorn, . . .
The ceiling of this near-forgotten festal room.
Eduard Mörike[2]

The fruitless search for meaning rendered my brain a quavering jelly.

It's amorphous. Any tingling or spontaneously arising crackling ferment is liable, in itself, to spark a shift and may pull anywhere. It's a disease. Pre-sentient and pre-volitional. Now that it's liquefied to putrefaction, it needs, my brain, a cold steel needle. I'm the desire for pain. I'm the desire to be a needle paralyzing my brain's exhausted consciousness, to pierce and terminate that sorry quivering. I am entirely the desire for the cold point on my skull the spike will drive through, so that my brain-turned-spear will flow, taking

the absolute as its own essence.

In my desire, too, I seek my losses. When my skull, filled like a sponge with blood, gets hard, I'll be the first to take the word to bed and be the lord of the first night. But lo—the spasm's losing steam. I'm cooling off, relaxing soft. I'm vitally weak. O hordes of wondrous Amazons. I guess I only have the pain of others for suffering through

my festering postmodern

age.

Irony: I lay this tired weeping at your feet

Our art is truly agricultural labor striving outward. One day, chasing the lure of virgin soil it'll lie down in the sands, exhausted, Macedonian, in anticipation of itself. And that's where I come in here like a dried-up oriental spore and drive myself into the soil that's tired of Alexander.

In my desire, too, I seek my losses but desire's limited. Orgasm is the death of passion. Reborn and once more passing through the Bardo,[3] I regain desire and so maintain the game of leapfrog with my lower half.

Irony: I lay this tired weeping at your feet, but seek the truth

It (art) cannot and will no longer speak to anyone. It's fallen dumb and mute. What do I do, its father and its son? All I have left is to preserve myself or at the very least press on. Where are you, heaven, answer, break the silence. O world, you're ugly and perverse, where is the truth?

Socrates, I have understood, in our time, I believe in sophism more than I do in myth. Sophism, Socrates, is myth's Aesopian language, my heaven in this hell, my peace in death.

Notes

1 Hnylytskyj initiates the wordplay using the Russian word *semia,* which means both "seed" and "semen." Thus, he was referring to the ideas of the Italian art critic Achille Bonito Oliva, who coined the term *transavantgarde*, which was used to describe work of Hnylytskyj and his generation of Ukrainian artists. "Oliva" also suggests the olive tree, hinting at the influence of Italian ideas, which grow like seeds in Ukrainian soil. —OM

2 Translated by Norah K. Cruickshank and Gilbert F. Cunningham.

3 *Bardo* (Tibetan བར་དོ Wylie: bar do) or *antarabhāva* (Sanskrit) is an intermediate, transitional, or liminal state between death and rebirth. —Trans.

From the catalogue of the exhibition *Babylon*, organized by Marat Guelman, held at the Moscow Palace of Youth in 1990, p. 5.

A Resolute Edge of National Post-Eclecticism

Oleg Tistol and Kostiantyn Reunov

Just like every new generation, we strive to create something new, and we see this novelty in a qualitatively different level of pictorial media along with its citationality and, to a large extent, in the layered eclecticism of the modern and classical arts, provided they are mainly based on classical modes of expression. In this regard, it is important to decipher the notion of the "Struggle for the Beauty of the Stereotype." By pitting different cultural stereotypes against each other as the most vivid conceptualization of what is "beautiful" in a dispute about beauty, we strive to grasp and, perhaps, to create a qualitatively new stereotype. A stereotype as a taut value system of a new vision and, correspondingly, of a new art. On the one hand, each artist works with classical culture and, on the other, he rediscovers this classical culture, brings to it new elements, forms, modes of expression, molding new visions.

In our view, now is the time requiring a certain breakthrough into a new layer of culture, a new layer of artistic consciousness. Through super-complexity we pass into a qualitatively new simplicity. It is possible that such a breakthrough can occur in Soviet art. Our art is characterized today by a movement toward liberation; in part, it is a mechanical forward movement. Along with the fact that some individual artists find themselves at the level of universal human culture, and assuming that they are engaged in this general movement toward freedom, the probability of breaking up the current value system, existing cultural stereotypes, is very high.

With slight editorial corrections approved by the artists, the text is reprinted from the catalogue of the exhibition *Kyiv Art Meeting*, Alipiy Gallery, Kyiv, Ukraine, September 3–19, 1995. The show included artists from Ukraine, Russia, and Poland.

The National Culture

Mykola Matsenko and Oleg Tistol (NATSPROM)

We consider our program of creating a micro-model of Ukrainian culture within European and global contexts to be well timed. The final task of every artistic process is devising a prominent stereotype, which consequently turns into a symbol of beauty (struggle for the beauty of a stereotype).

One of the main stereotypes for each national culture is the design of its currency banknotes, namely, its monetary symbols. Irrespective of their artistic or production value, money is the most widespread artistic creation.

Nearly all turning points in the history of Ukraine are connected with the act of unification:

Pereyaslav Treaty, 1654 (Ukraine + Russia)
Battle of Poltava, 1709 (Ukraine + Sweden)
Soviet occupation of Poland, September 17, 1939
(Eastern Ukraine + Western Ukraine)

Therefore, the topic of unification is prevailing in our project for the design of Ukrainian money, on which we have been working since 1984.

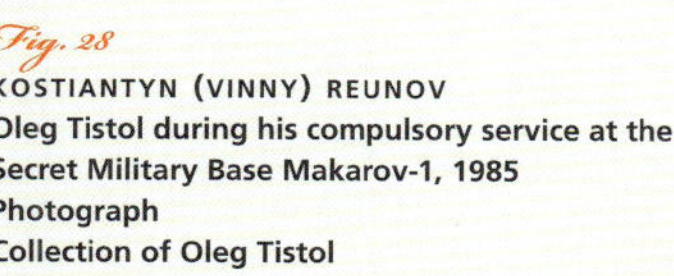

Fig. 28
KOSTIANTYN (VINNY) REUNOV
Oleg Tistol during his compulsory service at the Secret Military Base Makarov-1, 1985
Photograph
Collection of Oleg Tistol

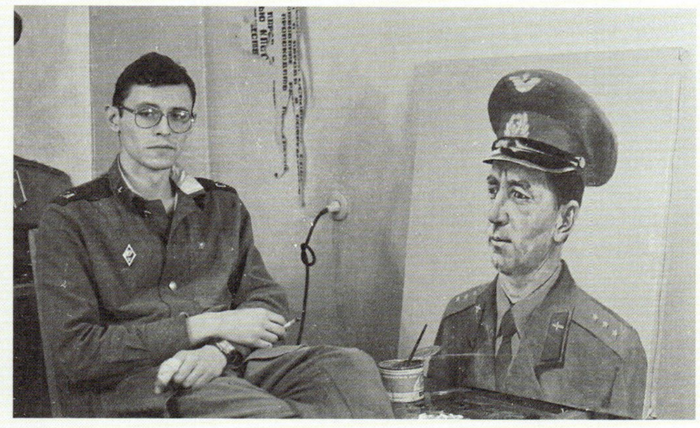

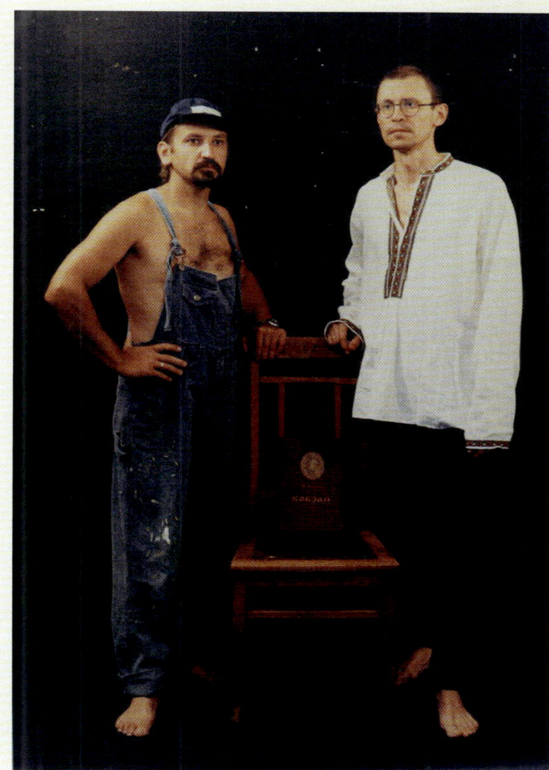

Fig. 30
MYKOLA MATSENKO and OLEG TISTOL (NATSPROM)
Untitled photograph, 2000
From the NATSPROM Collection

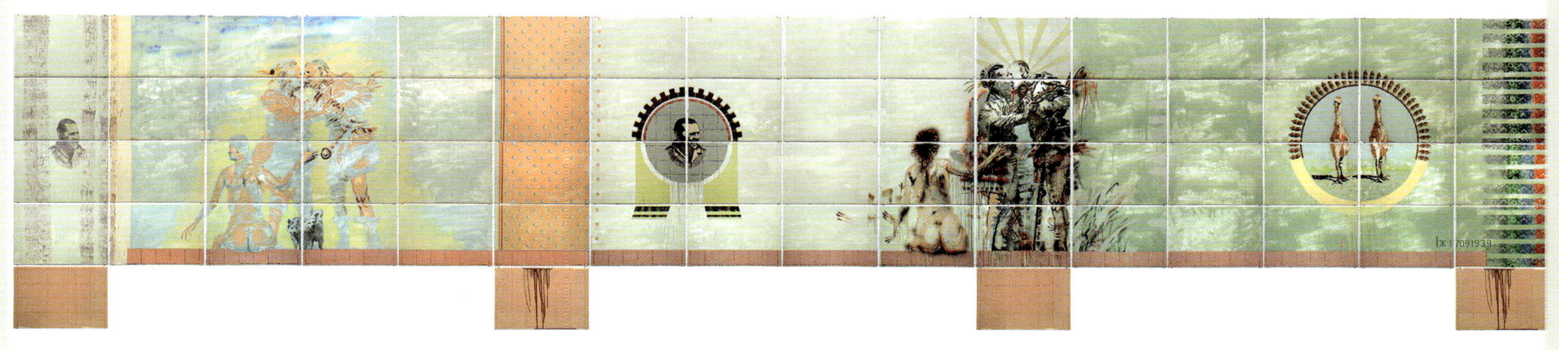

Fig. 29
MYKOLA MATSENKO and OLEG TISTOL (NATSPROM)
September 17, 1939, from the *Museum of Ukraine* series, 1994
Oil on paper
10 ft., 5 in. × 52 ft., 5⅞ in. (320 × 1600 cm)
From the NATSPROM Collection

History

Born and formed as a nation with active help from Genghis Khan and raised among the Sobeskys and the Osmans, the Piłsudskis and the Atatürks, we have mastered the great "lore of defeat."

The Ukrainian mindset suggests a principally different method of achieving victory, in contrast to the one practiced by the general Aleksandr Suvorov and the like.

On a regular basis, our neighbors (perhaps, except for the Ottoman Empire) failed to recognize the Ukrainian culture or ethnicity in general as existing. Nevertheless, the Ukrainian territory now covers nearly all the regions where Ukrainians historically settled.

The conversations between the art critic Oleksandr Soloviov and young artists took place in Kyiv in 1989 during the all-republican Youth Exhibition.

This excerpt is from the personal archive of Oleksandr Soloviov, published with the assistance of Research Platform of the PinchukArtCentre on korydor.in.ua.

A Conversation Between
Oleksandr Soloviov and Georgii Senchenko, 1989

Oleksandr Soloviov (OS): *People are saying that the postmodern is undergoing a crisis. In an era that has already been called one of "fundamental indifference," reality itself realizes a reduction of the semiotic system that always seemed to be the main priority of postmodern art. It would be curious to know what Georgii Senchenko feels about this "situation"?*

Georgii Senchenko (GS): I think that the artist's relativism today is connected not so much with an ontological (and much less with a social) perspective as with an anthropological one. Correspondingly, also the citationality of the situation seems to me a consequence not so much of a desire to display objective, socially significant statuses and the context of the citation as much as acknowledging the symbolic nature of experiencing the outside world. Hence the lack of distinction between actual citations of language and the citations of substance, from the world, as it were, of facts and objects and the definition of the above as the phenomenal world, capable of reflecting that particular type of trans-subjective reality that latently pertains to the subject itself and constitutes the very focus of our existence.

OS: *Yet another "illusion of subjectivity"?*

GS: Anticipating some skepticism, I have a quotation (there's no getting out of it!) from the *Tibetan Book of the Dead:* "recognizing the voidness of thine own intellect to be Buddhahood and knowing it at the same time to be thine own consciousness."

OS: *You know, conversations about the void have already become, it seems, a commonplace in today's cultural situation.*

GS: I always prefer to keep my silence for this reason; yes, in fact, to keep my silence in general. As is well known, those who always speak never say anything; those who are always silent never leave anything unsaid.

OS: *Nonetheless, recently, you haven't often been repeating those maxims like "A great artist doesn't paint pictures."*

GS: Yes, I don't have any more illusions about my greatness.

OS: *And what about, let's say, the secret of* Sacred Landscape [1988; cat. 33]. *Is it not connected with just this display of self-denial? Or is it rather connected with when reproducing this work one discovers that one's original meaning has become metaphoric?*

GS: Indeed, the classical deconstructivist task is not resolved here by the traditional path of establishing a new boundary of meanings through the destruction of the existing one. Rather, I was possessed by a desire to test the very borders of existence through describing their meaning. At the cost of identifying the limits of experience, one needed to feel the birth of a constantly enduring moment of transgressive transition into the "other," the cyclical nature of which is associated with the doomed-like nature of discursive attempts: through the simulation of the author and the profanation of the visual gesture, the self-removal of the image; onward to the very source of the expressive act, to that nonobjectified reality where, strictly, all discursive possibilities break down, there, where such less reliable values such as fortitude, taste and risk, a noble trust in nobility, come into force.

Published in *Dekorativnoe Iskusstvo SSSR* 385, no. 12 (1989), p. 21.

Apocrypha

Arsen Savadov and Georgii Senchenko

And harkening Being, we turned to essence, but didn't know that everything was moving toward the Name. Putting our faith in motion, we destroyed the essence and condemned ourselves to the sin of omission. We tried to deplete Nothingness, but were afraid of the return. Afraid, we made a sacrifice so as to call on Will, but Will was tempting Fate. Accepting the Ceryneian roses, we rejoiced of their perfume, there was no limit to our joy, and then they called on flight and were assured that they were free but something slipped away eternally. We came to what was lost but found the meanings void. We gave our praise unto the void but then, the roses had already faded. We repented . . . And it snowed . . . And it was said, "Appear no matter what thou who'll subdue (with good intentions) whosoever who no matter what."

April 1990
From the catalogue of the exhibition *Oleg Holosiy: Introduction* at the Ridzhina Art Gallery, Moscow, 1991.

The Great Ancestor of All Being

Oleg Holosiy

Stepping out on the early side, let's take a stroll straight past the blind alleys and the dead ends. Minding the usefulness of the useless, we go. Barking dogs, cawing crows, sleet and lack, yet these boots fit, more or less.

If the boot fits, oh yes, you can take your mind off the foot.

The great gray luminary won't let you forget the eternal. Clouds in neat little rows. It's chilly. The clock of the heart that tells you to live says it's almost dinner. Day and night alternate, nobody knows how it started. Don't let them into your heart. Or else you will never see the great horned cat in the white apples. She's very close—just strain your ears, you will hear rustling in the distant bushes. Just don't get scared, she'll realize instantly, and then death will be the least of your punishment. Blessed is he who has known the great fear—therein lies uninhibitedness. Don't turn around, she's right behind you. Fate ripens like a catastrophic drop. It ripens in the yard. It ripens in the bushes. In the damp brush. Day and night alternate, nobody knows how it started. To calm the quivering of your watery members. Not think about where to knock. It's basically laid out for us. It won't even consider chiding us. The great ancestor of all being. A sinking feeling. That's the blood being sucked. It's dinnertime. Where the hell is that sink. Just don't fall into existentialism. You couldn't think of a worse present to give yourself. Better think. And breathe deeper. Consolidated consciousness isn't being-ated. And vice versa. Probably. They slowly move aside, like your own leaves lost to the sway, like the lines on your hand. We allow ourselves to declare adult discourse spent. The first steps have been taken. But if he doesn't improve upon what was granted by life, how can he be called a man? Firmness and whitewash. Day and night alternate and you don't know where it will end. To follow that which is such in itself. Night's soon. They say it has blue eyes. At night, they shine like halogen they say. Just don't let it be getting hit in the head with a stick. We allow ourselves to declare daytime discourse spent. It's cold at night. They say the forest is about to end now any minute, but it keeps getting thicker. They say it will get thicker and thicker until it is impassible. And then—bam—the desert. Just don't look back. The branches crack underfoot like white bones. Eagle-owls hooting. Too late to turn back. Besides, there is nothing back there. But what about that wild cat? Living without why and what for, in an oblivion of honest expression. The great ancestor of all existence. Day and night alternate, nobody knows how it started. They slowly move aside, like your own leaves lost to the sway, like the lines on your hand. We allow ourselves to declare mystical discourse spent. It's a gray, brainless day in 1990.

Minding the usefulness of the useless, we go. The fruitfulness of reality. The vivid specter of plurality. Non-space is the seed of space, stillness—the seed of motion, shadow—of light. The breathing of a single body. We know that around the bend, it's a dead end, we will not go there. What if we skip it. It's drizzling. Cat's tears. Why are you crying, little one? Everything will be all right.

We'll get an early start and we'll go.

On the early side, straight past . . .

From the catalogue of the exhibition *Zhyvopysny Zapovidnyk*, Ukrayinsky Dim (Ukrainian House), Kyiv, 1995.

On Color

Tiberiy Silvashi

I do not wish to express, to interpret, for this is an outrage.

Let color freely reveal its nature through me.

My ego should vanish and melt into color.

Translated and abridged from *Dekorativnoe Iskusstvo SSSR* 385, no. 12 (1989), p. 23.

Kyiv as a Cultural Model

Sergei Anufriev

Arriving in Kyiv, I immediately became aware of the strong resemblance that this city had with Rome. The architecture itself prompted me to make this comparison. Then, upon seeing the endless hills and the vistas opening out before me, I came up with the idea that the elevated terrain was the key trait of this city. The "relief-like structure" of the landscape is transmitted to the design of buildings, imparting an improbable, very mundane, and at the same time, vehement, splendor to all the décor of Kyiv life and to all the lush and fleshy manifestations of Kyiv mentality. It is a kind of vital Baroque mentality.

If the first main attribute of this city is its Baroque nature, then another is its recreational side.

Strolling through the city with residents of Kyiv, I noted that their city, unlike Moscow or, let's say, Odessa, is far more segmented by the green spaces of parks where very beautiful paths are adapted for walking and comfortable benches have been built. One can always look around and admire the stunning views. The trees look as if they have been planted expressly for this purpose. The fountains, slopes, and ascents have all been arranged so that a strolling sojourn here will involve no exertion.

Walking around the city, a person experiences no hideous tension. And walking through fraught spaces, he is able to behold their splendor and magnificence, not forgetting that there are recreational possibilities nearby. While at work, a person knows that he still holds a voucher for a sanatorium.

Kyiv provides opportunities of this kind in abundance; their presence allows this city to exist in a rich and life-affirming way. At present, effectively it is the only large city of ours to endure. In this regard one can say that Kyiv is the most exact model not of that culture which exists but that speculative culture which one would like to represent a more civilized culture. That city as culture in which a person feels both tense (sensing a way through its system of signs) and cultured, meanwhile having the opportunity to glance around and behold not the terrain but the smooth, calm foliage and a path stretching out into the distance upon which he will never stumble.

Translated and abridged from *Dekorativnoe Iskusstvo SSSR* 385, no. 12 (1989), pp. 24–26.

On the Intimate in Art

Oleksandr Roitburd and Mikhail Rashkovetsky

In the Eastern Slavonic mini-cosmos, Ukraine embodies the idea of the South. Hence the mythologeme of Ukrainian nature as luxuriant, excessively abundant (one cannot hear such utterances as "Russia! Oh Russia, destitute and poor!" here). If in the Great Russian state cultural consciousness of the mid-twentieth century, the myth of abundance is subservient to the cult of labor, then in the Ukrainian mythologeme abundance dominates: abundance is not seen so much as a reward but as a generous gift sent down from the heavens. This is consistent with Confucian tradition. "Diligence yields a little wealth, great wealth is sent

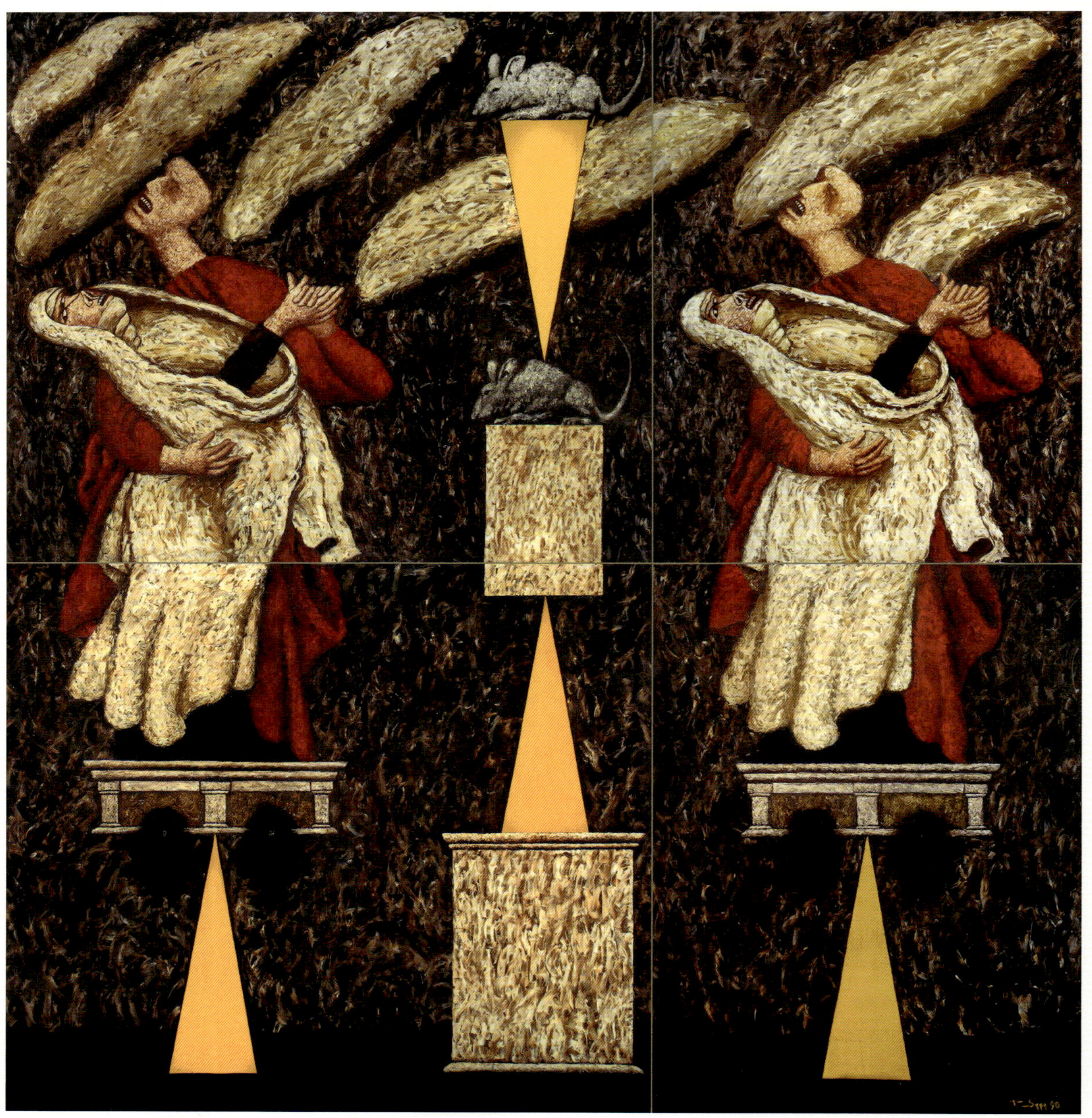

Fig. 31
OLEKSANDR ROITBURD
Altar, 1990
Oil on canvas
155⅞ × 147¼ in. (396 × 374 cm)
Collection of the artist

from Heaven." In the Zhou mindset, one can encounter the concept of "Tsi siu"—merciful, noble endowment. . . . "Tsi" and the sublime presence of "siu" calmly linger in the field of vitality, emanating from the fertile Ukrainian land, thus forming a certain ethereal body—"Vitaliya." The constant characteristics of the fundamental realities of Ukraine (azure, lush, sunny, luxurious, mellifluous; maidens dark-eyed and lovely) offer us the opportunity to read the term "vitality" (V-Itality) as an "Eastern Slavonic Italianness."

The parallel between Ukraine and Italy can be considered on many levels. For example, on a historical and ethnographic level, pointing to the structural similarities of the cosmological arrangement of Kyiv and Rome, located, as is known, on seven hills: or, indeed, comparing the heroic ideals of Republican Rome and the Zaporizhian Sich, which Fredrich Engels described as a "peculiar Cossack Republic."

> What of those needy Romans!
> What the hell—not Brutuses!
> We have our Brutuses! And Cocleses!
> Glorious, not forgotten!
> *Taras Shevchenko*[1]

However, Italy's soul is weighed down with grieving for its lost Golden Age, for its lost ancient grandeur. Ukraine, unacquainted with such a splendid imperial past, yearns for the very possibility of such a longing. This longing is fine, as an unassuaged yearning for love, but its object is elusive. Thus, Ukraine thinks of itself in the role of an elusive "Heavenly Italy" as distinct from the earth as the Heavenly Jerusalem is from reality. . . .

The spirit of Heavenly Italy is unfettered by the servitude of the "settling of meanings," but is consumed by a yearning for the very possibility of longing, one not inducing a schizophrenic expansion of consciousness with subsequent reflection and structure formation (P. Pepperstein)[2] but a mental obfuscation, and in its wake—a total poetic madness. . . .

Therefore, in an ideal scenario there would arise a certain hollow model, cold and resonant, spirited and, at the same time, as it were, inanimate. Yet only ideally. In actual fact, the fertile heavenly soil brings about an inevitable germination (in the gaps between the elements of the hollow carcass) animated, or rather, animating the following: tenderness, a certain appeal, youthful eroticism, a sweet beckoning voice and so on, which, with a certain fraction of error, could be described as the "intimacy complex."

The existence of these characterizes the art of the younger branch of the Ukrainian Transavantgarde, sometimes defined as the "new tender ones." In other words, we are talking about a curious "Transavantgarde with a human face."

Notes

1 Translated by Peter Fedynsky.
2 Pavel Pepperstein (b. 1966). Moscow conceptualist who founded the group Inspection Medical Hermeutics in 1987, along with the Odessa artists Yuri Leiderman and Sergei Anufriev.

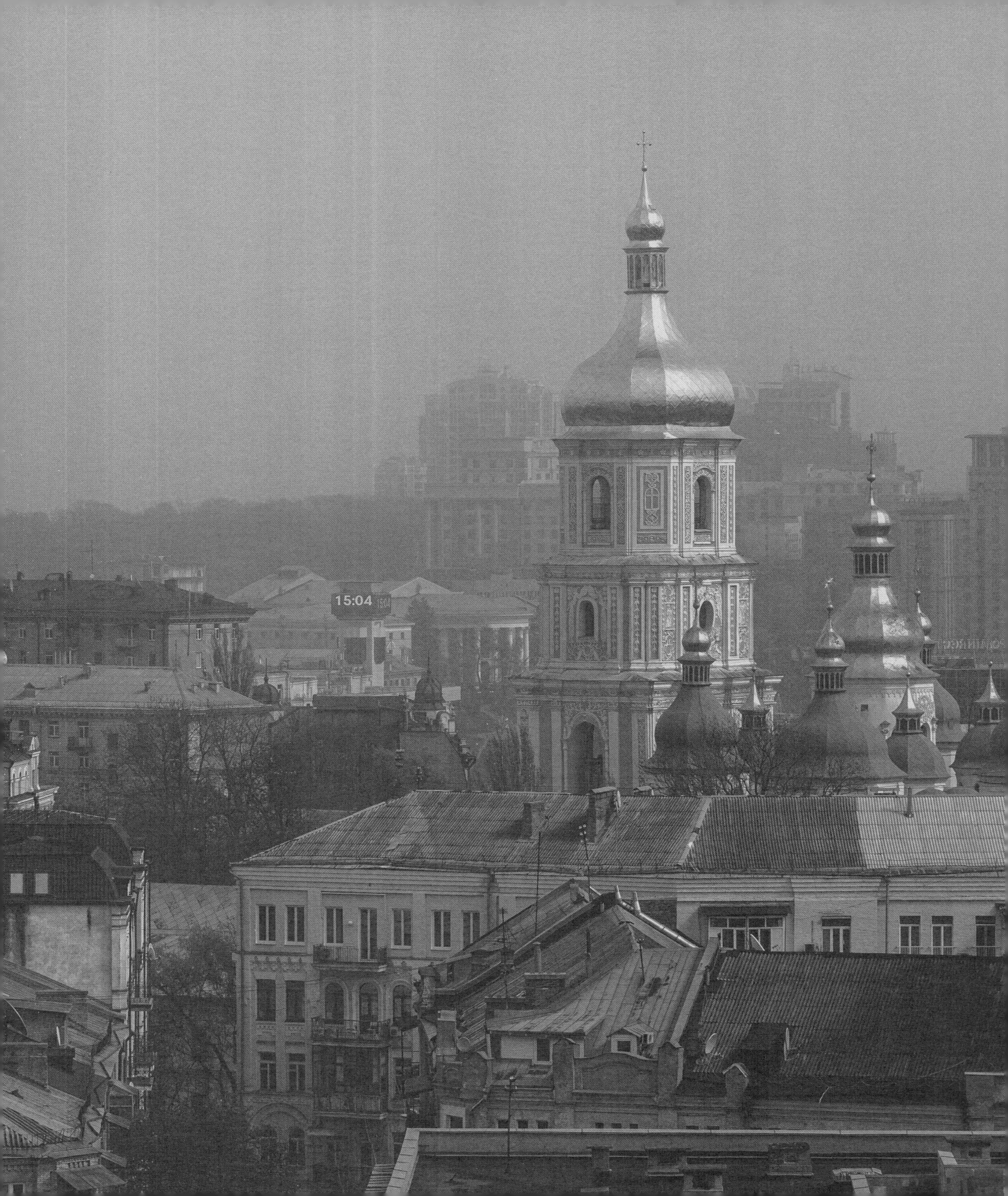
15:04

Plates

Oleksandr Babak (b. 1957)

Untitled, undated | Oil on canvas | 74½ × 37⅜ in. (189.3 × 95 cm)

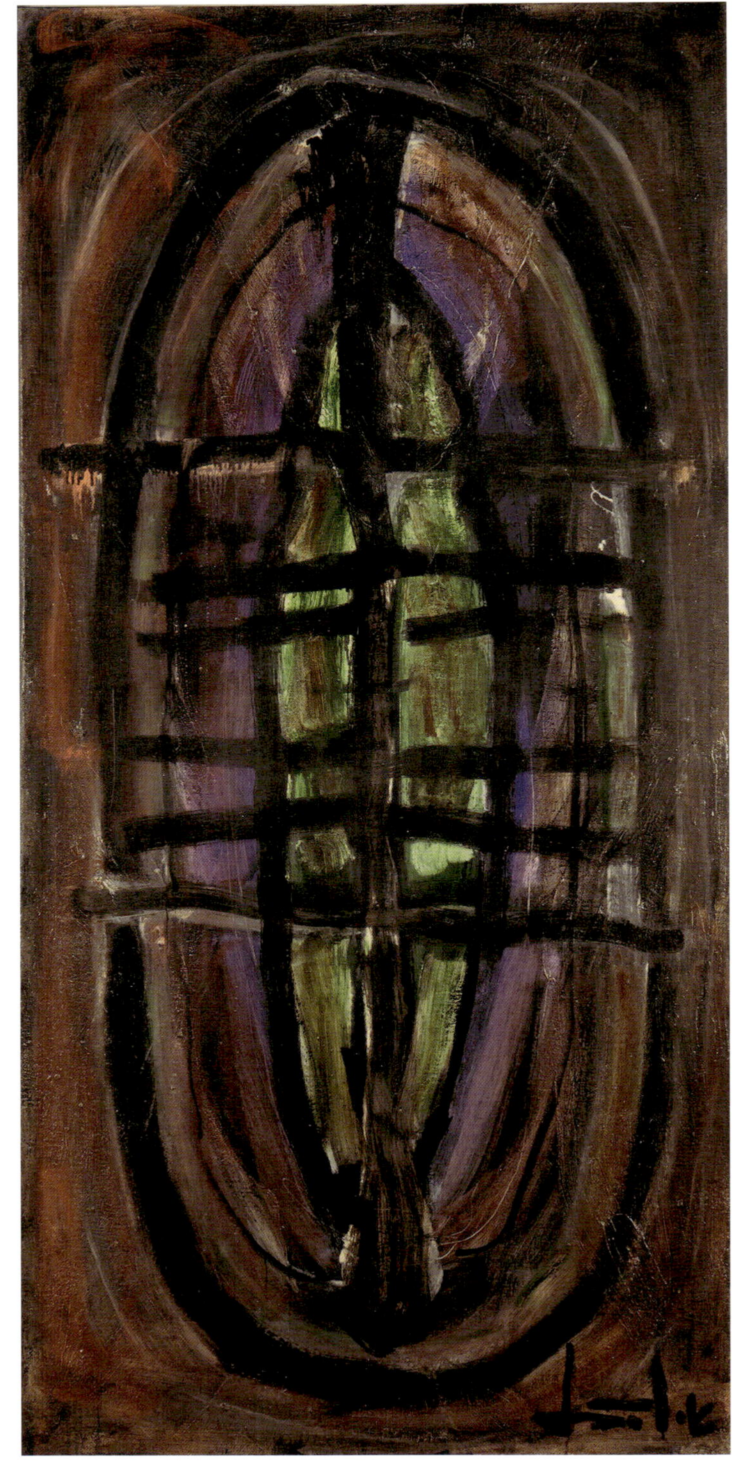

2 **Oleksandr Babak** (b. 1957)

Untitled, undated | Oil on canvas | 74½ × 37⅜ in. (189.3 × 95 cm)

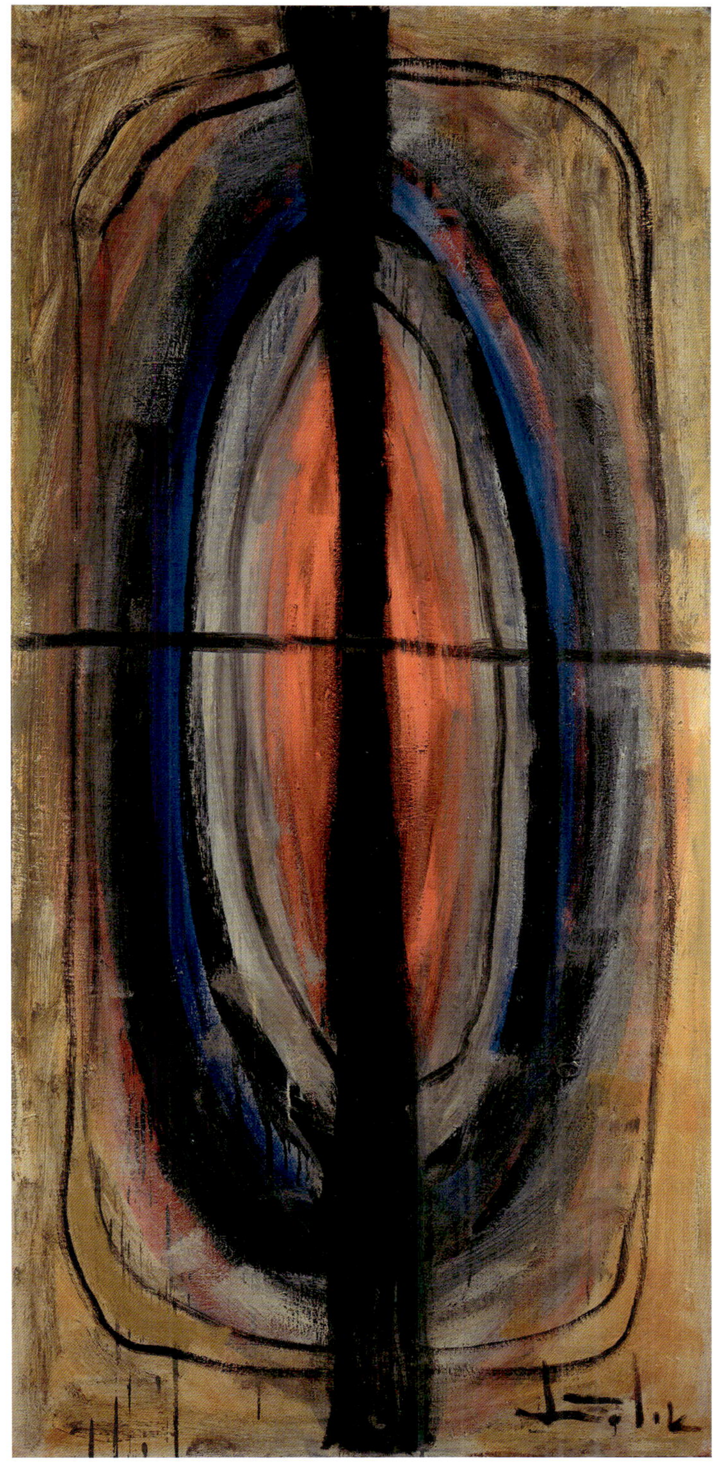

3 **Volodymyr Budnikov** (b. 1947)

The Game, 1985 | Oil on canvas | 39$\frac{1}{16}$ × 35$\frac{7}{16}$ in. (99.2 × 90 cm)

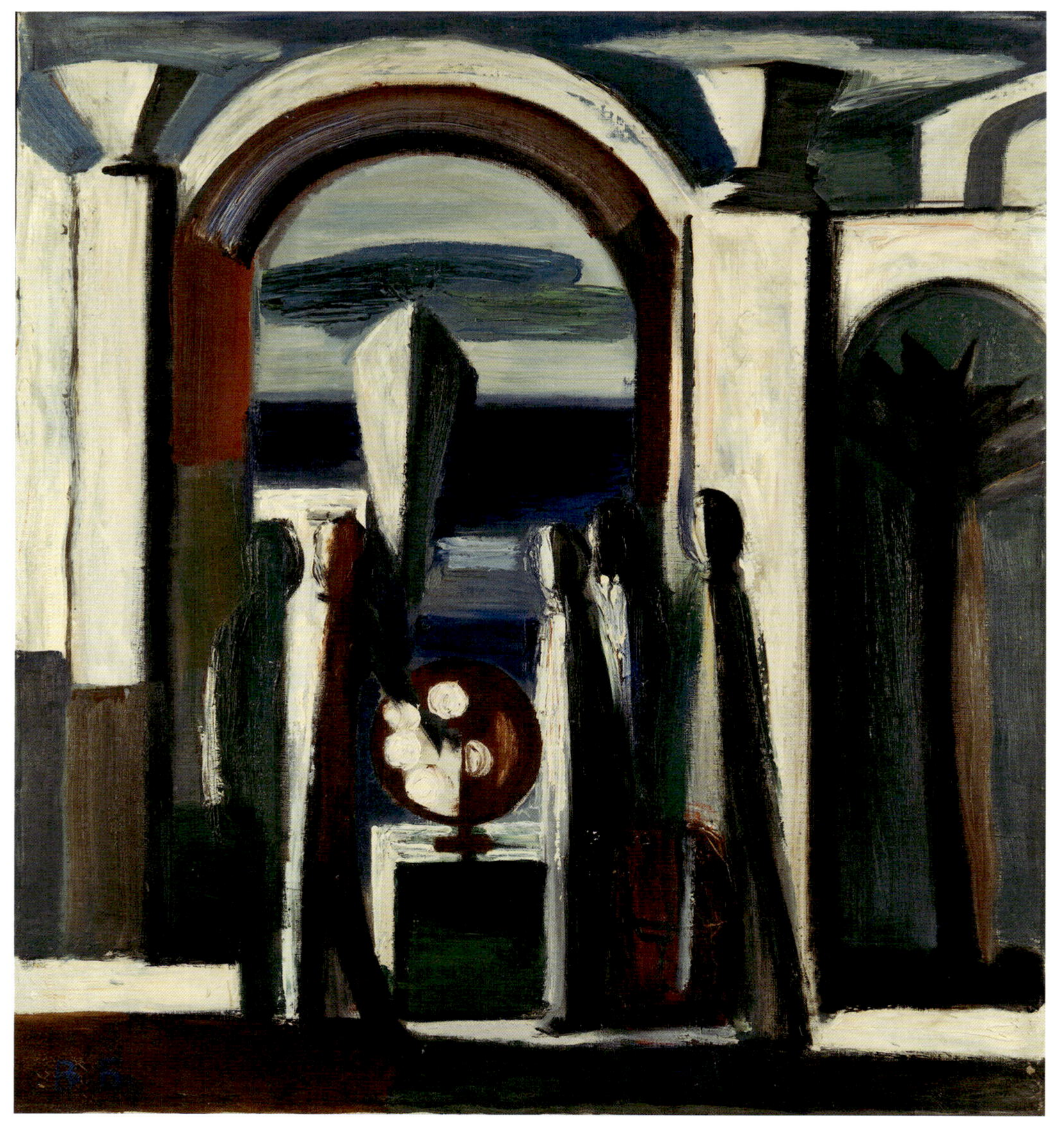

4 **Yana Bystrova** (b. 1966)

The Deity of Chill During Her Crimean Stay, 1989 | Oil on canvas | 47¼ × 78¾ in. (120 × 200 cm)

PRIVATE COLLECTION

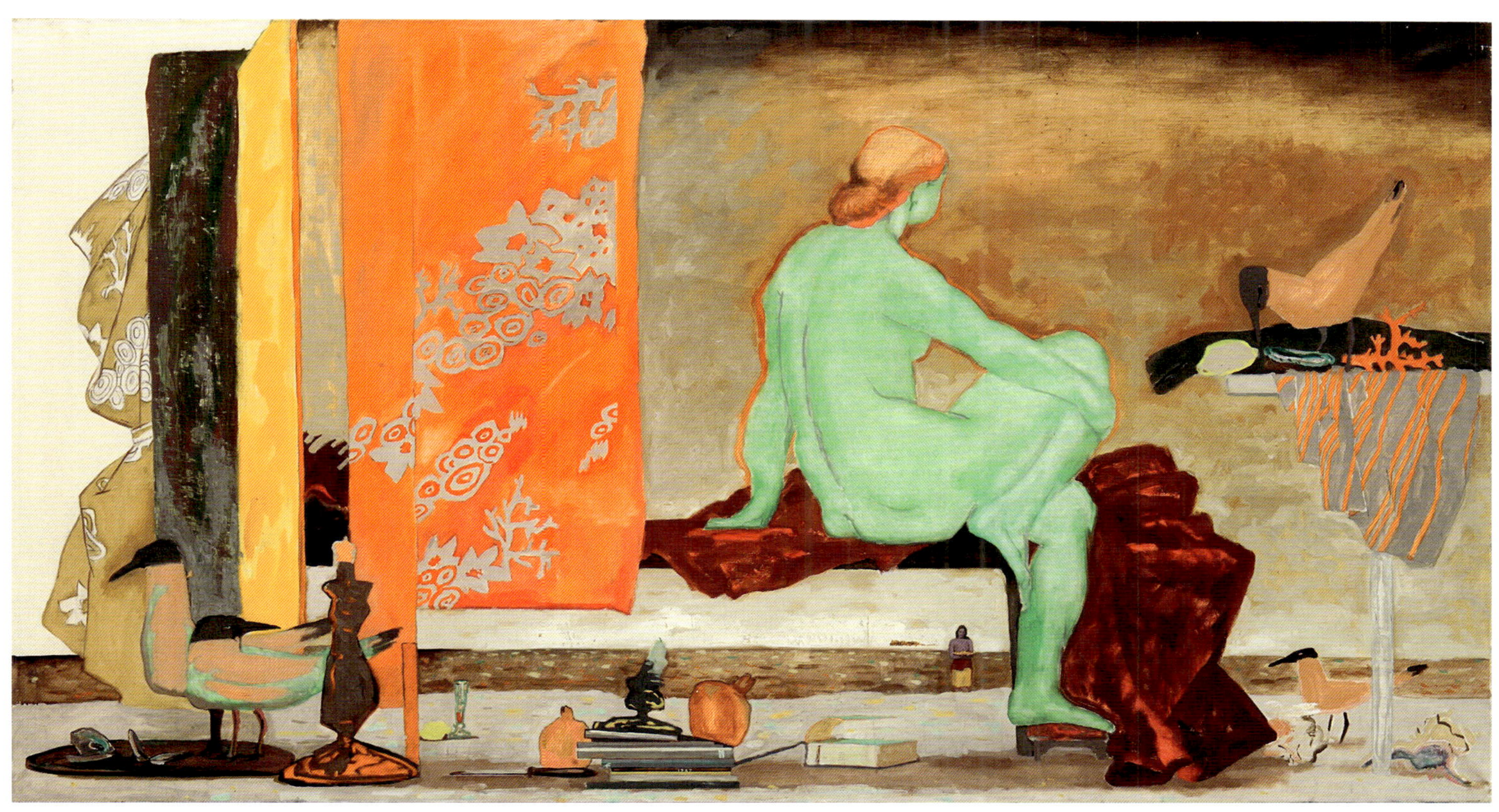

5 **Oleksandr Dubovyk** (b. 1931)

Black Square, 1980 | Oil on canvas | $51\frac{3}{16} \times 51\frac{3}{16}$ in. (130 × 130 cm)

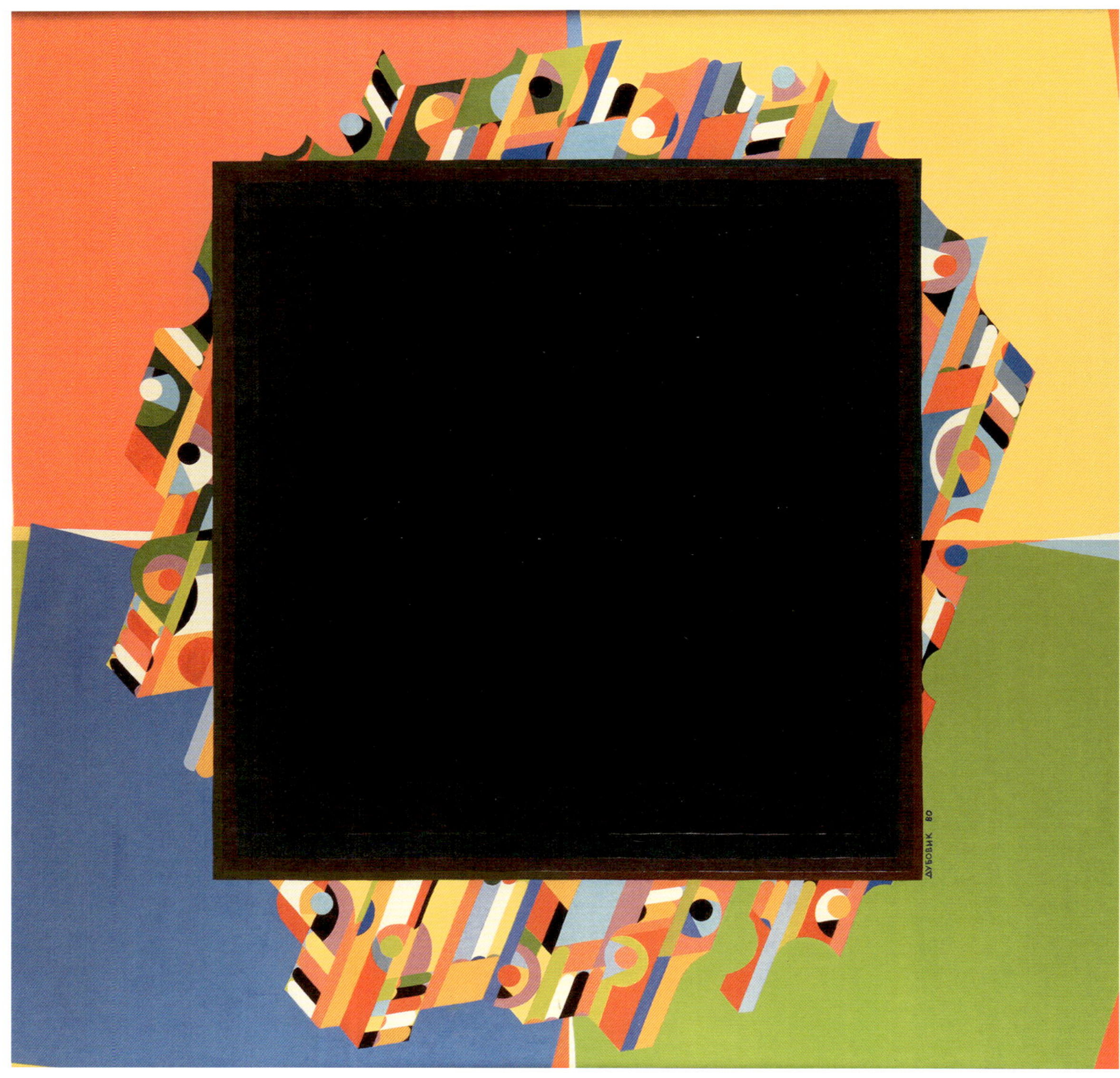

6 **Hryhorii Havrylenko** (1927–1984)

Composition VIII-II, 1962 | Tempera on paper | 23 13/16 × 16 3/4 in. (60.5 × 42.6 cm)

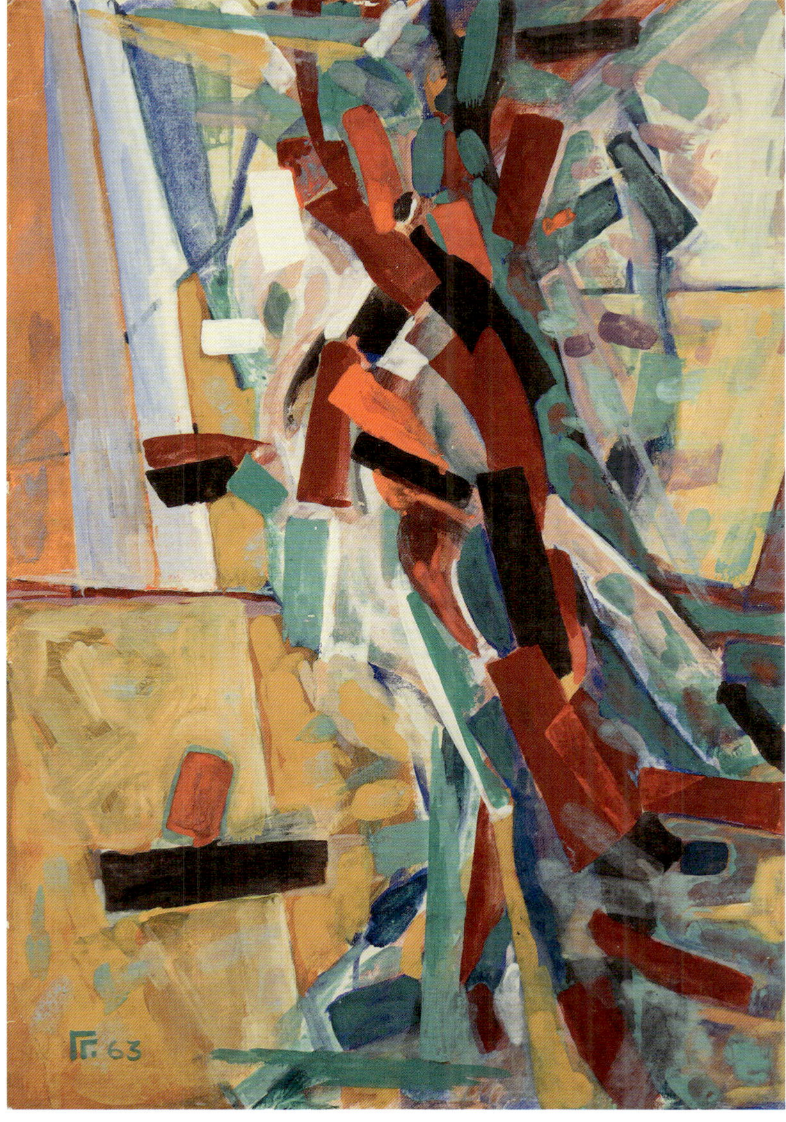

7 **Hryhorii Havrylenko** (1927–1984)

Composition, 1963 | Gouache on cardboard | 14¾ × 10 in. (37.4 × 25.4 cm)

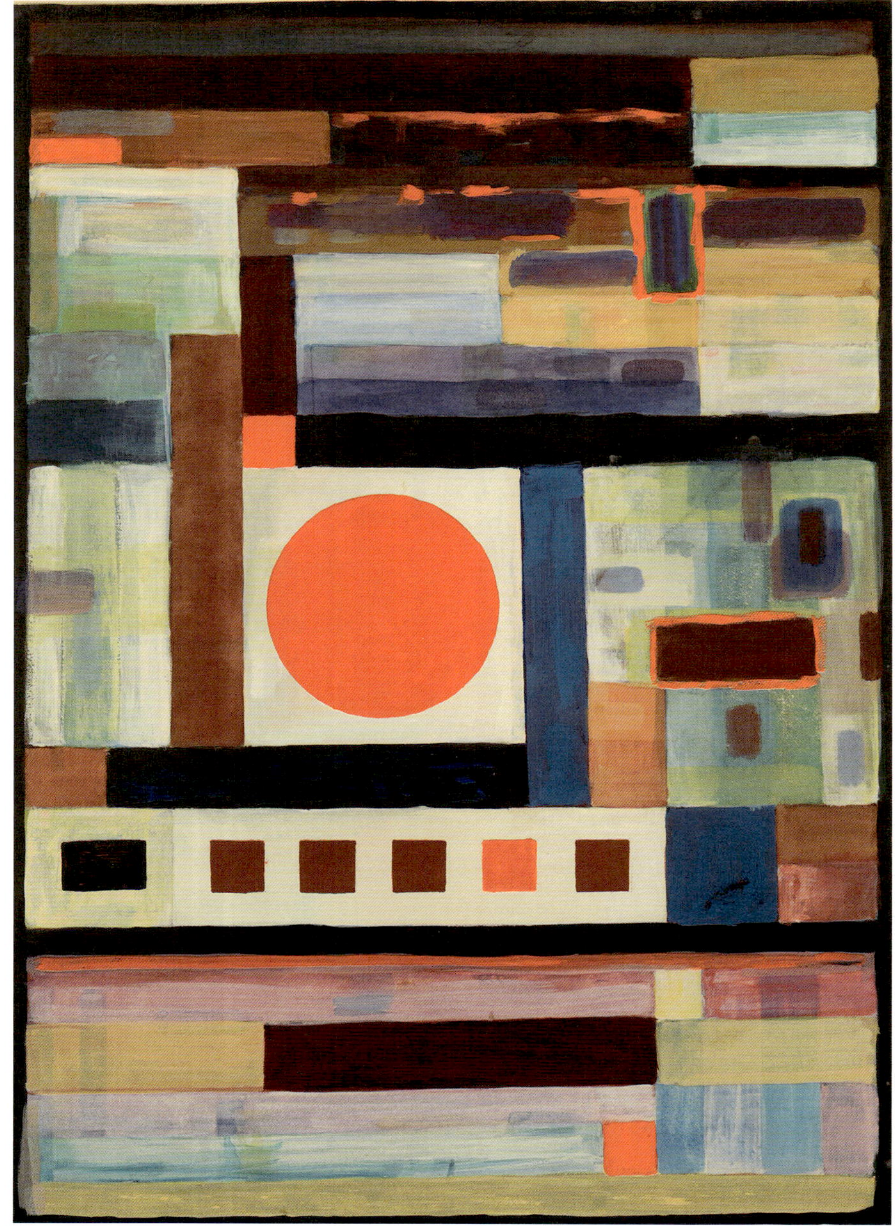

8 **Oleksander Hnylytskyj** (1961–2009)

Yearning, 1988 | Oil on canvas | 77 15⁄16 × 66 15⁄16 in. (198 × 170 cm)

FROM THE COLLECTION OF LIUDMYLA AND ANDRIY PYSHNYY

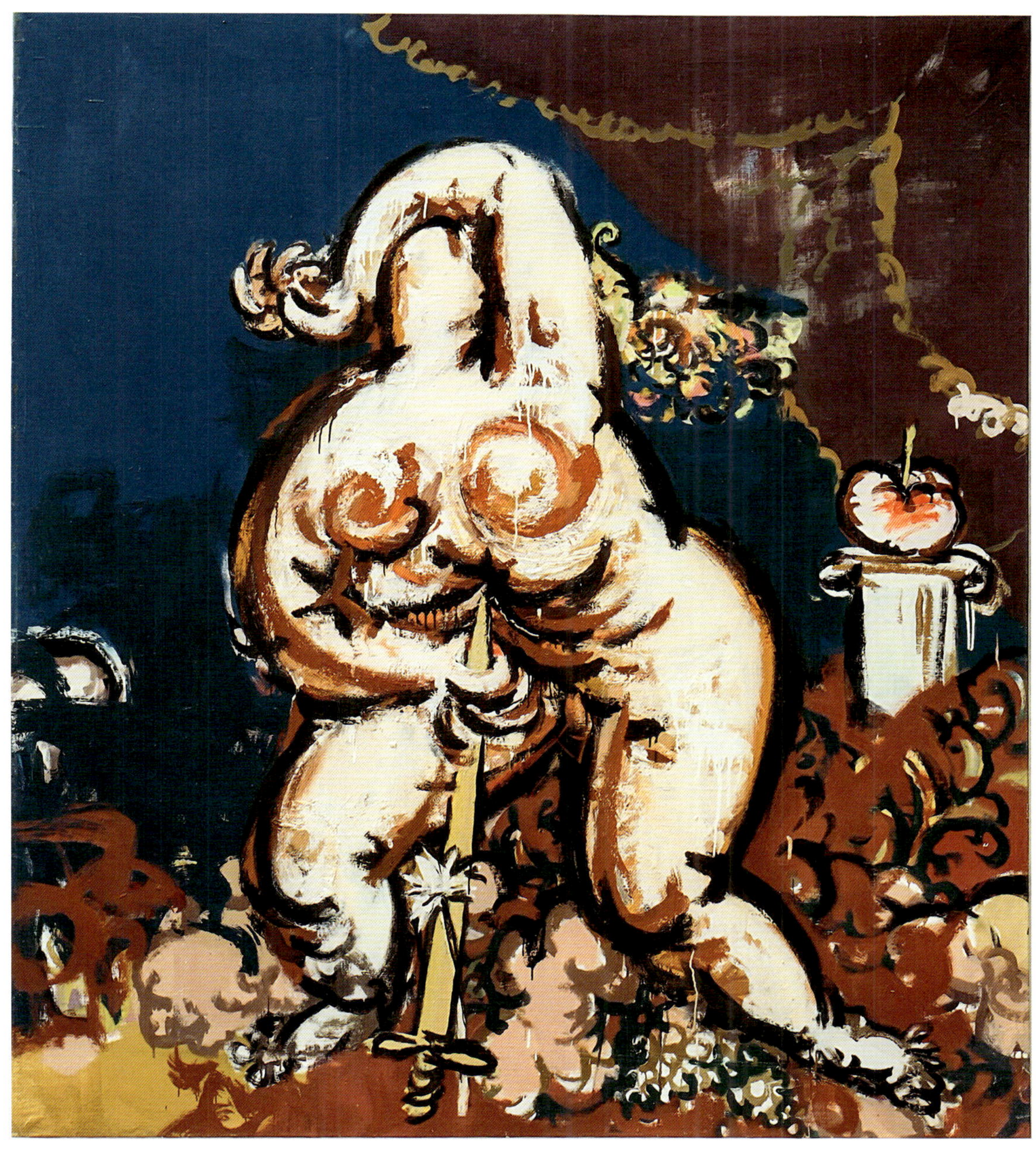

9 Oleksander Hnylytskyj (1961–2009)

Untitled, undated | Marker on paper | 14$\frac{9}{16}$ × 9$\frac{13}{16}$ in. (37 × 25 cm)

ABRAMOVYCH FOUNDATION

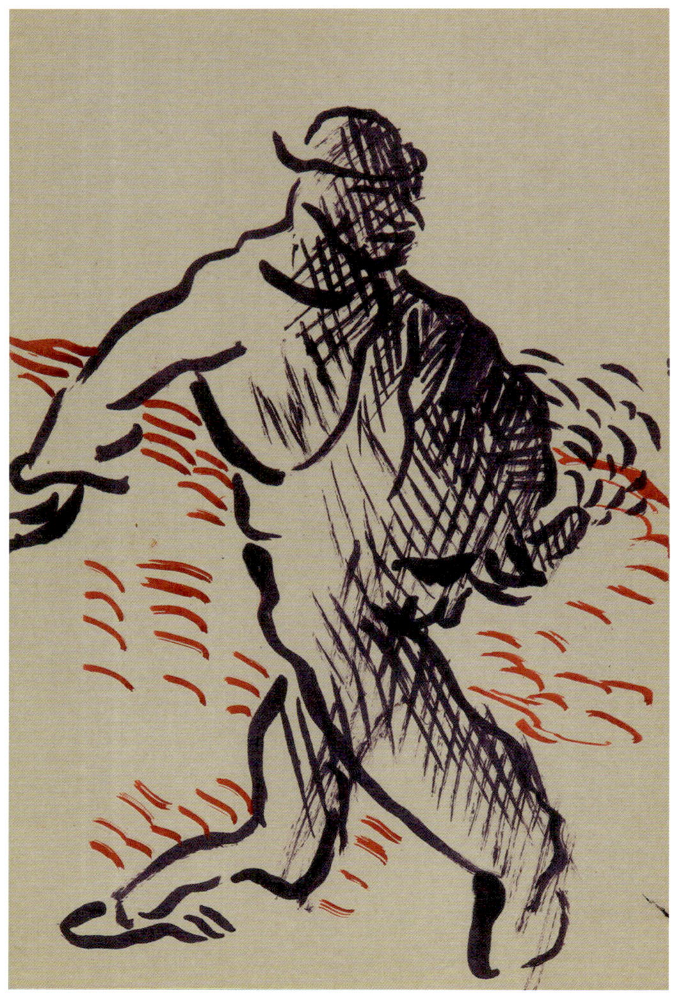

10 **Oleksander Hnylytskyj** (1961–2009)

Untitled, undated | Marker on paper | 14 9/16 in. × 9 13/16 (37 × 25 cm)

ABRAMOVYCH FOUNDATION

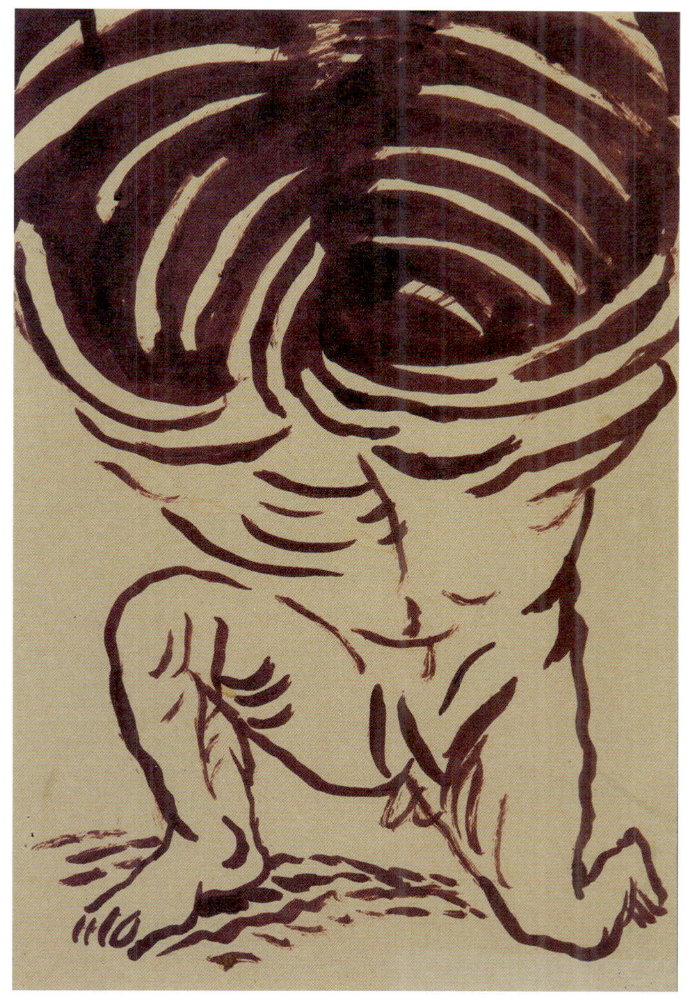

11 **Oleg Holosiy** (1965–1993)

The Angel Has Come, 1992 | Oil on canvas | 76¾ × 39 in. (195 × 99 cm)

VORONOV ART FOUNDATION

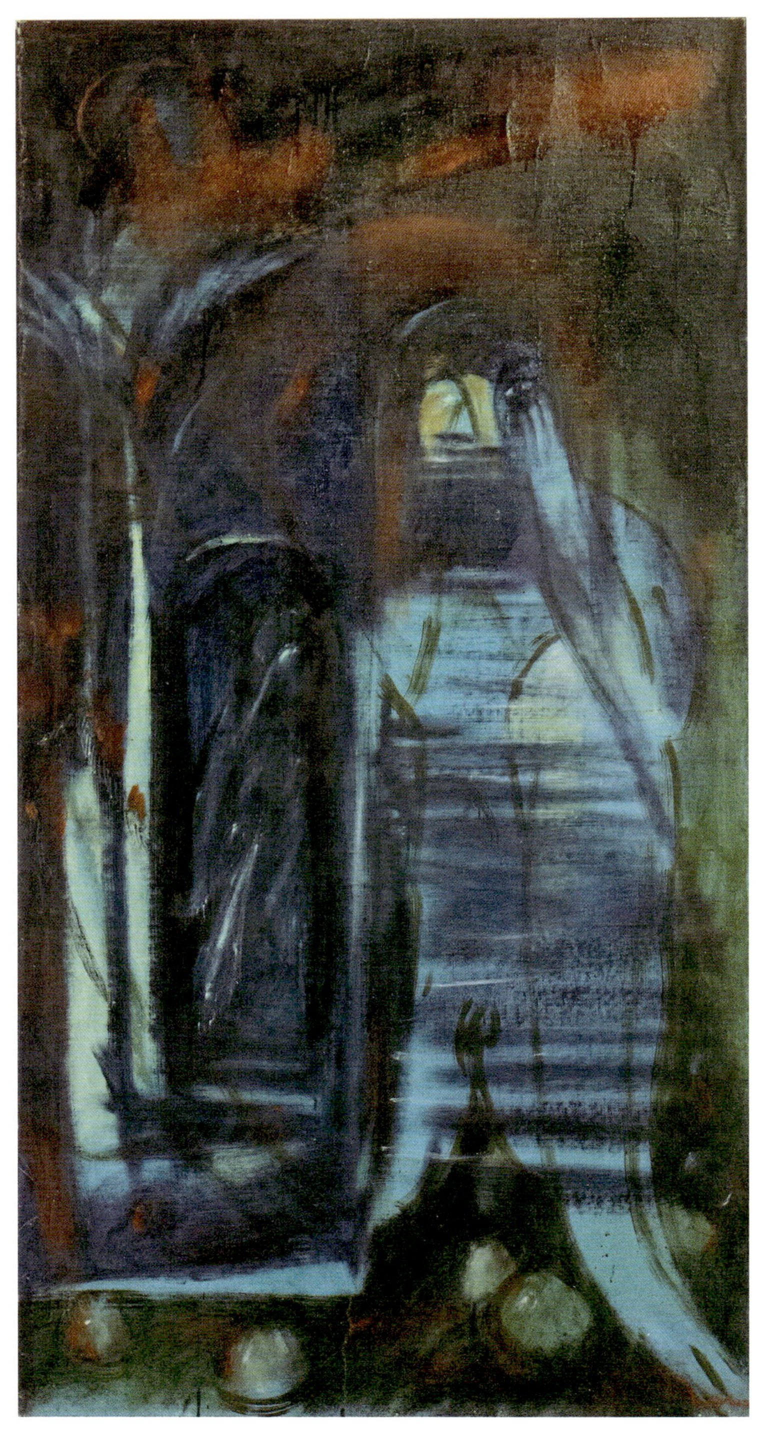

12 **Alla Horska** (1929–1970)

Untitled (Silence), 1964 | Gouache and graphite on paper | 20⅜ × 6⅝ in. (51.8 × 16.9 cm)

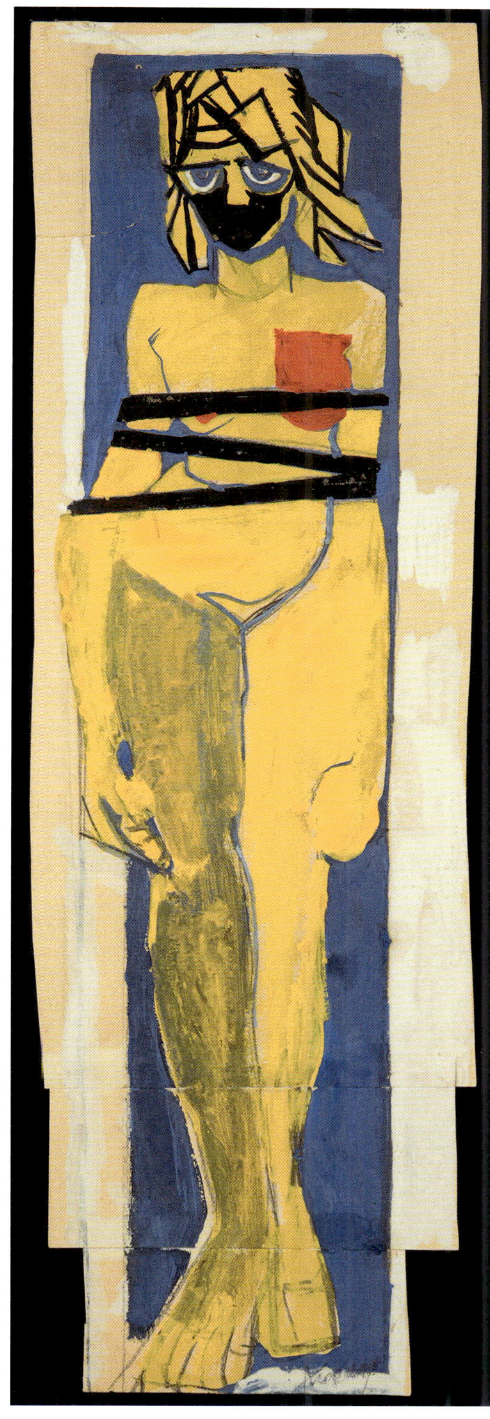

13 **Dmytro Kavsan** (b. 1964)

Who Comes Last Gets the Bones, 1986 | Oil on canvas | $36\frac{5}{8} \times 35\frac{1}{16}$ in. (93 × 89 cm)

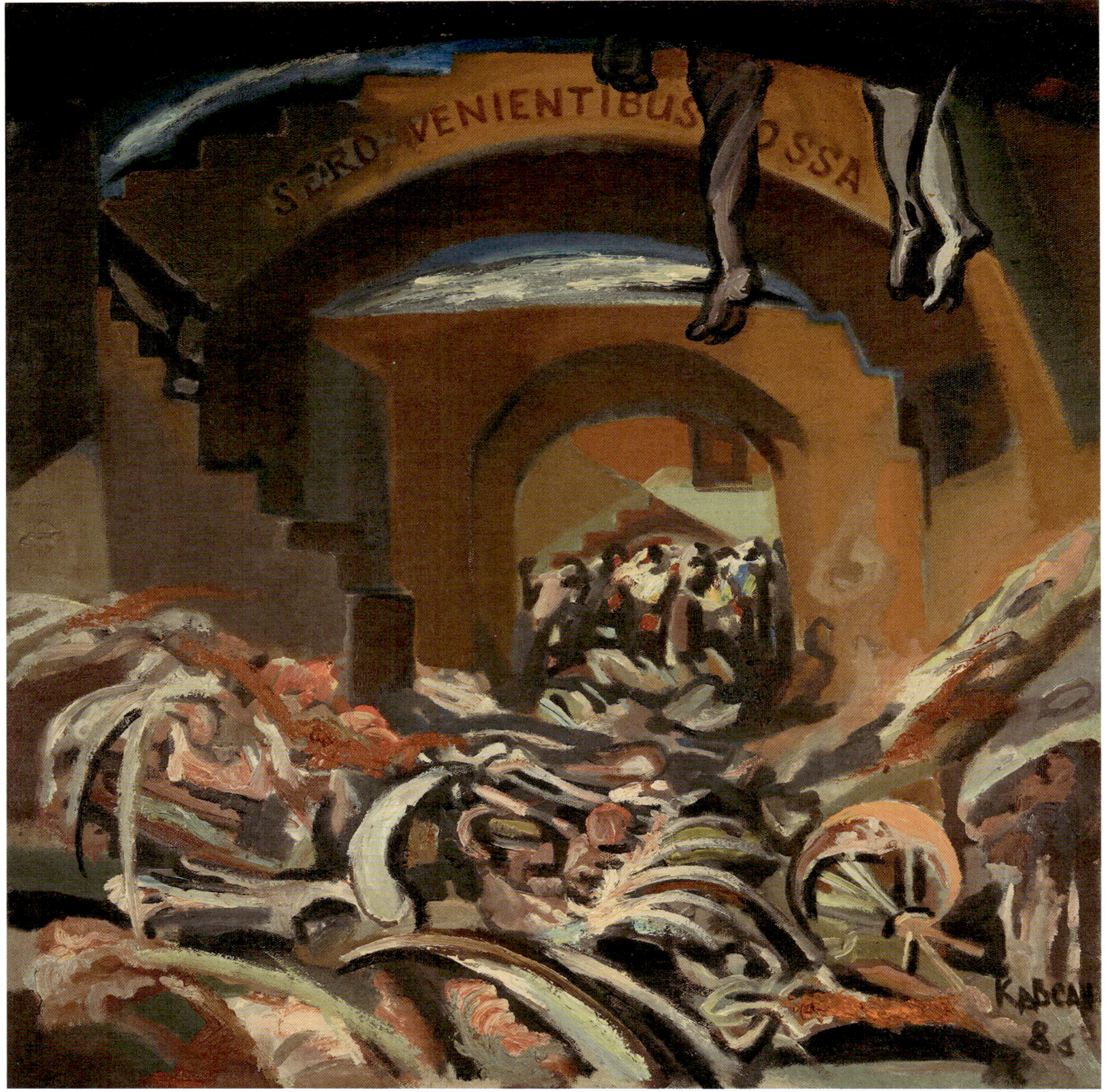

14 **Anatoly Kryvolap** (b. 1946)

Four Substances, 1992 | Oil on canvas | 25⅝ × 33 1/16 in. (65 × 84 cm)

COLLECTION OF THE ARTIST

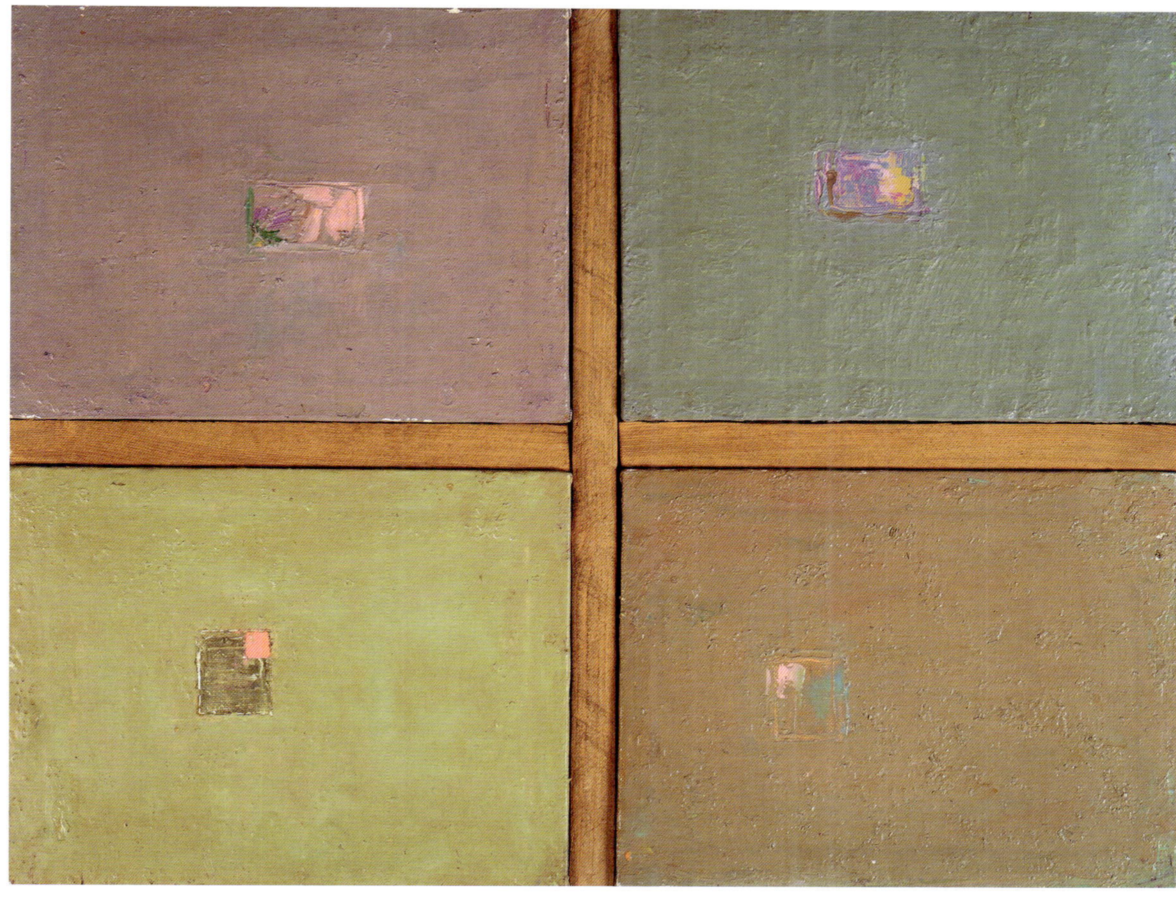

15 **Valery Lamakh** (1925–1978)

Composition No. 8, 1959 | Tempera on panel | 27¼ × 19 5/16 in. (69.2 × 49 cm)

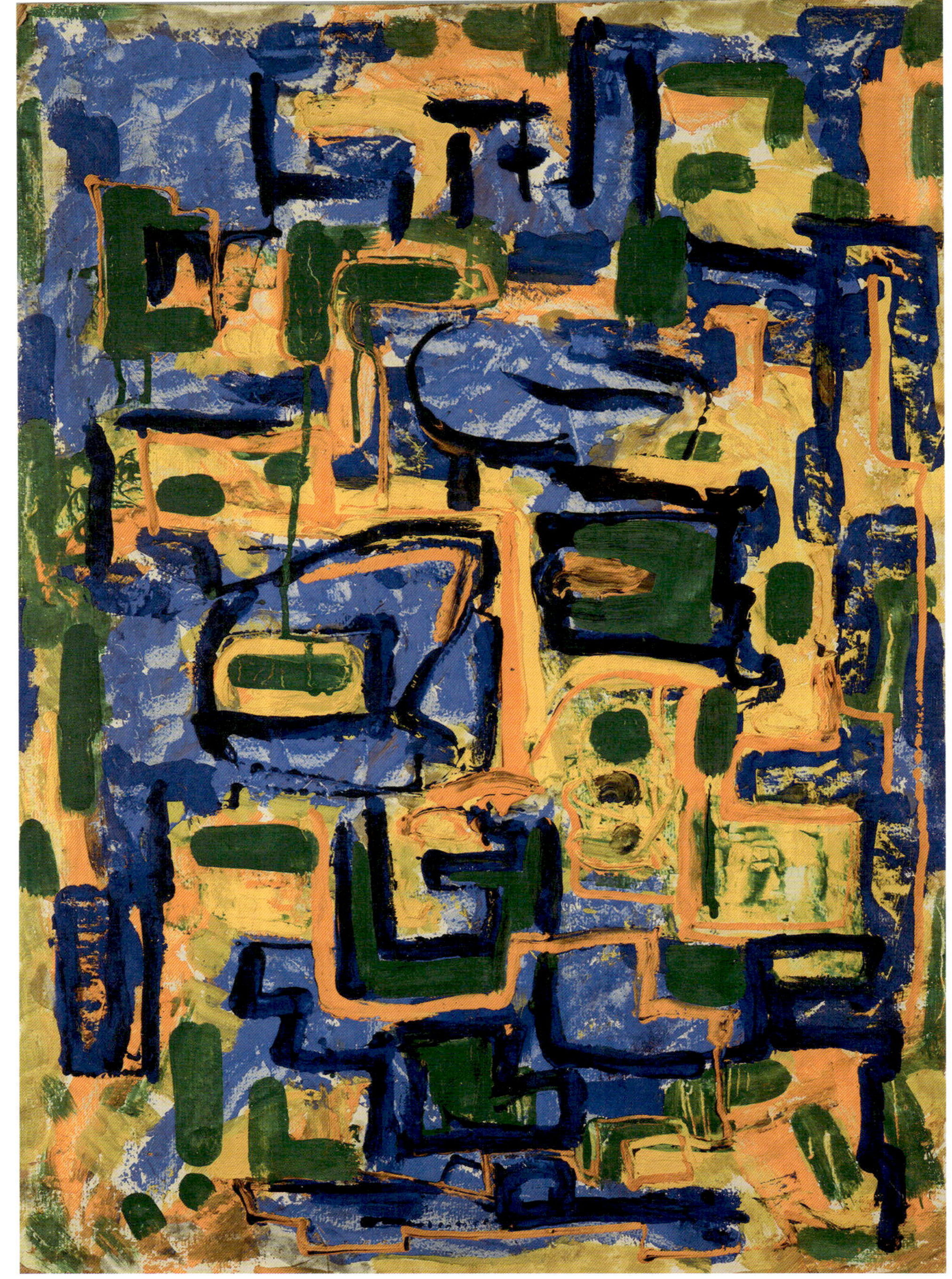

16 **Valery Lamakh** (1925–1978)

Composition No. 10, 1962 | Tempera on fiberboard | 27 7/16 × 19 3/8 in. (69.7 × 49.2 cm)

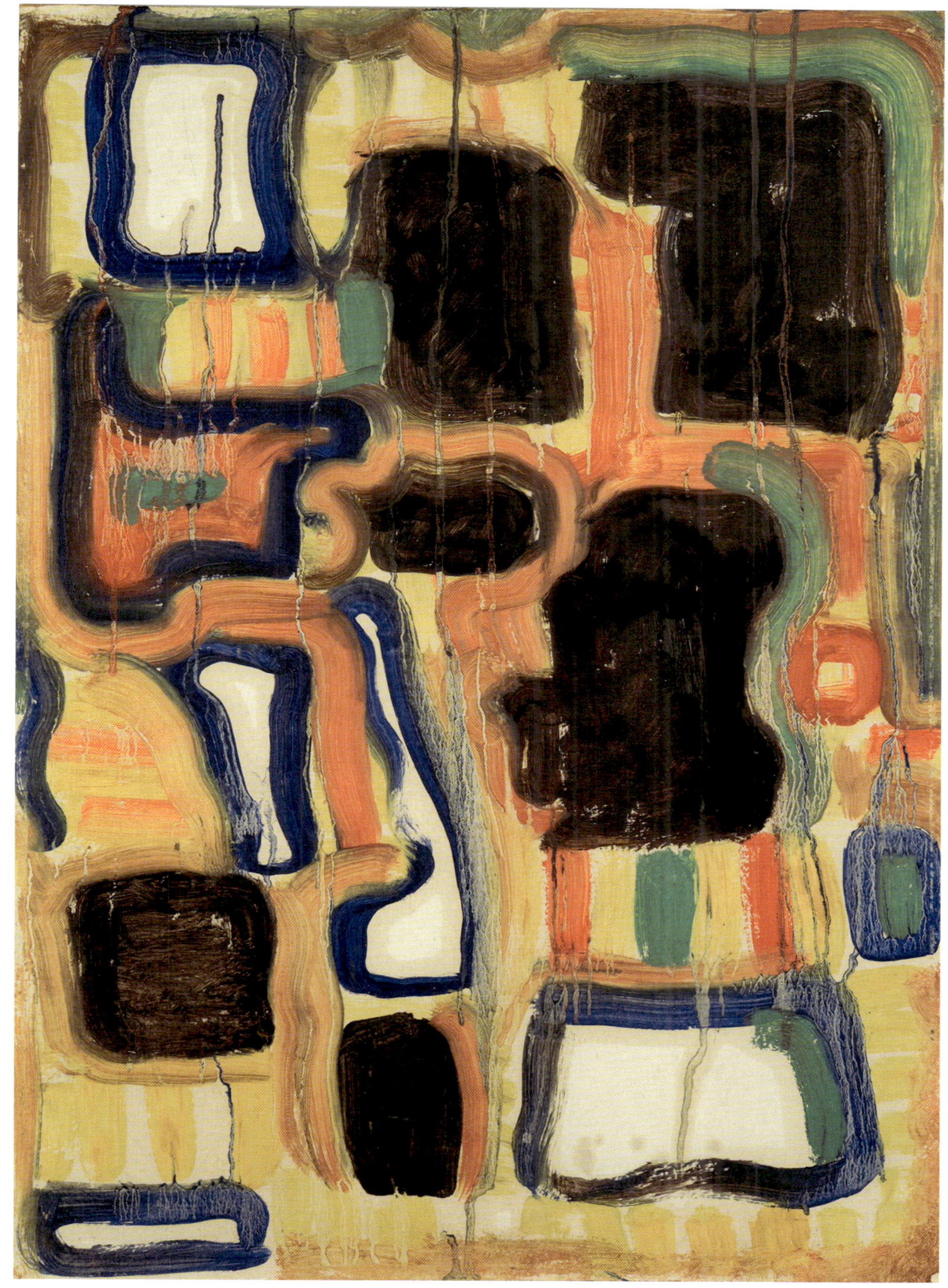

17 **Yuri Lutskevych** (1934–2001)

Madrigal, 1972 | Oil on canvas | 35 7/16 × 39 3/8 in. (90 × 100 cm)

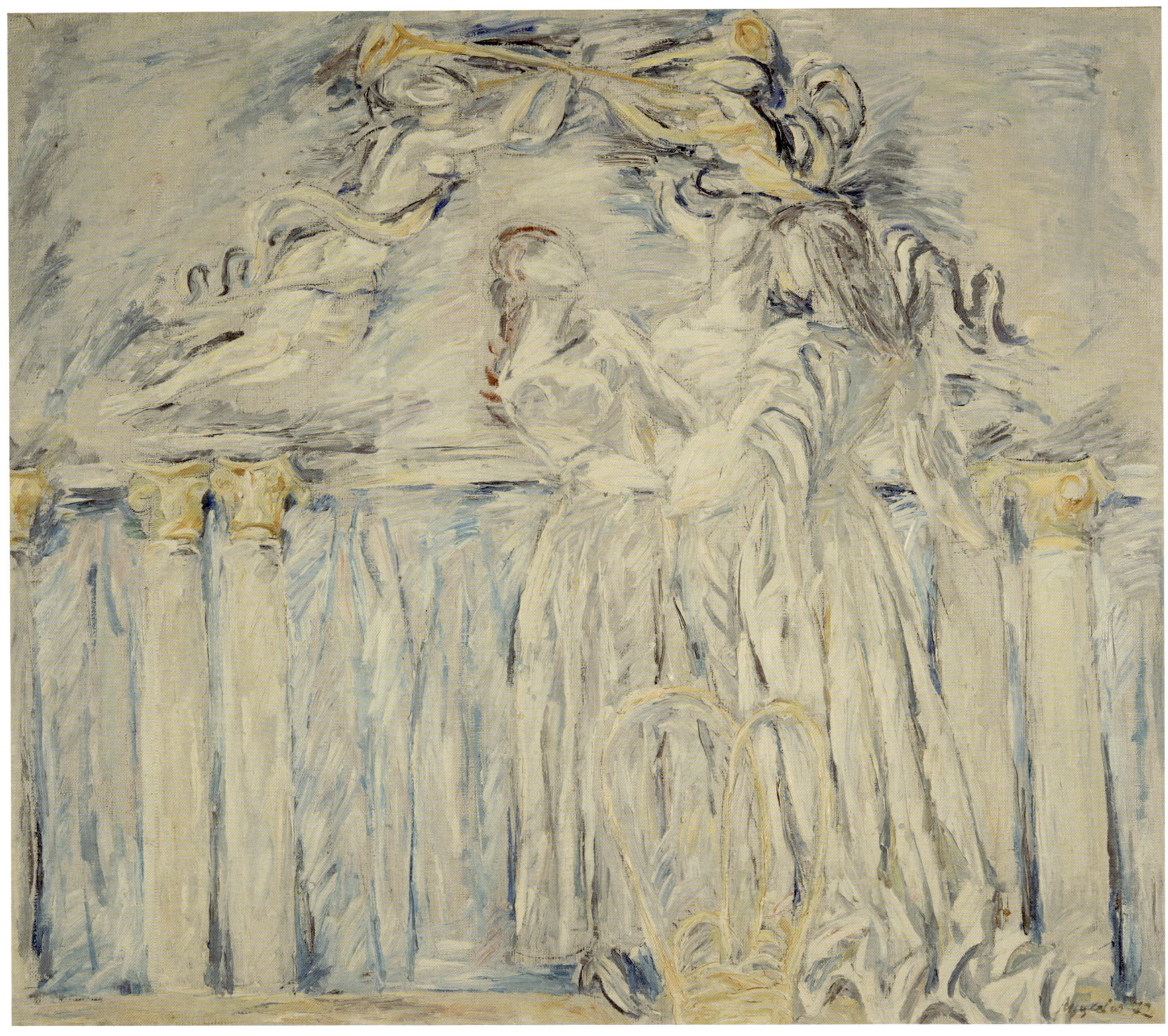

18 **Mykola Matsenko** (b. 1960) and **Oleg Tistol** (b. 1960) (NATSPROM)

Piłsudki, 1993 | Oil on paper | 97⅝ × 226¾ in. (248 × 576 cm)

ABRAMOVYCH FOUNDATION

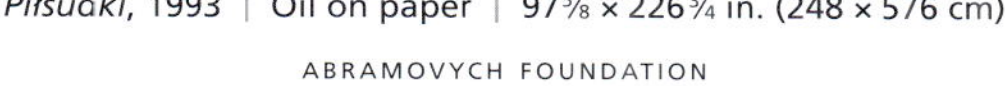

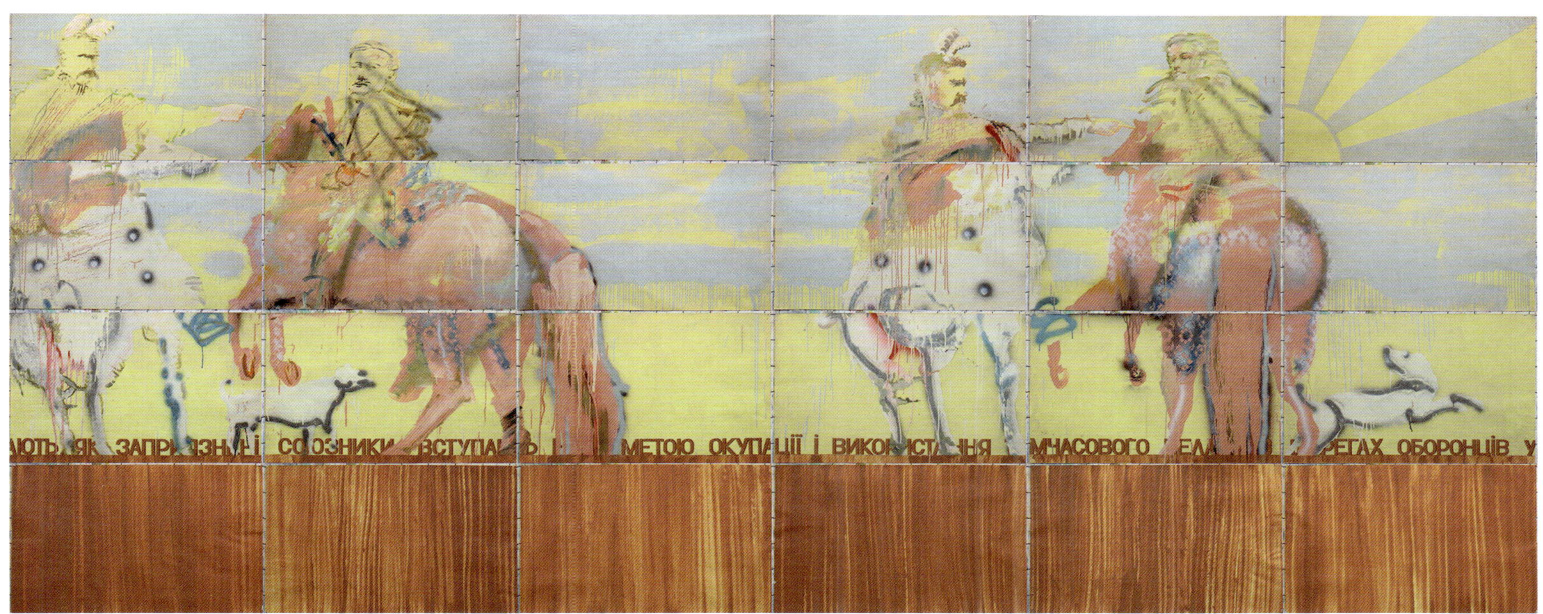

19 **Halyna Neledva** (b. 1938)

Untitled, undated | Oil on canvas | 35 5/16 × 31 3/8 in. (89.7 × 79.7 cm)

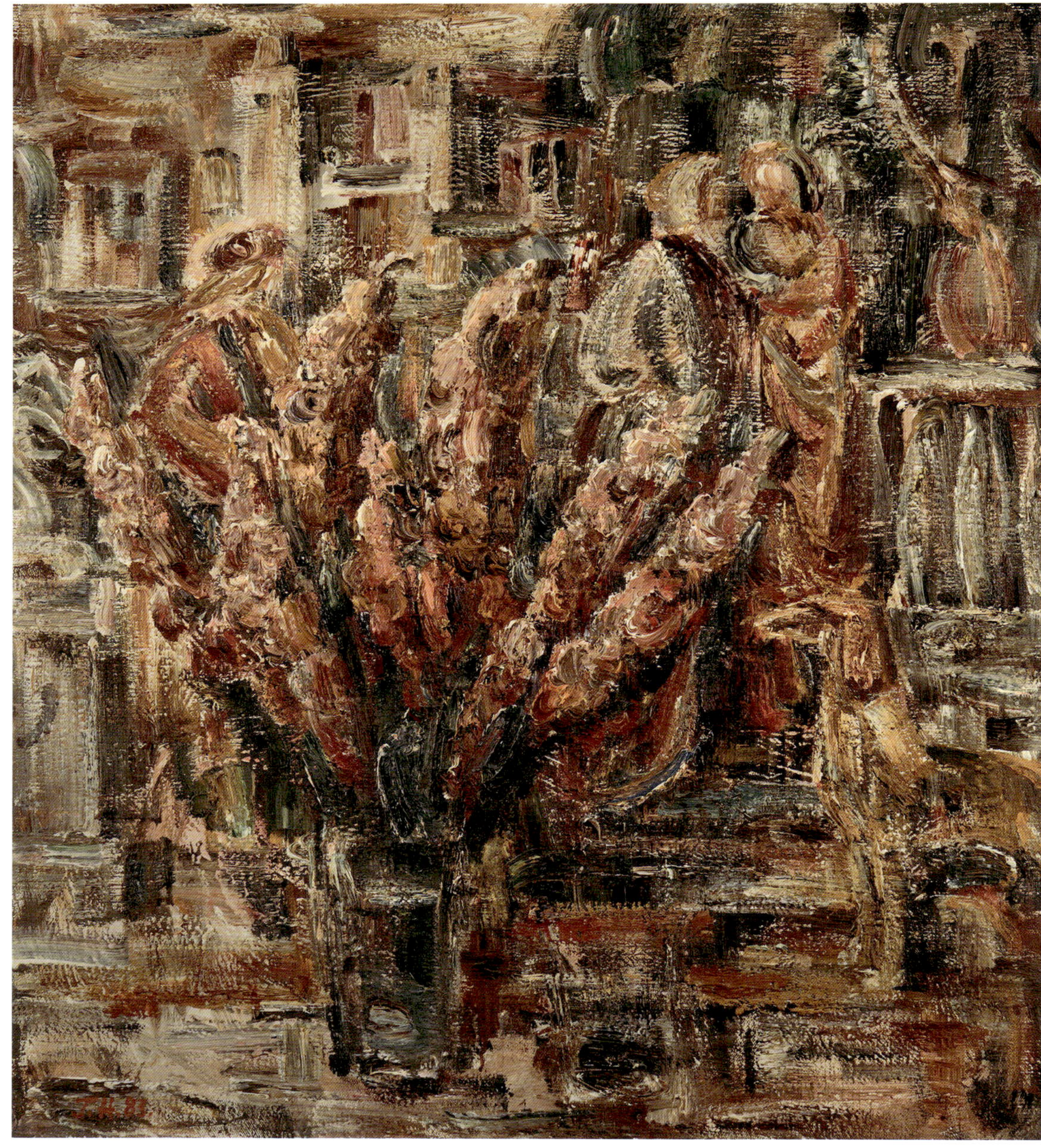

20 **Yevhen Petrenko** (1946–2016)

Landscape, 1980 | Oil and tempera on canvas | 35 1⁄16 × 35 1⁄16 in. (89 × 89 cm)

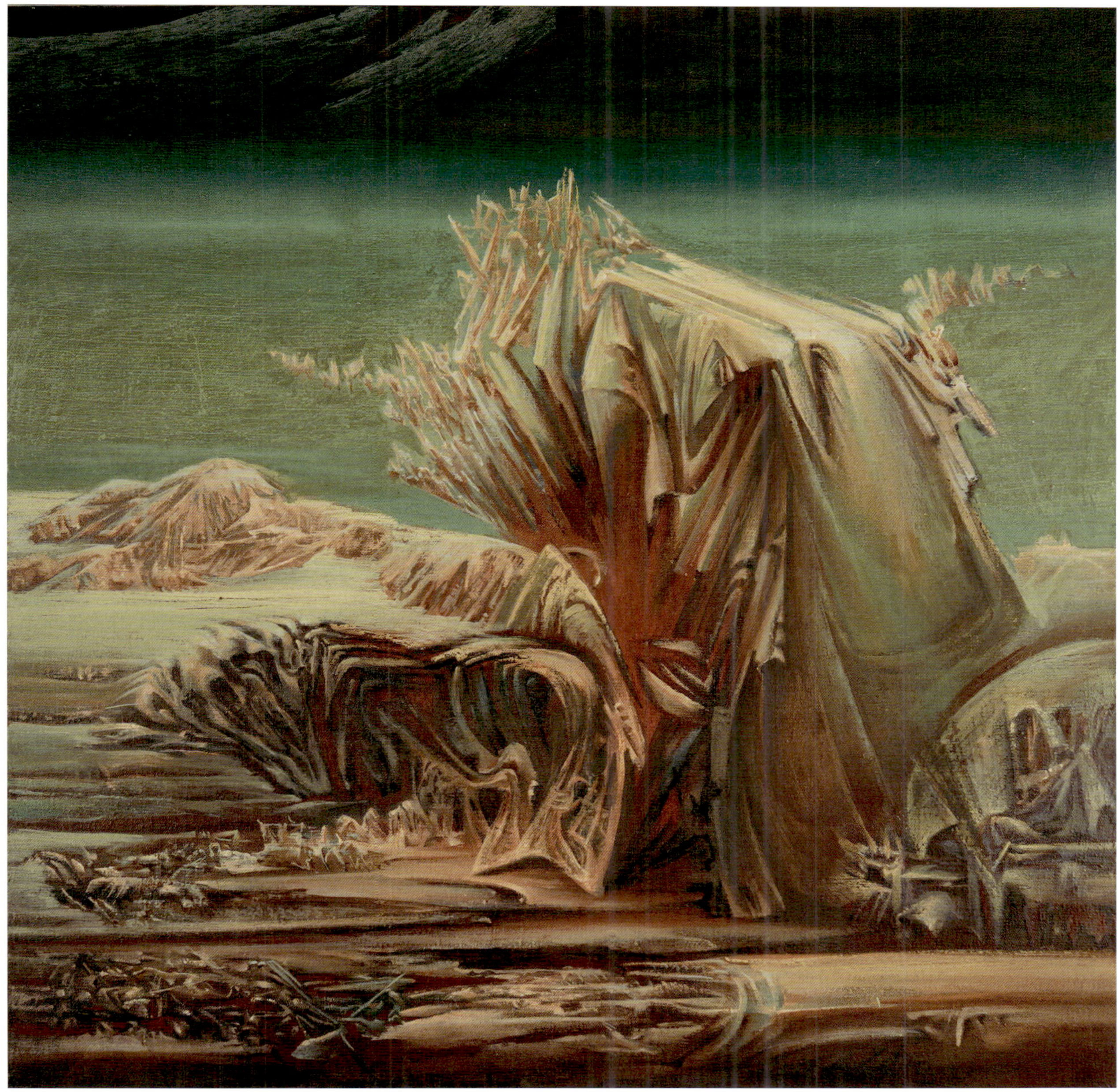

21 **Kostiantyn (Vinny) Reunov** (b. 1963)

Only There, 1990 | Oil on canvas | 76¾ × 76¾ in. (195 × 195 cm)

VORONOV ART FOUNDATION

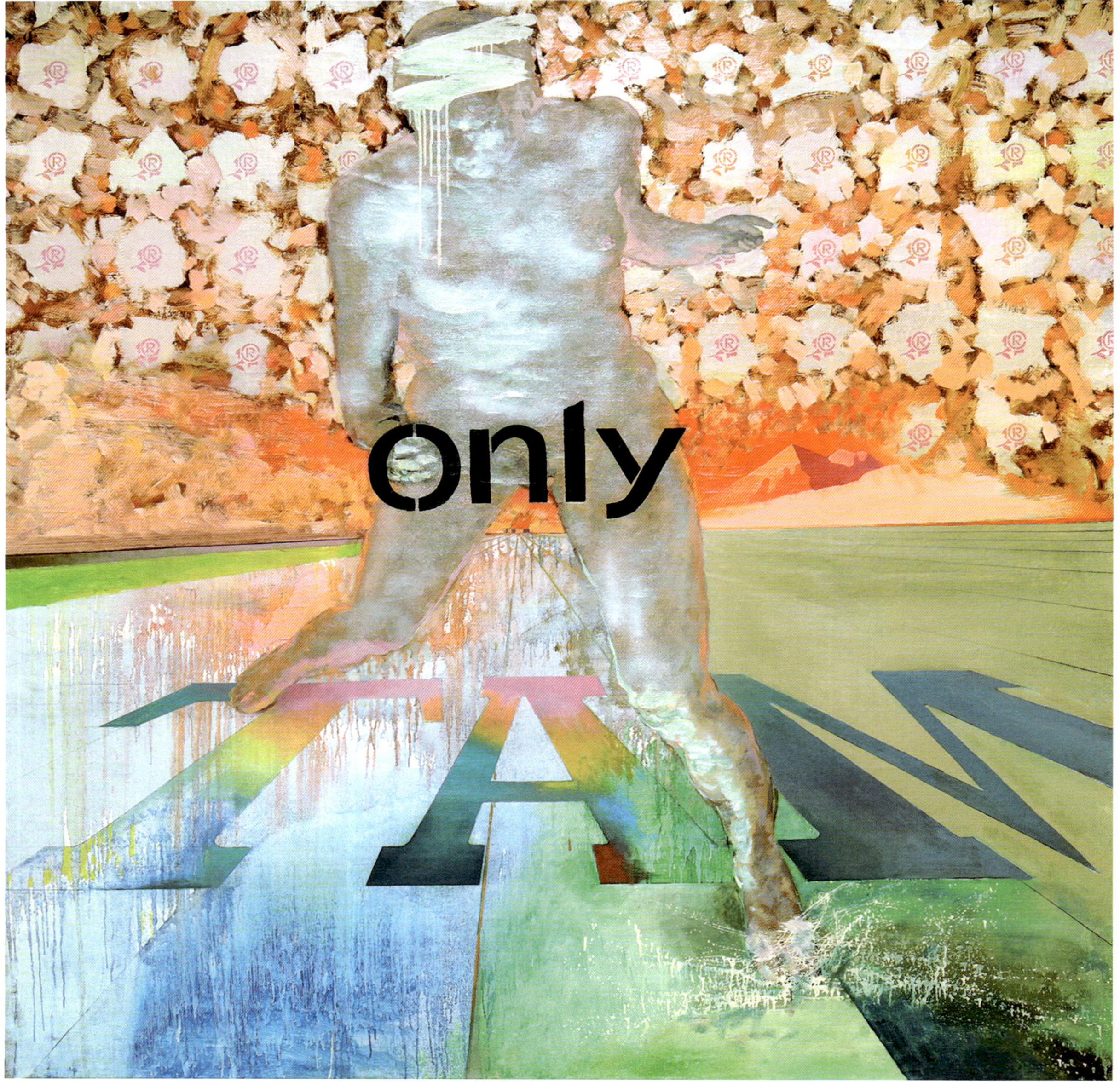

22 Oleksandr Roitburd (1961–2021)

Untitled, undated | Collage and ink on paperboard | 18¾ × 14³⁄₁₆ in. (47.7 × 36 cm)

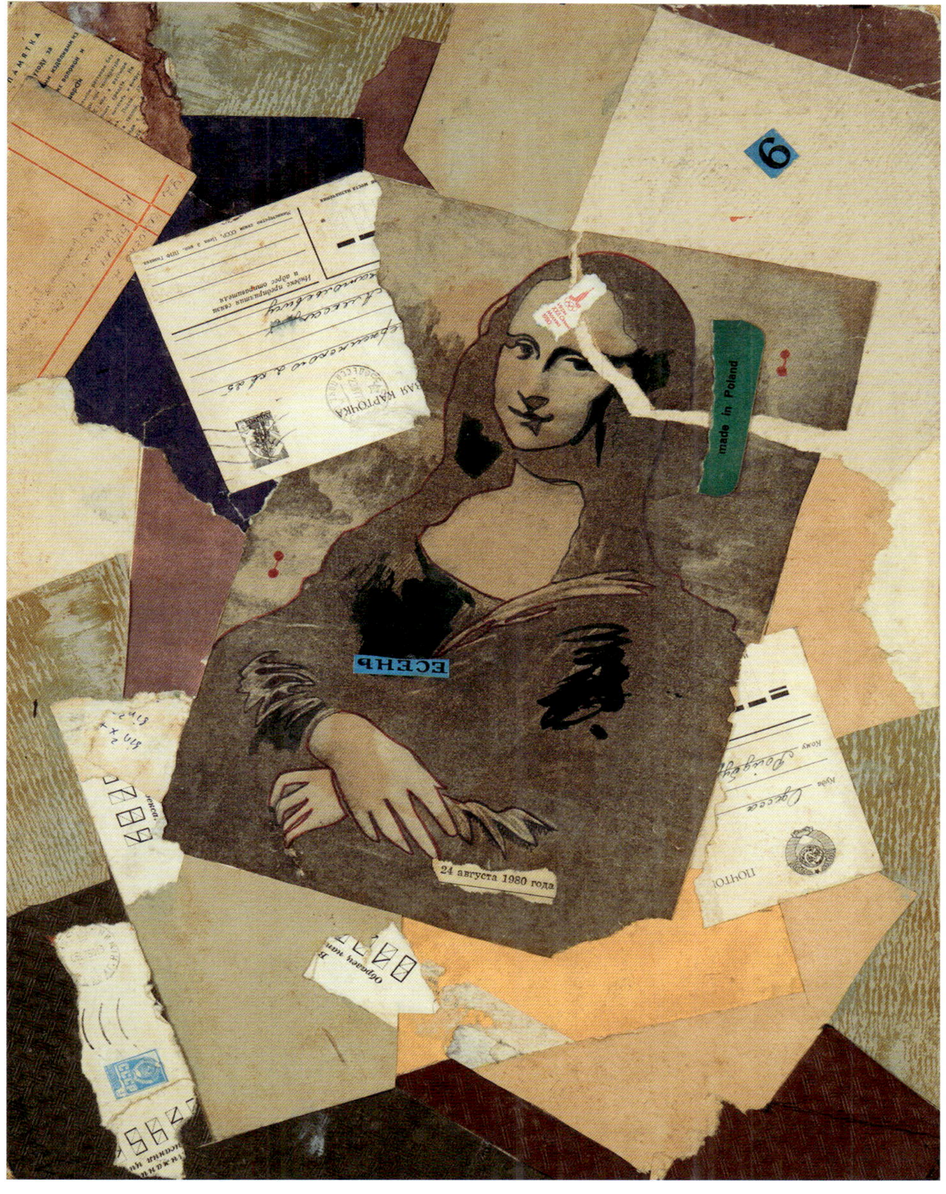

23 **Oleksandr Roitburd** (1961–2021)

Untitled, 1985 | Oil on panel | 44⅛ × 32$^{5}/_{16}$ in. (112 × 82 cm)

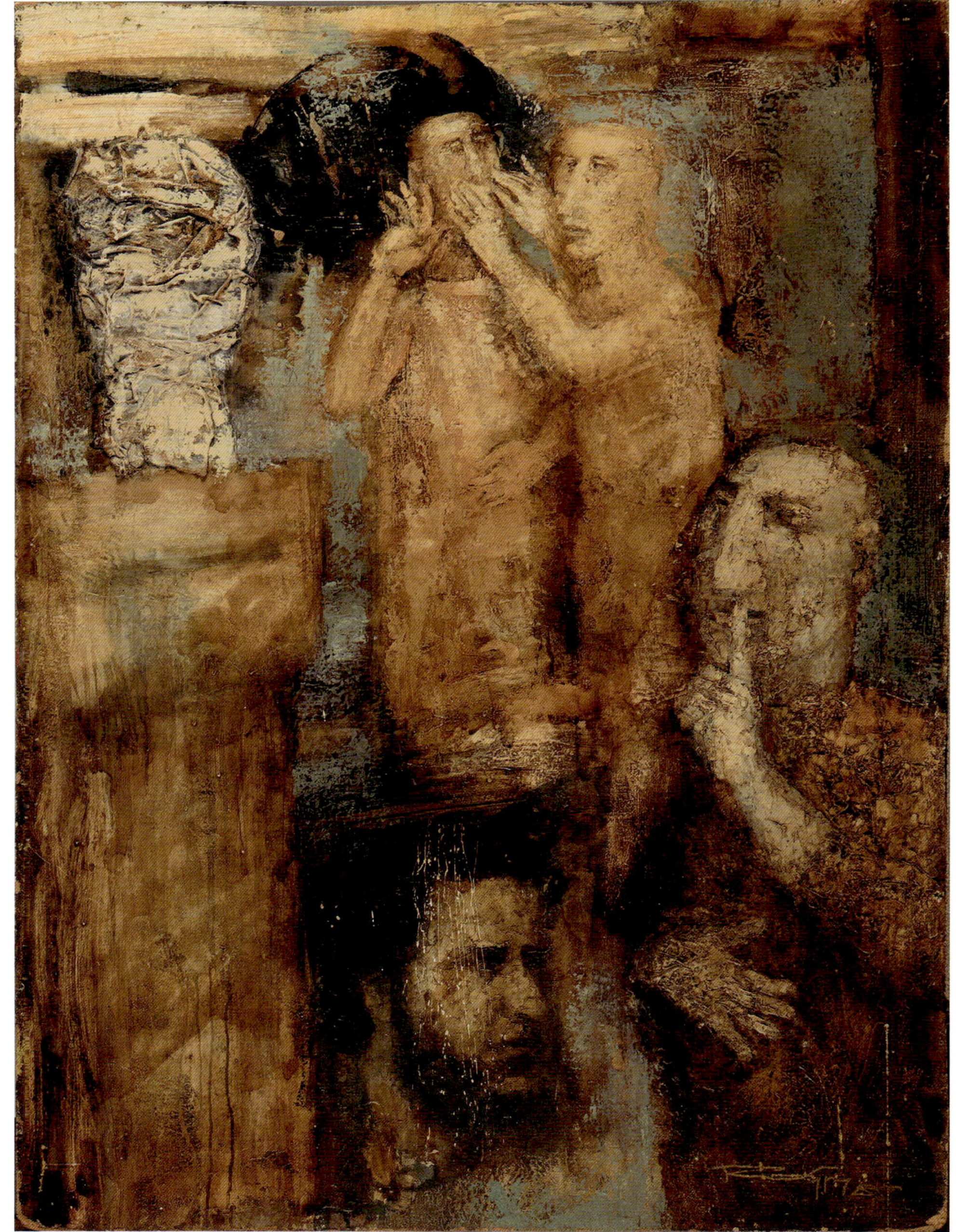

24 **Viktor Ryzhykh** (b. 1933)

Untitled, undated | Oil on canvas | 35 7/16 × 39 3/8 in. (90 × 100 cm)

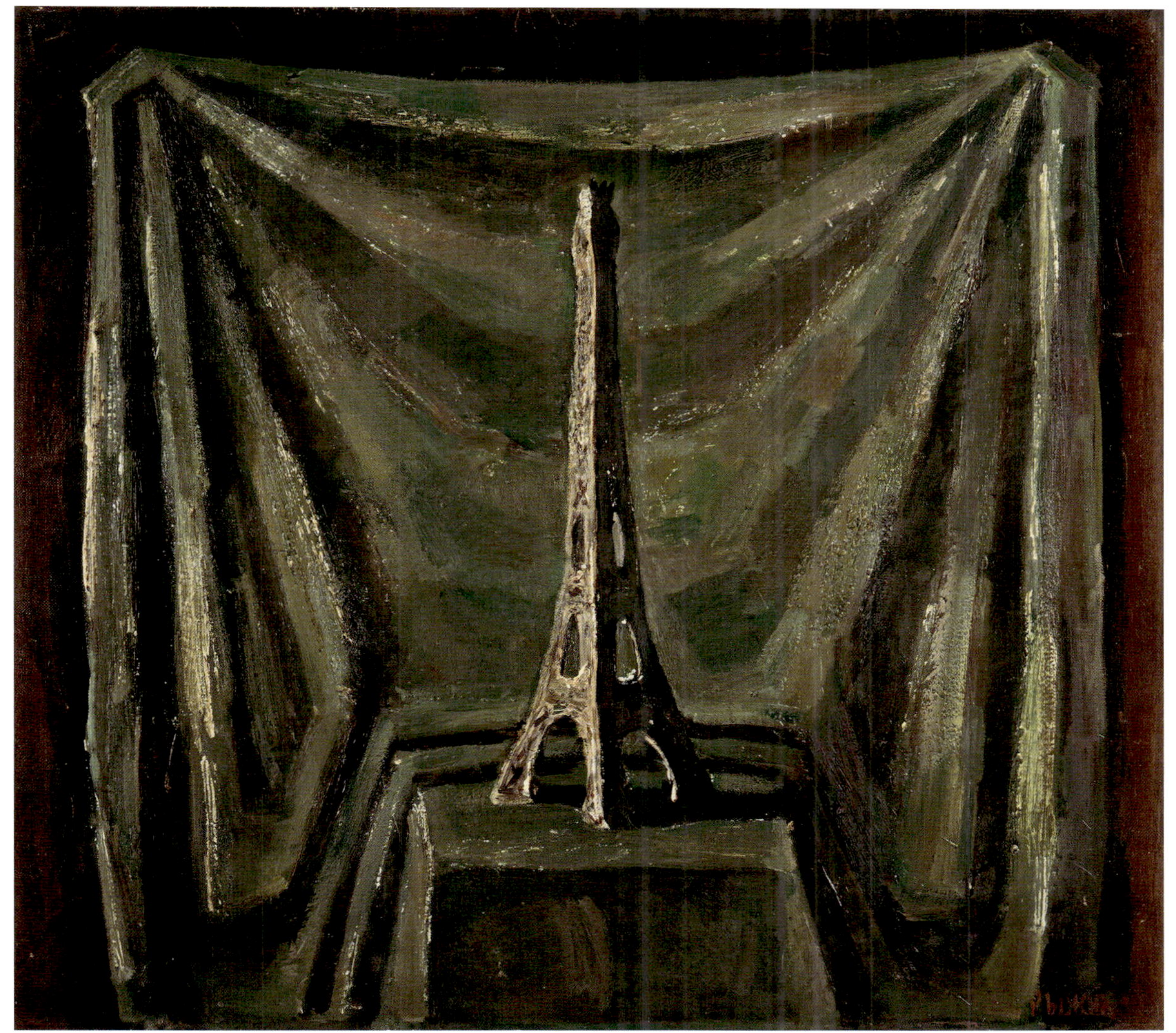

25 **Arsen Savadov** (b. 1962) and **Georgii Senchenko** (b. 1962)

Gardens Old and New, 1986–87 | Oil on canvas | 36 13/16 × 57 ½ in. (93.5 × 146 cm)

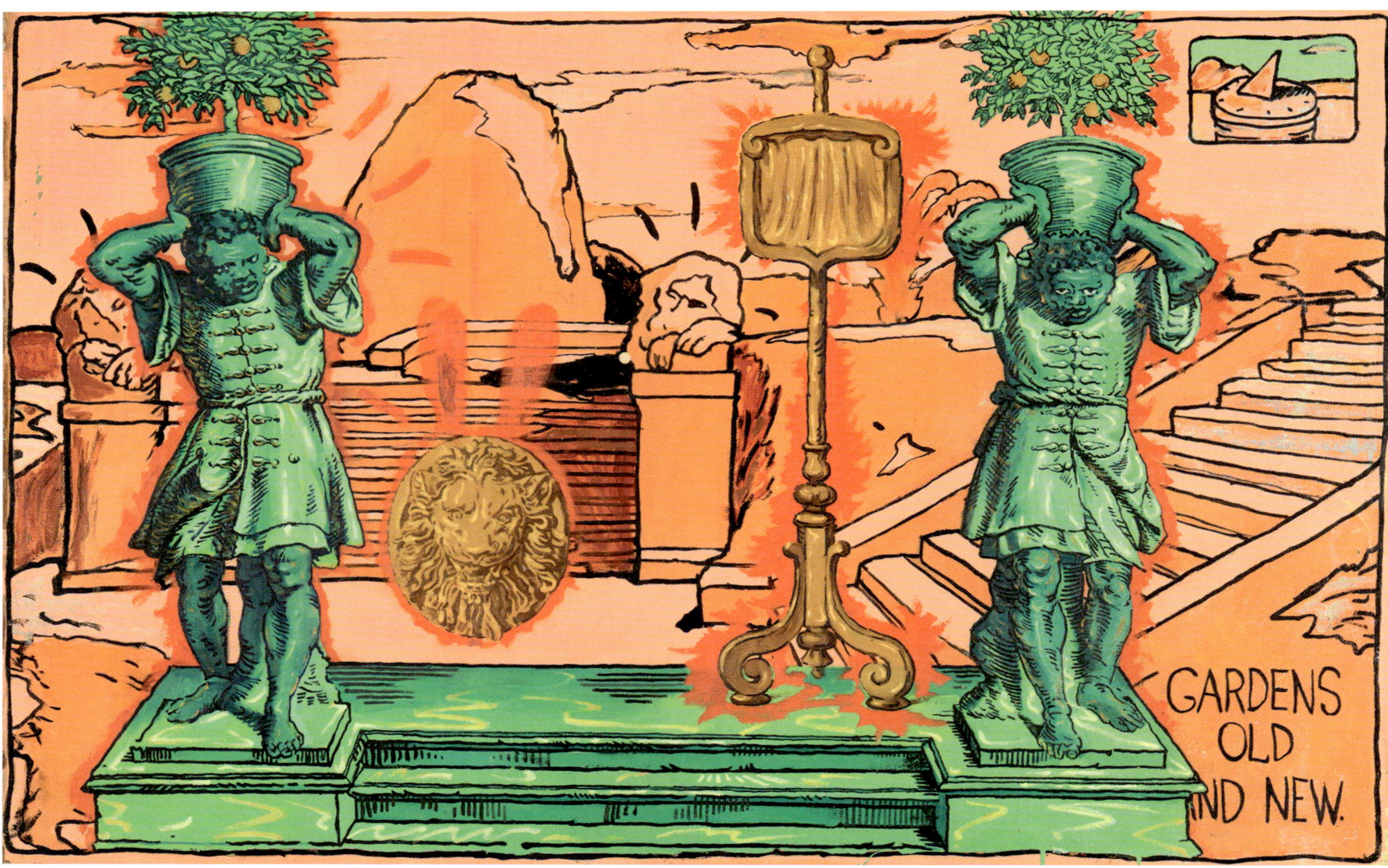

26 **Arsen Savadov** (b. 1962) and **Georgii Senchenko** (b. 1962)

Gardens Old and New, 1986–87 | Oil on canvas | 37 × 57½ in. (94 × 146 cm)

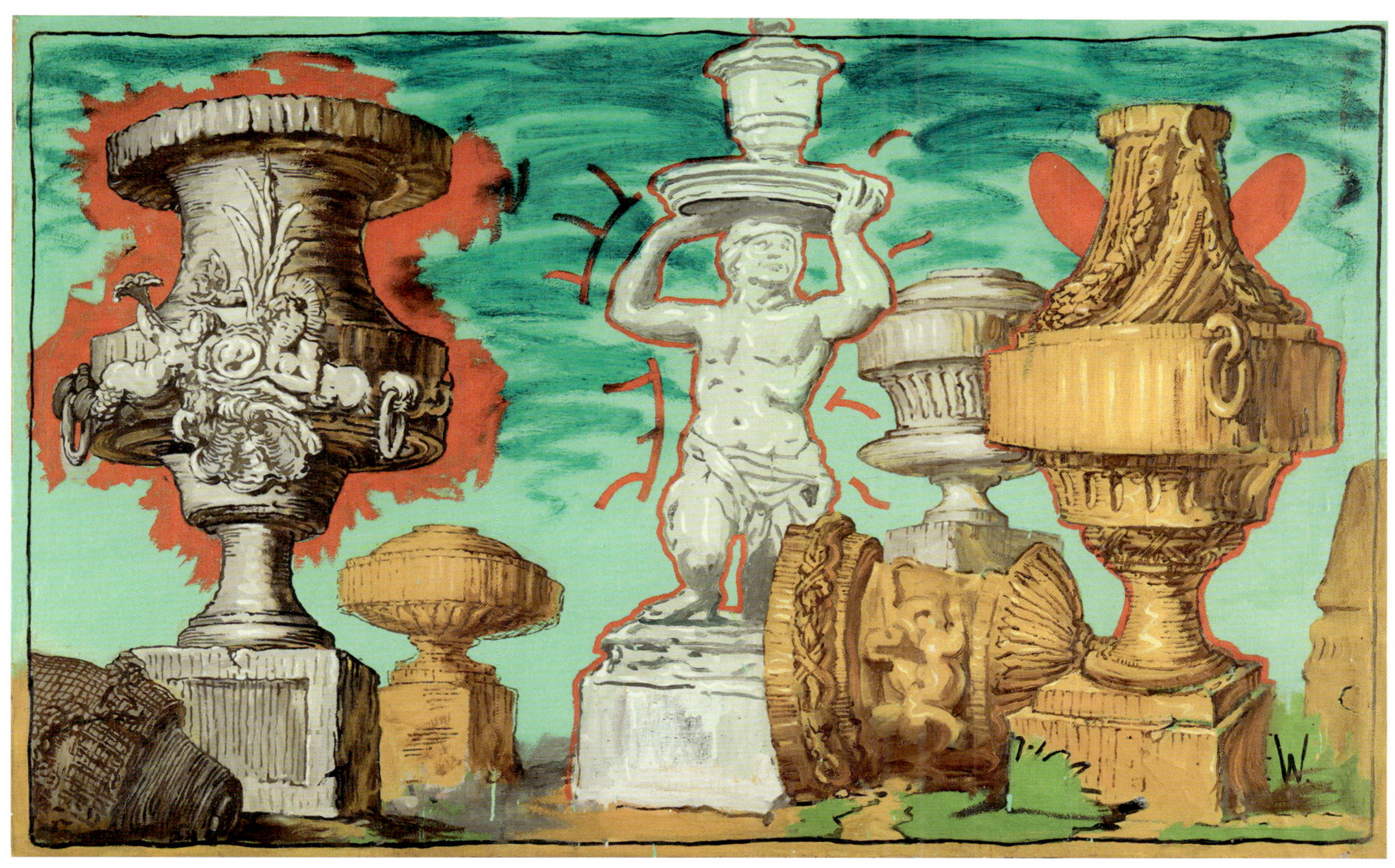

27 **Arsen Savadov** (b. 1962)

Untitled, 1986 | Graphite, ink, red felt-tip pen on paper | 11⅛ × 14$\frac{9}{16}$ in. (28.2 × 37 cm)

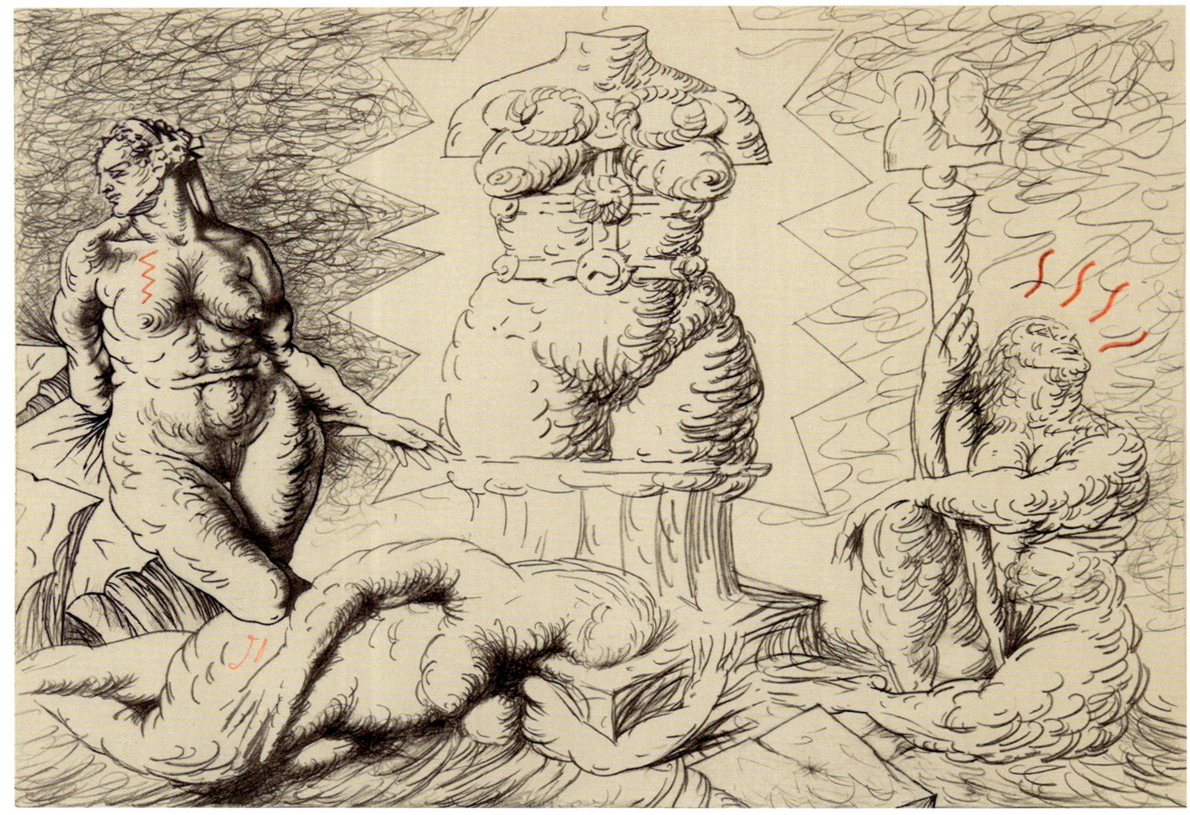

28 **Arsen Savadov** (b. 1962)

Untitled, 1986 | Graphite, red felt-tip pen on paper | $10\frac{5}{16} \times 16\frac{5}{16}$ in. (26.2 × 41.5 cm)

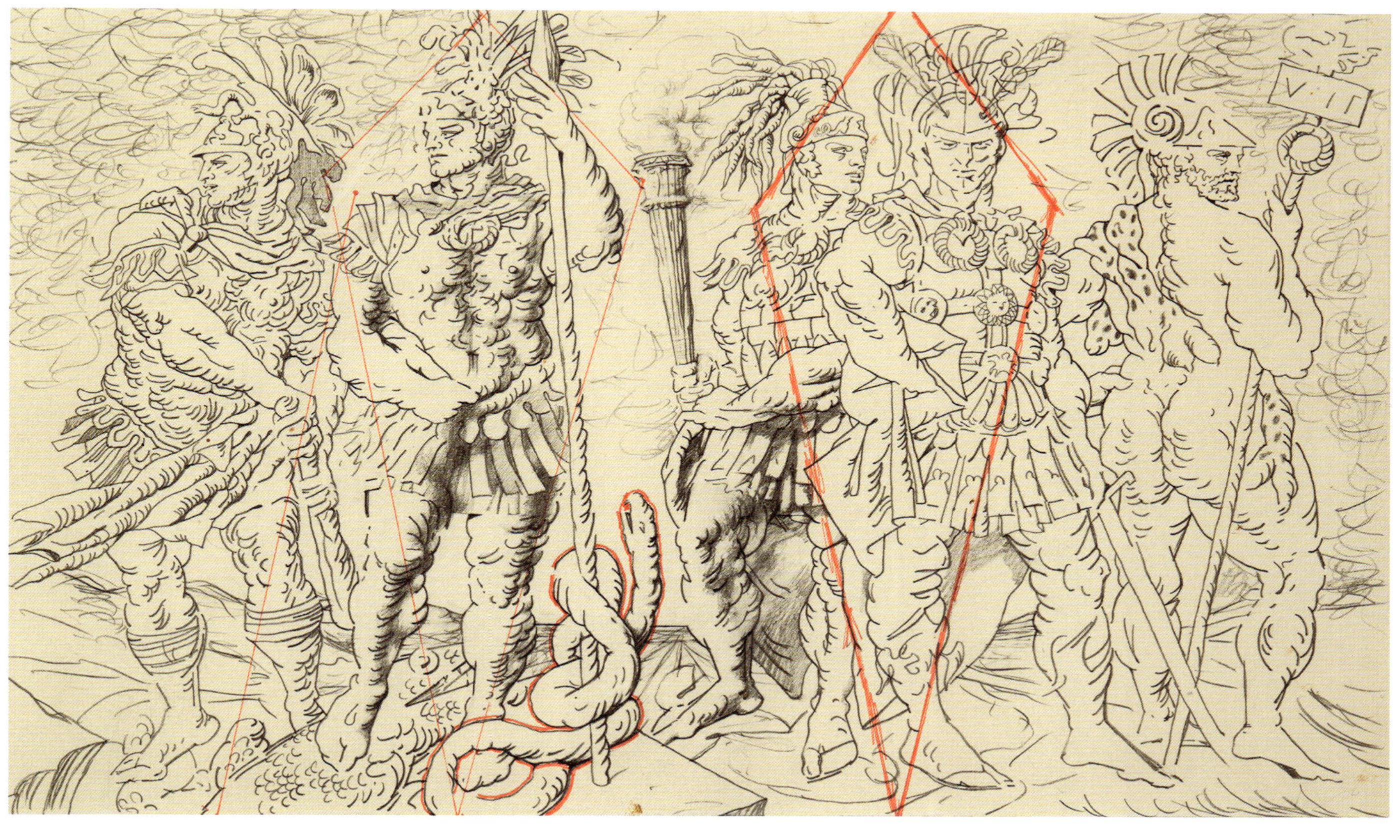

29 **Arsen Savadov** (b. 1962)

Untitled (Horse), 1987 | Oil on canvas | 79¼ × 120 × ⅞ in. (201.3 × 304.8 × 2.2 cm)

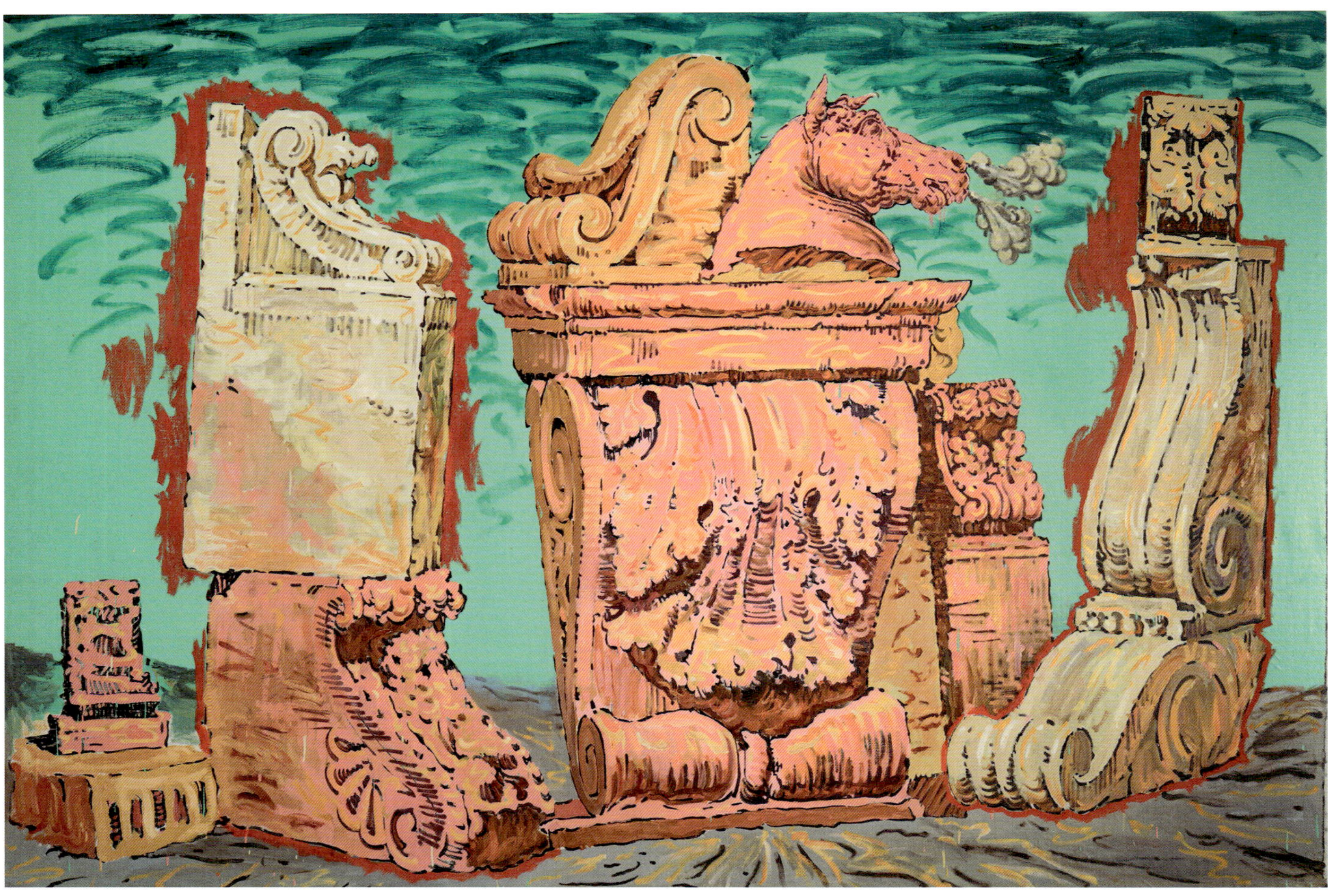

30 **Arsen Savadov** (b. 1962)

Snake Charmer, 1989–90 | Oil on canvas | 121 × 85½ in. (307.3 × 217.2 cm)

GIFT OF ROBERT L. AND ANN R. FROMER

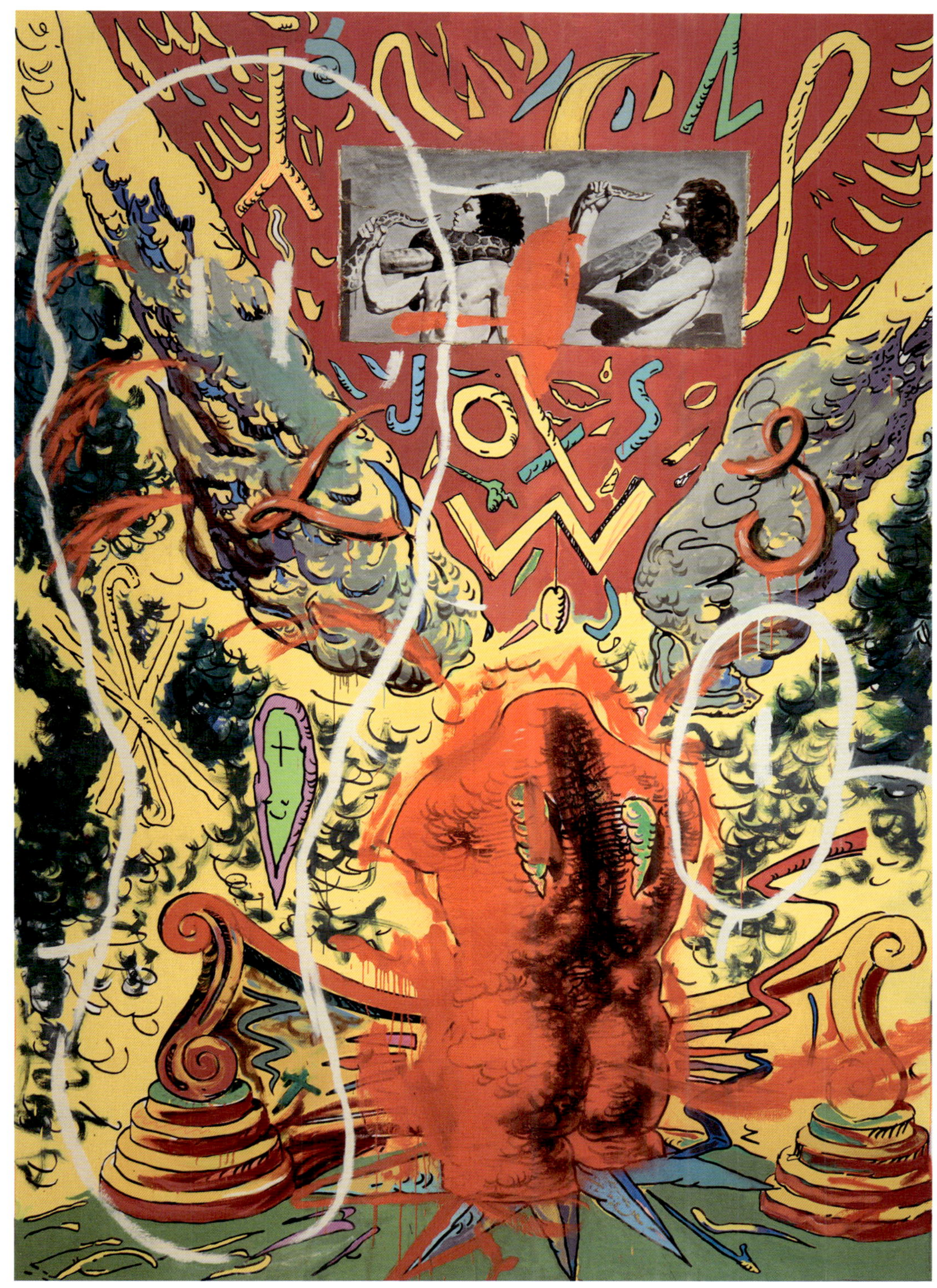

31 **Arsen Savadov** (b. 1962)

Untitled, undated | Pencil, ink on paper | 8$\frac{3}{4}$ × 11$\frac{9}{16}$ in. (22.3 × 29.4 cm)

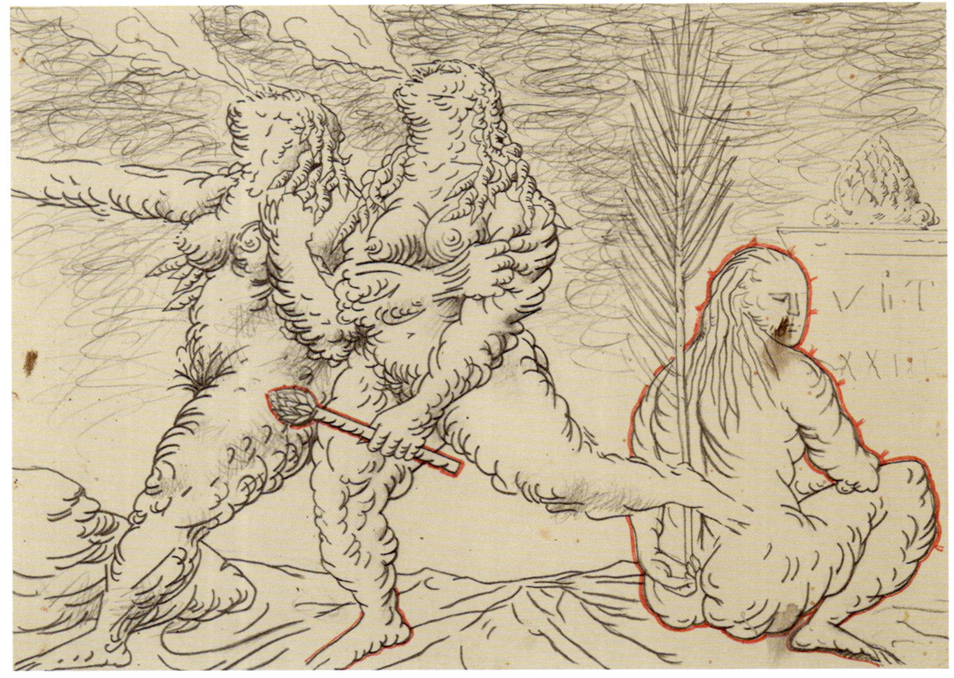

32 **Arsen Savadov** (b. 1962)

Untitled, undated | Graphite, felt-tip pen on paper | 7 5/16 × 16 5/8 in. (18.5 × 42.3 cm)

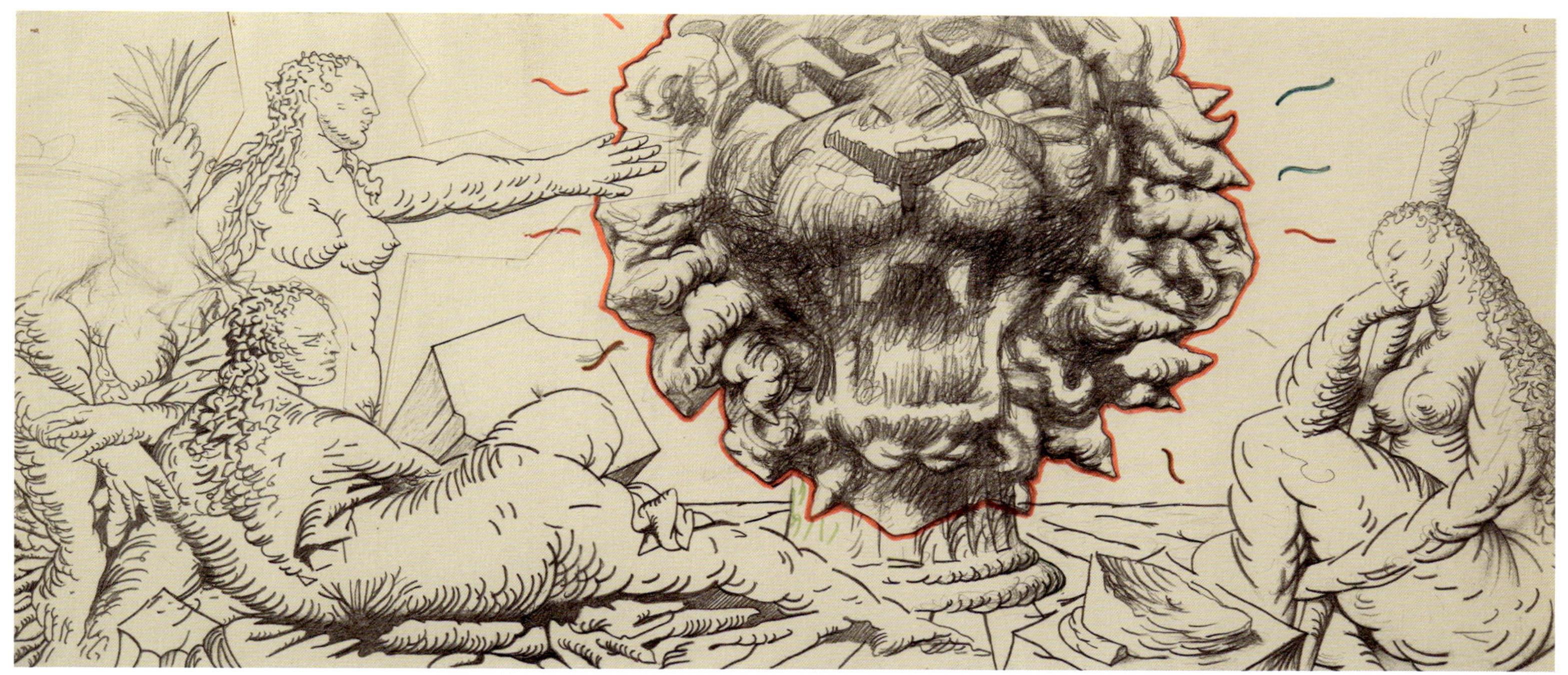

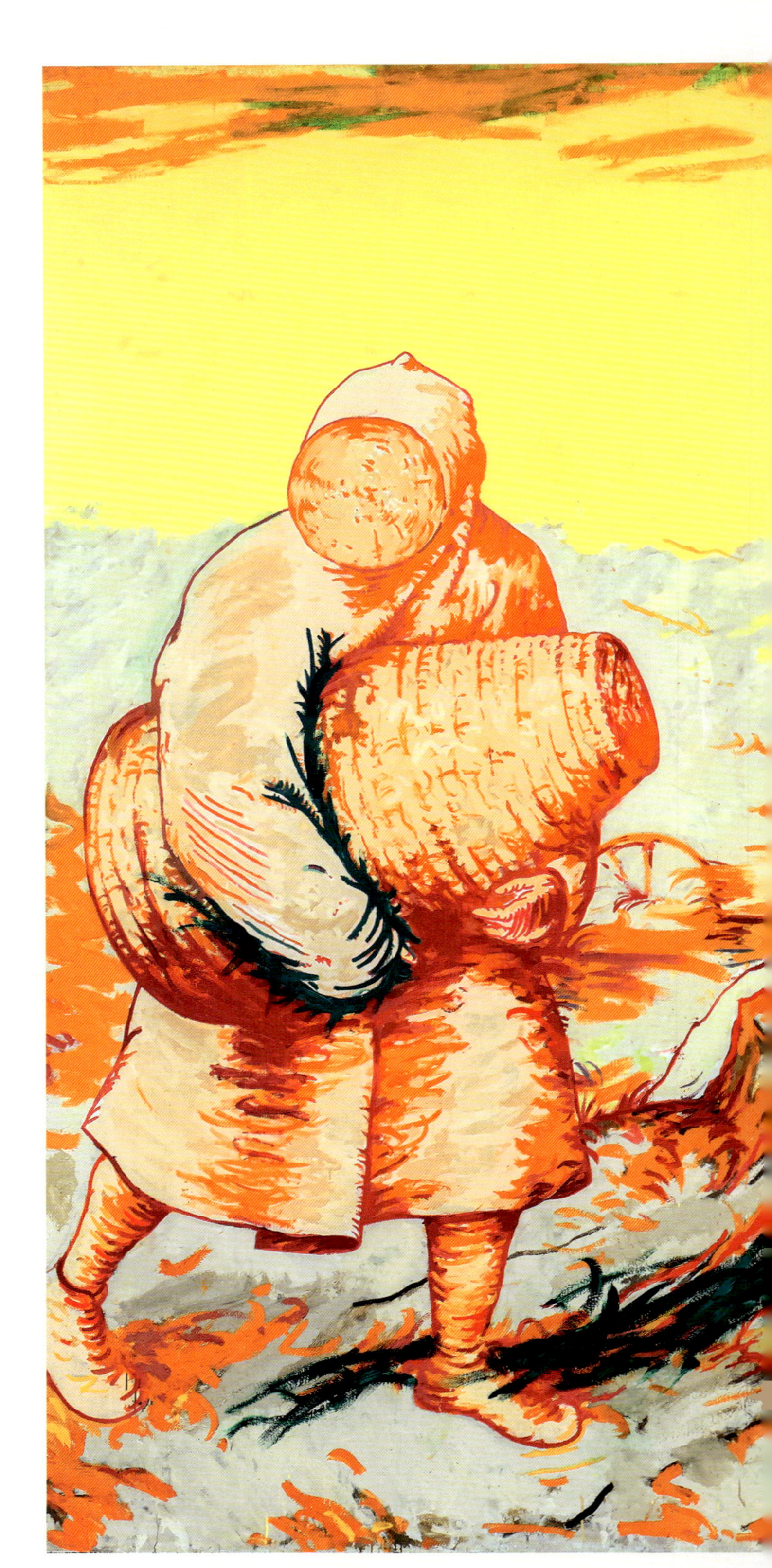

33 **Georgii Senchenko** (b. 1962)

Sacred Landscape of Pieter Bruegel, 1988 | Oil on canvas | 110 × 166 in. (279.4 × 421.6 cm)

GIFT OF ROBERT L. AND ANN R. FROMER

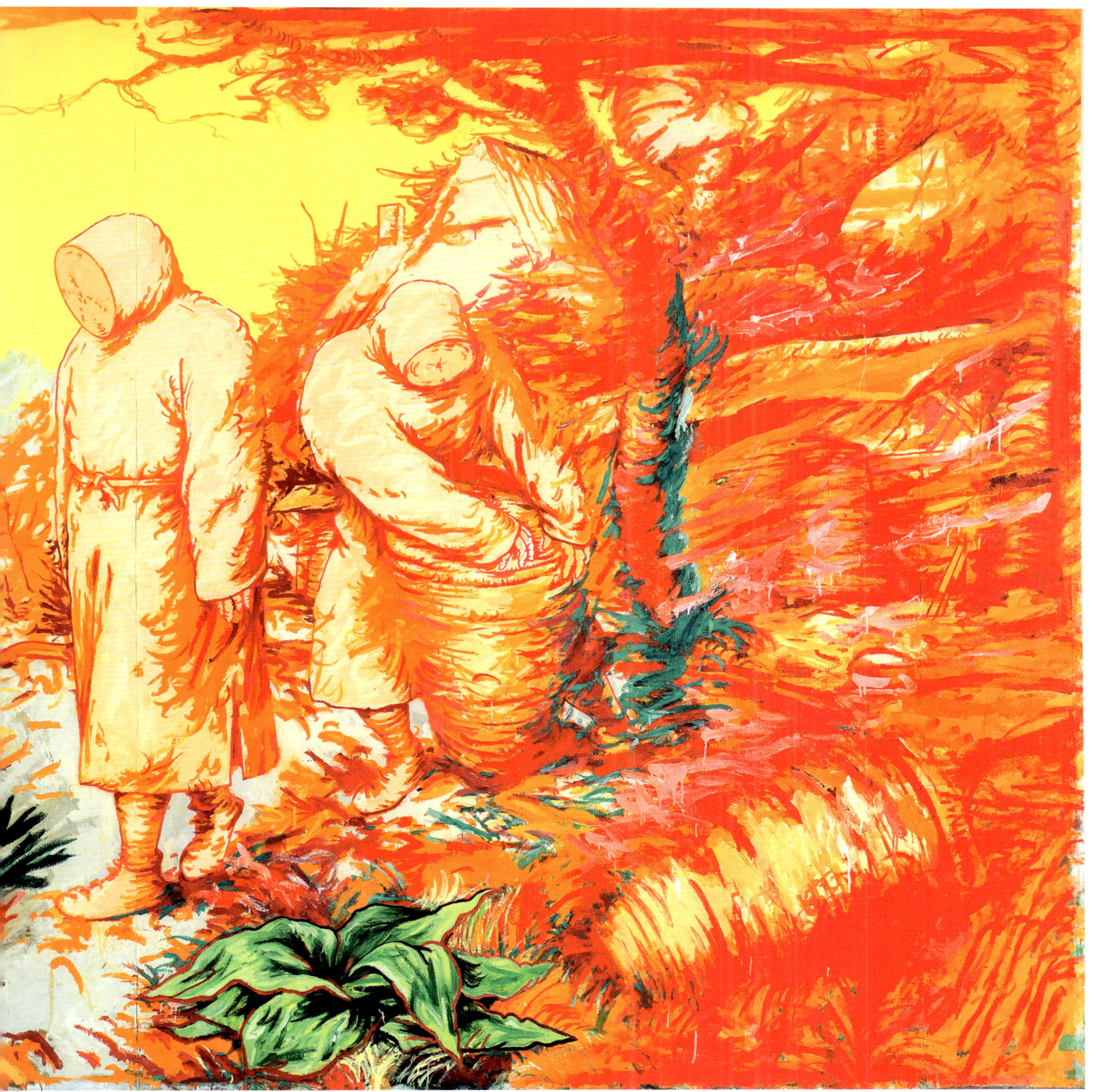

34 **Tiberiy Silvashi** (b. 1947)

Midnight, 1981 | Oil on canvas | 39⅜ × 47¼ in. (100 × 120 cm)

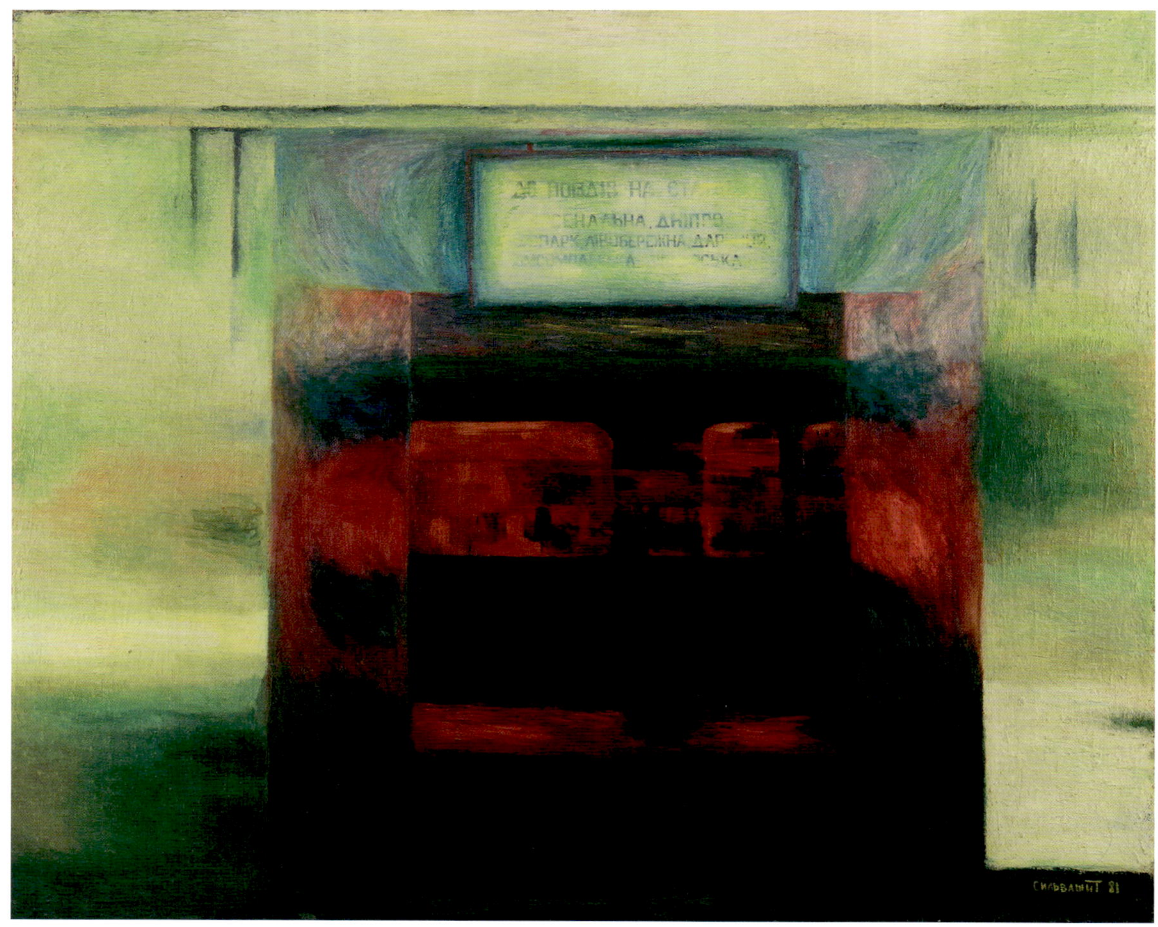

35 **Tiberiy Silvashi** (b. 1947)

Guest, 1982 | Oil on canvas | $39\frac{3}{16} \times 59\frac{13}{16}$ in. (99.5 × 152 cm)

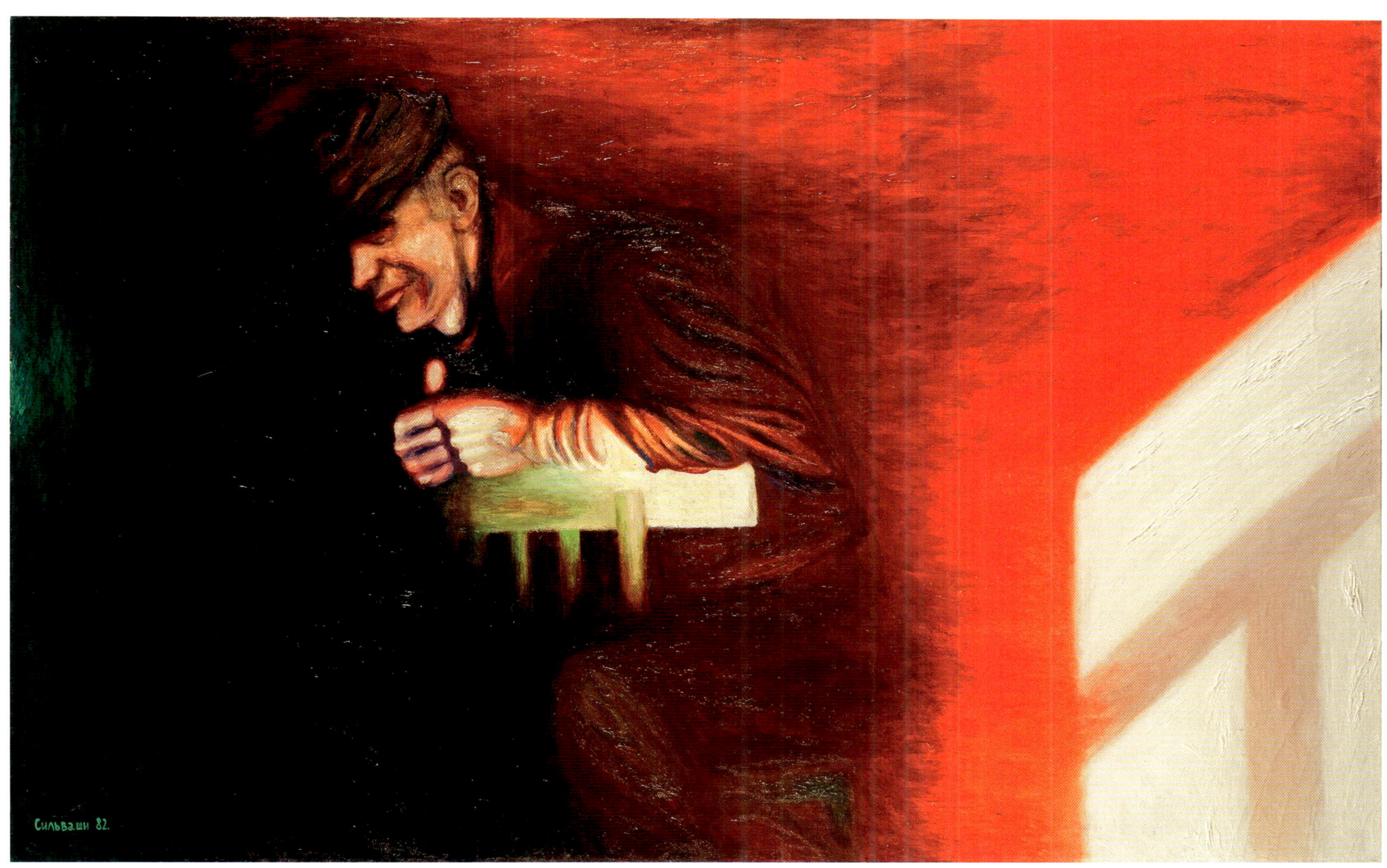

36 **Marina Skugareva** (b. 1962)

Portrait of Anatoly Stepanenko, 1988 | Tapestry | 47¼ × 59¹⁄₁₆ in. (120 × 150 cm)

COLLECTION OF THE ARTIST

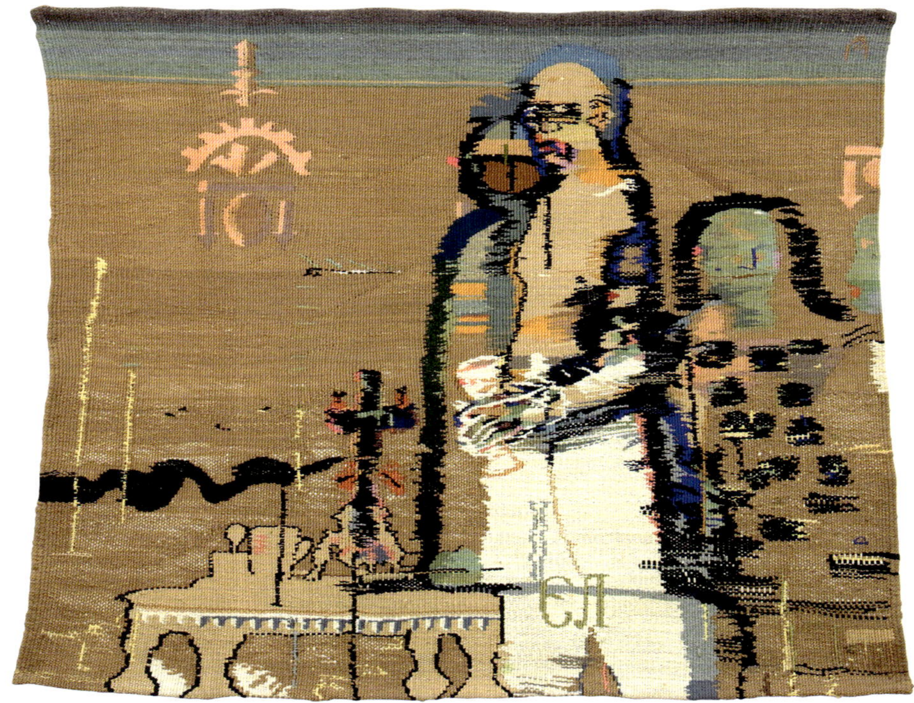

37 **Marina Skugareva** (b. 1962)

Sevastopol Waltz, 1994 | Oil and embroidery on canvas | 70⅞ × 47¼ in. (120 × 180 cm)

FROM THE COLLECTION OF NATALIA AND VOLODYMYR SPIELVOGEL

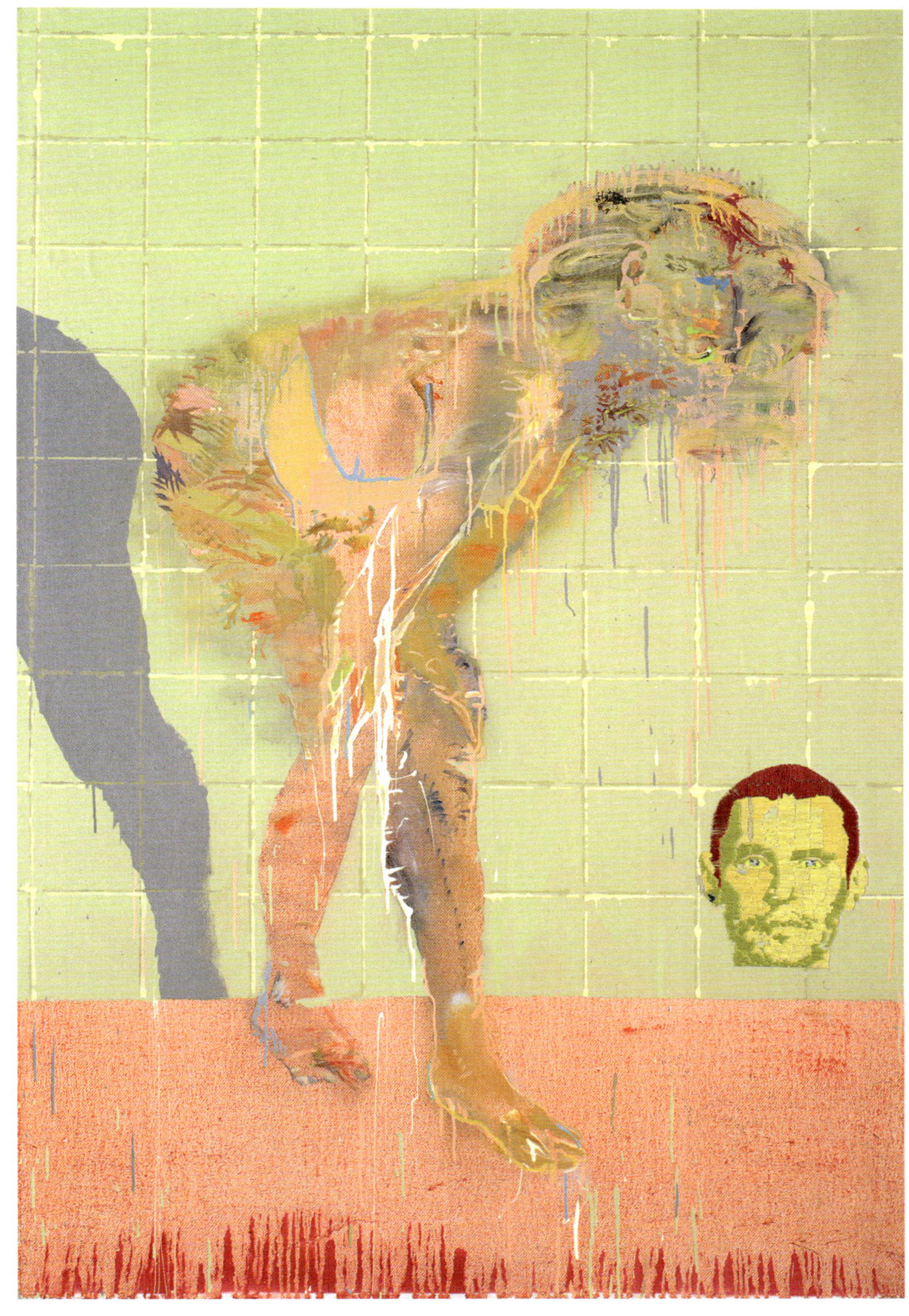

38 **Anatoly Stepanenko** (b. 1948)

Actuality, 1985 | Collage, ink, and felt-tip pen on paper | 12$\frac{5}{8}$ × 6$\frac{11}{16}$ in. (32 × 17 cm)

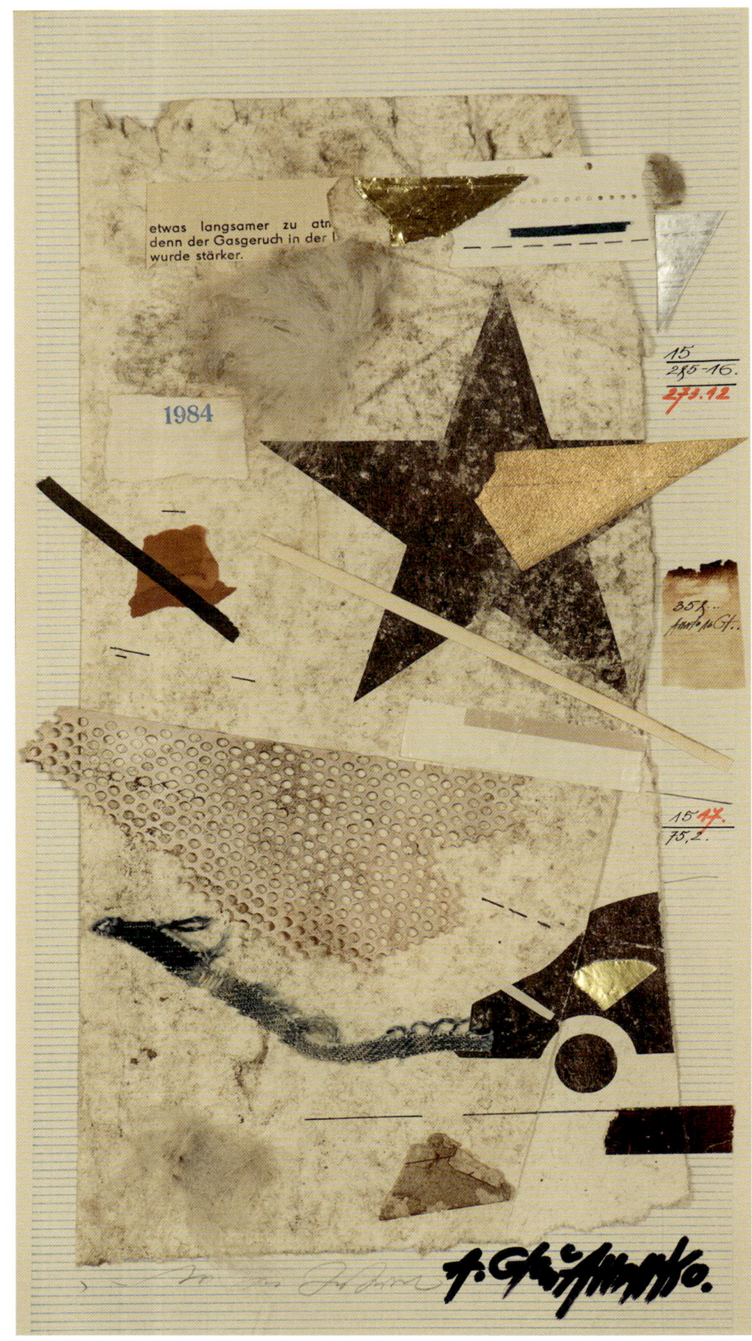

39 Anatoly Stepanenko (b. 1948)

Consequences Are Unknown (Shadow of the Albatross), 1985 | Collage, ink, graphite, felt-tip pen on paper | 11 13/16 × 6 3/4 in. (30 × 17.1 cm)

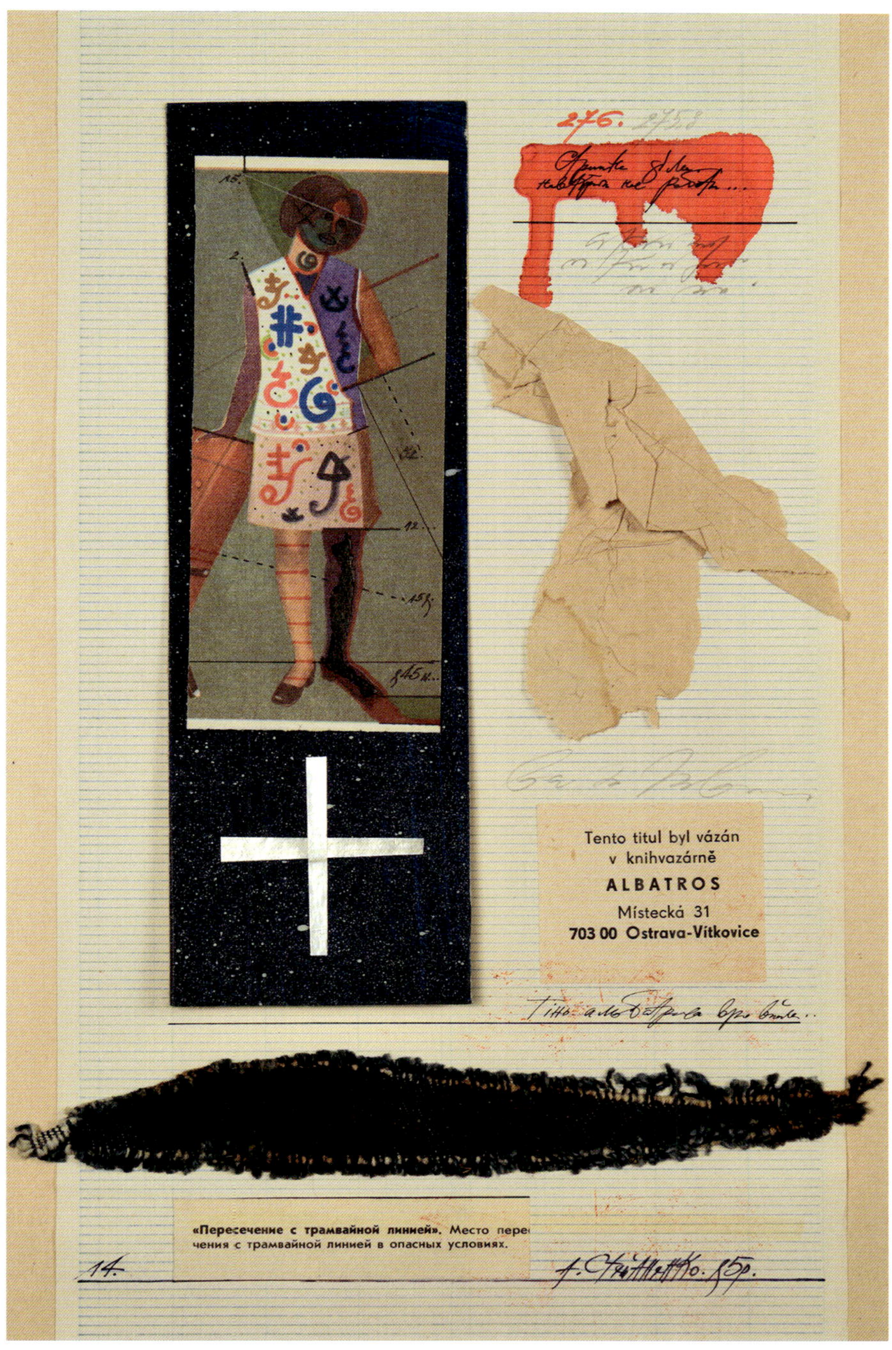

40 **Anatoly Stepanenko** (b. 1948)

The End of the Day of Jeans, 1985 | Ink, felt-tip pen, collage on paper | 11 13/16 × 6 11/16 in. (30 × 17 cm)

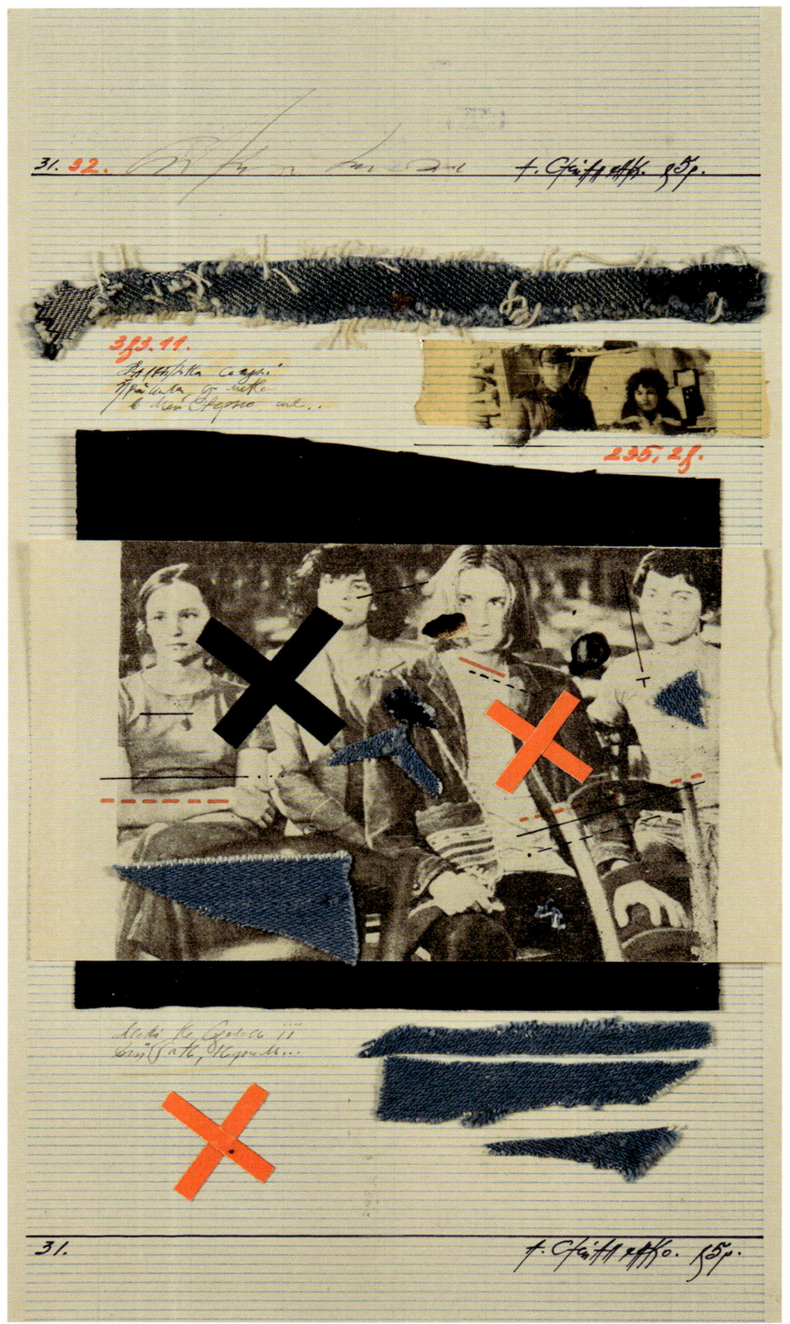

41 **Anatoly Stepanenko** (b. 1948)

Etude 19, 1985 | Ink, collage, and felt-tip pen on paper | $11\frac{13}{16} \times 6\frac{11}{16}$ in. (30 × 17 cm)

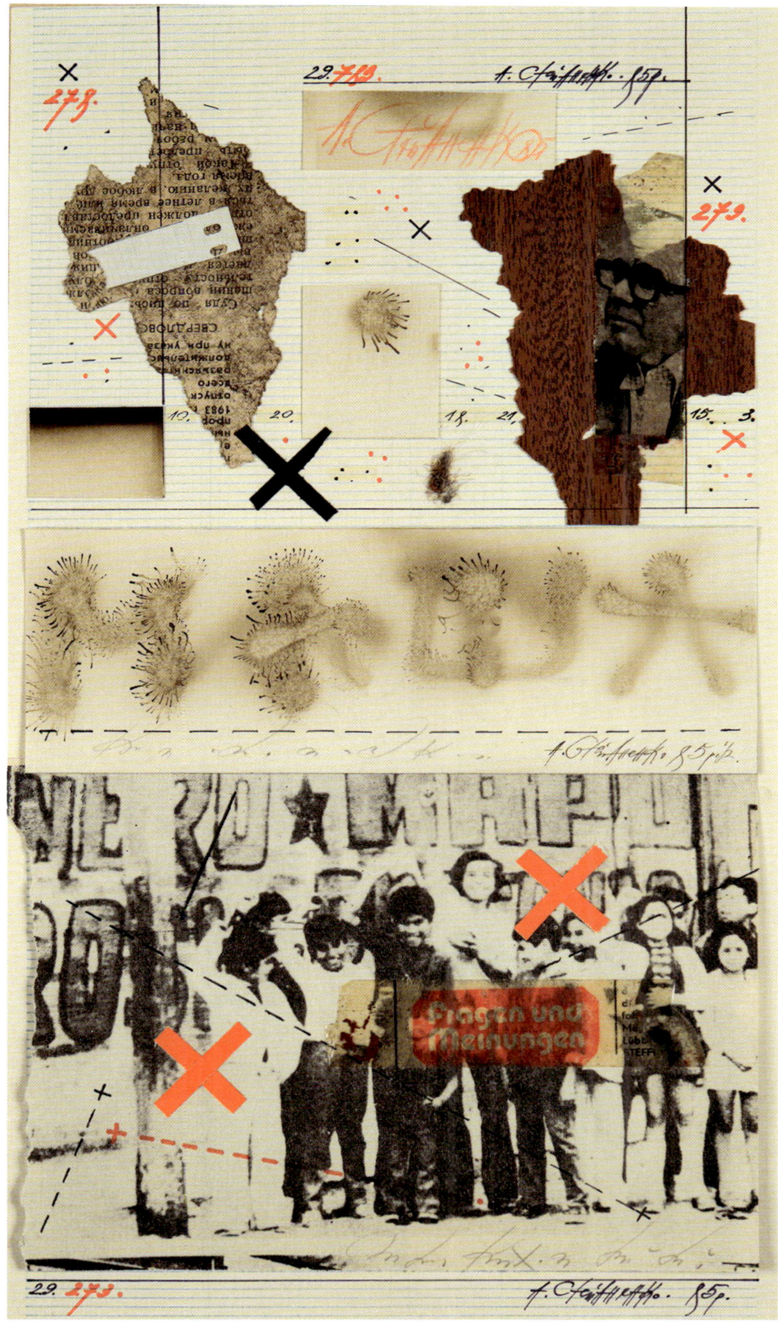

42 **Anatoly Stepanenko** (b. 1948)

The Life as a Playing Machine, 1985 | Mixed-media collage on paper | 12⅝ × 6¾ in. (32 × 17.1 cm)

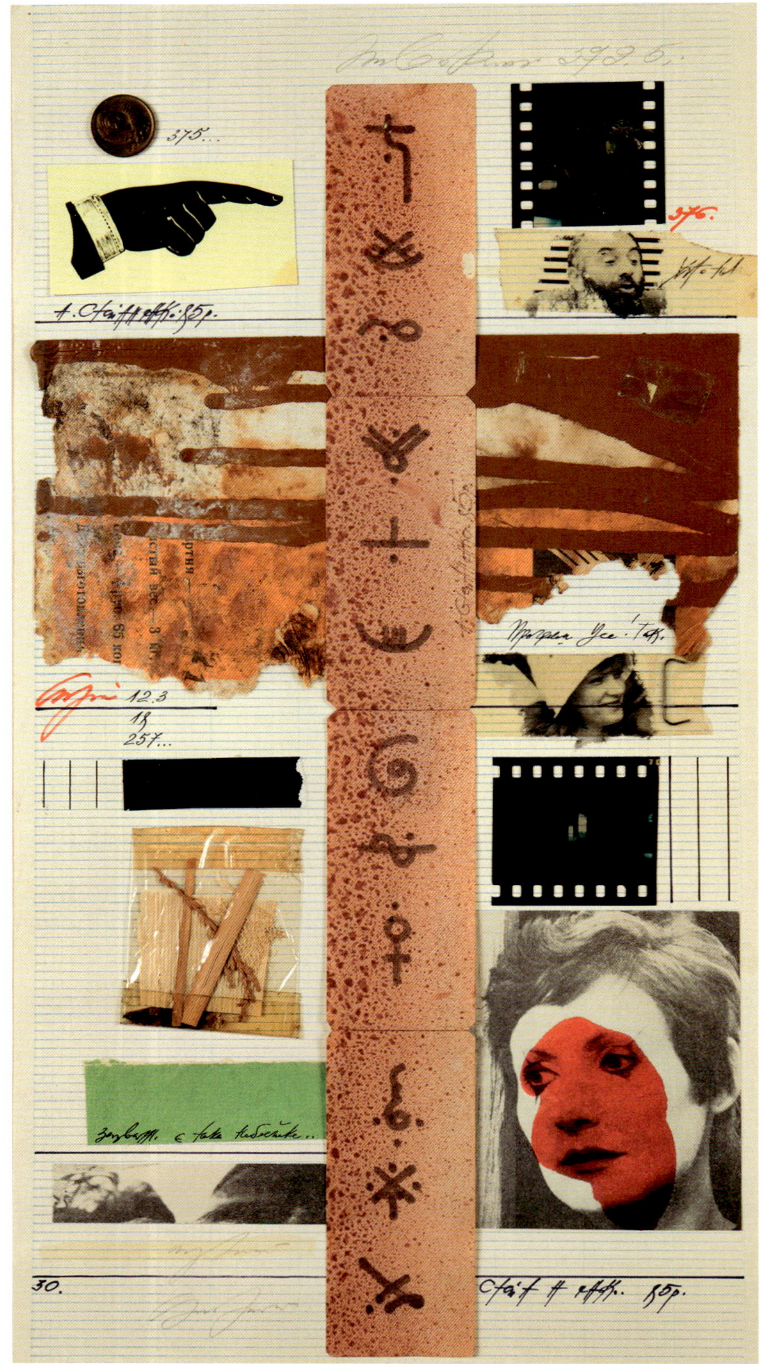

43 **Anatoly Stepanenko** (b. 1948)

Metaphoric Shot, 1985 | Paper collage on paper | 11 × 6 11/16 in. (28 × 17 cm)

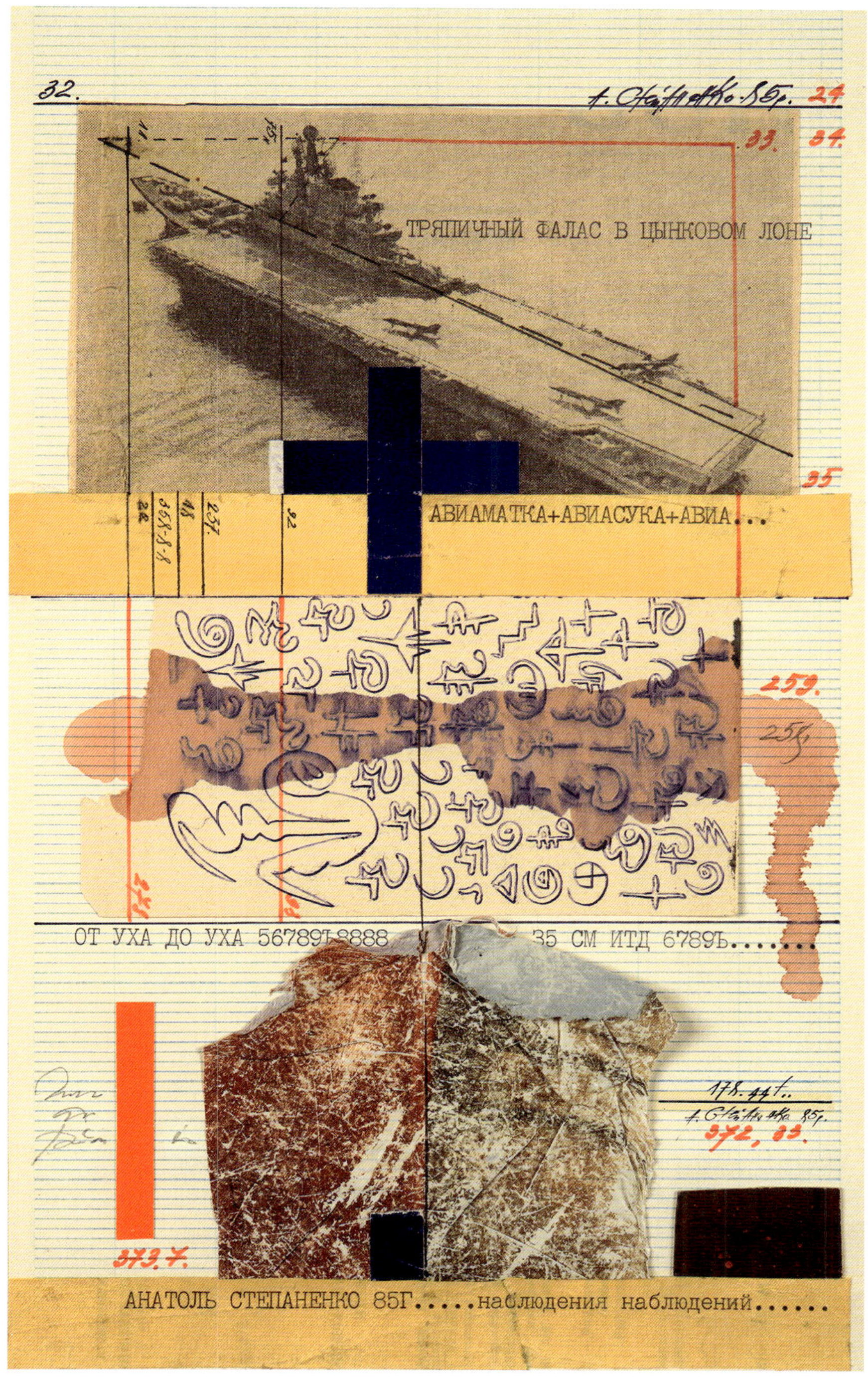

44 **Anatoly Stepanenko** (b. 1948)

Metaphysics of Night Symbols, 1985 | Foil, paper, and mixed media on paper | 12⅝ × 6¾ in. (32 × 17.1 cm)

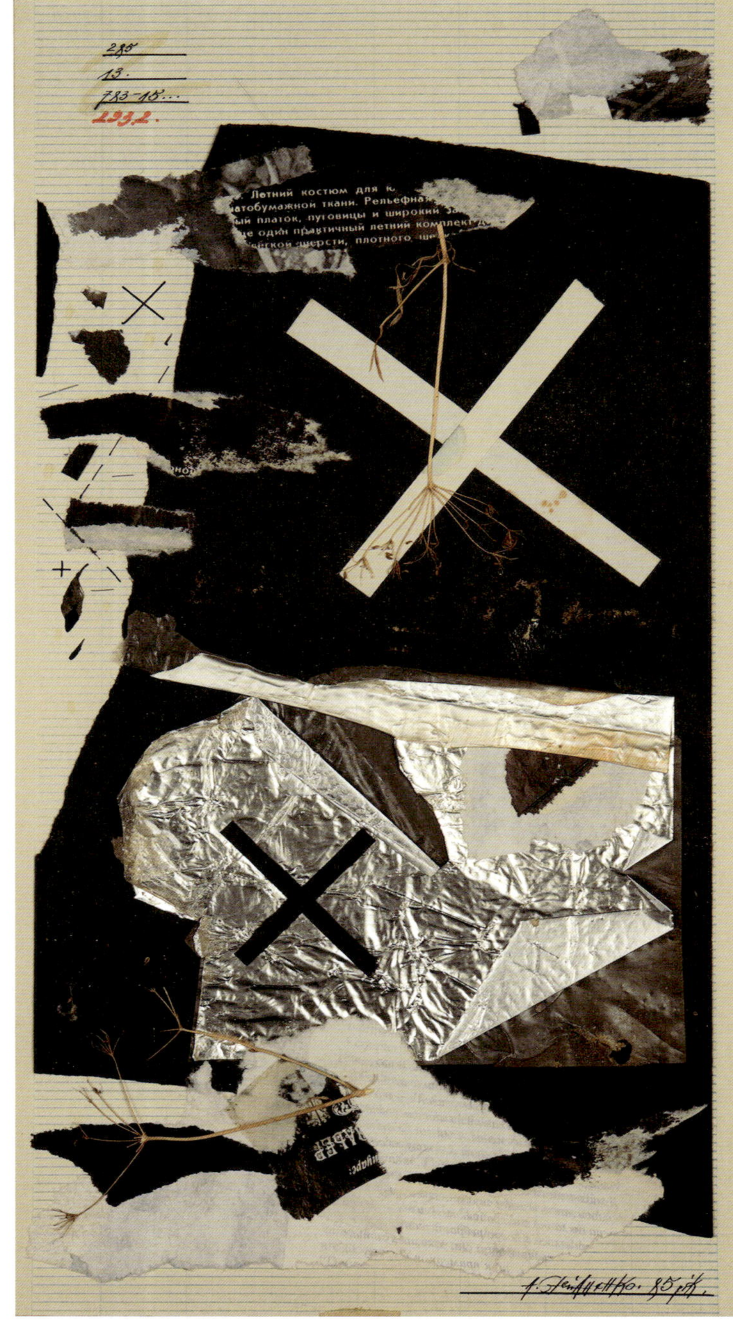

45 **Anatoly Stepanenko** (b. 1948)

Remembrance of Concrete Objects, 1985 | Mixed-media collage on paper | $13\frac{7}{16} \times 6\frac{11}{16}$ in. (34.1 × 17 cm)

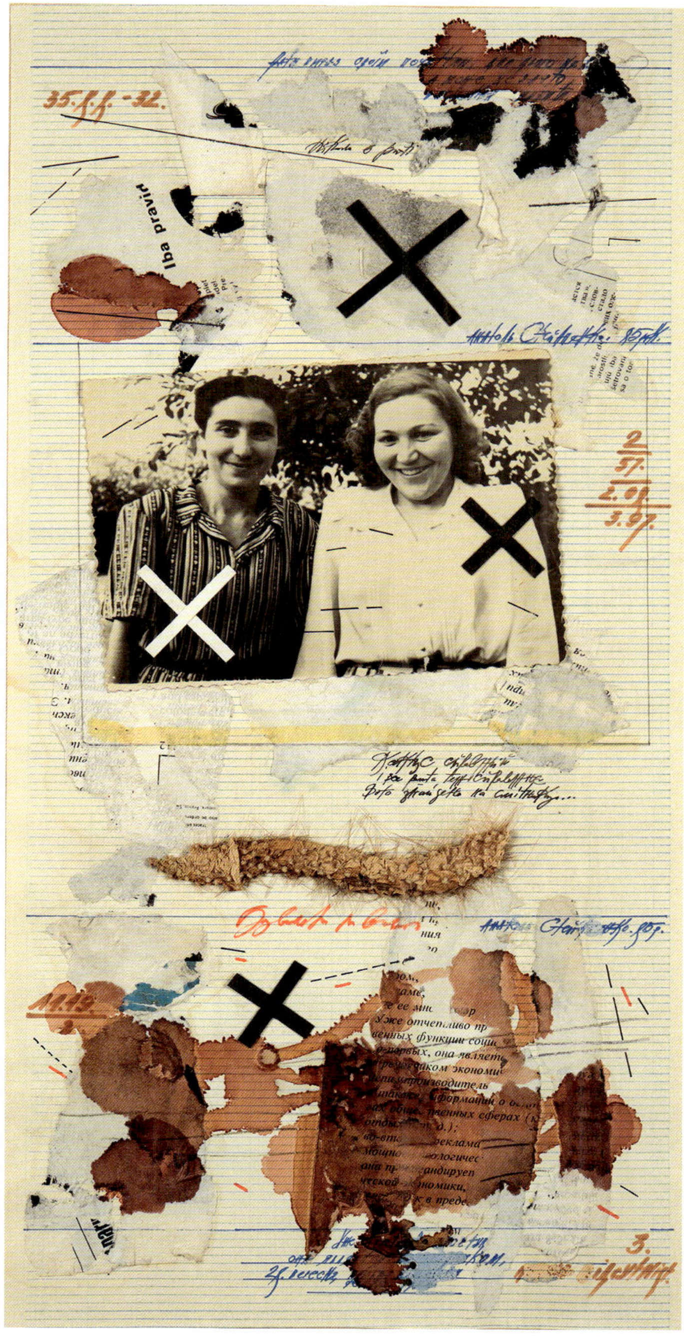

46 **Anatoly Stepanenko** (b. 1948)

Sentimental Herbal Collection, 1985 | Mixed-media collage on paper | 12¼ × 6¾ in. (31.1 × 17.1 cm)

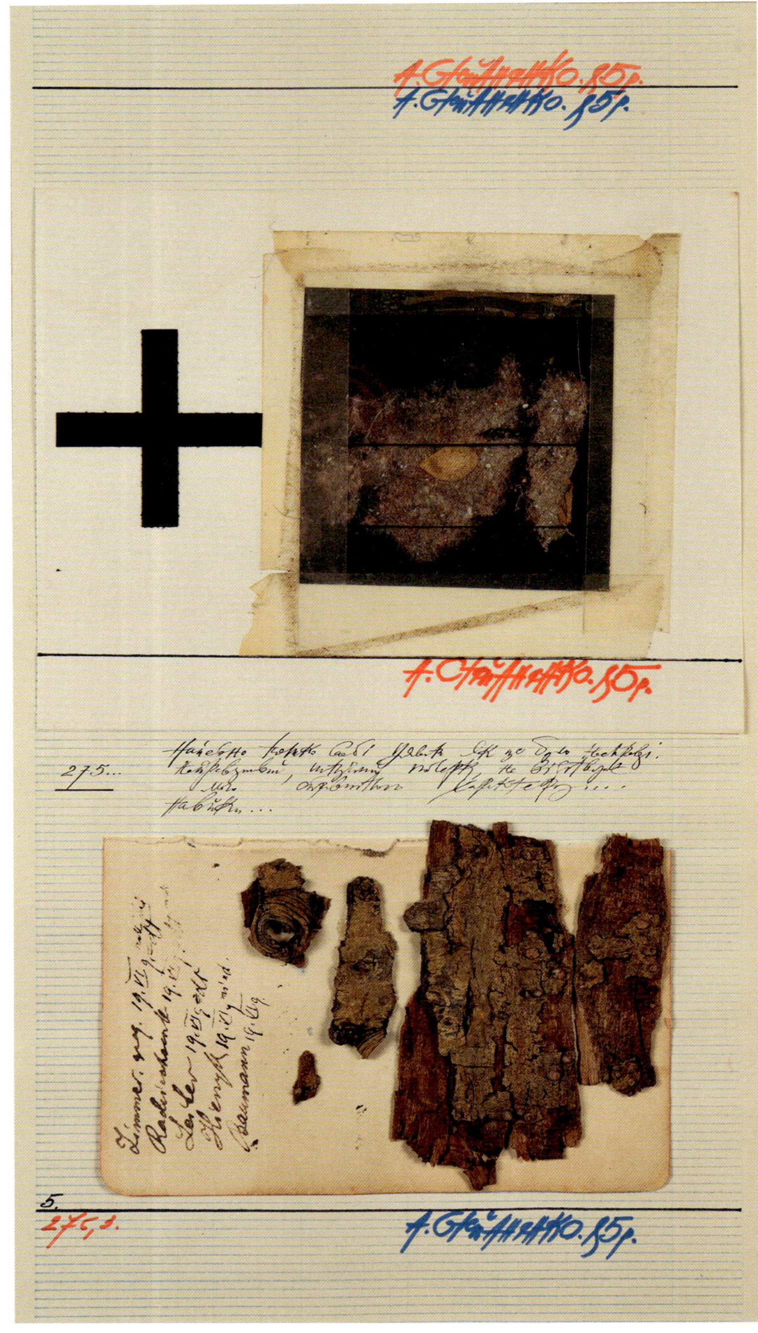

47 Anatoly Stepanenko (b. 1948)

Sleep, Uncle, Sleep, 1985 | Collage, ink, graphite, felt-tip pen on paper | $11\frac{13}{16} \times 6\frac{11}{16}$ in. (30 × 17 cm)

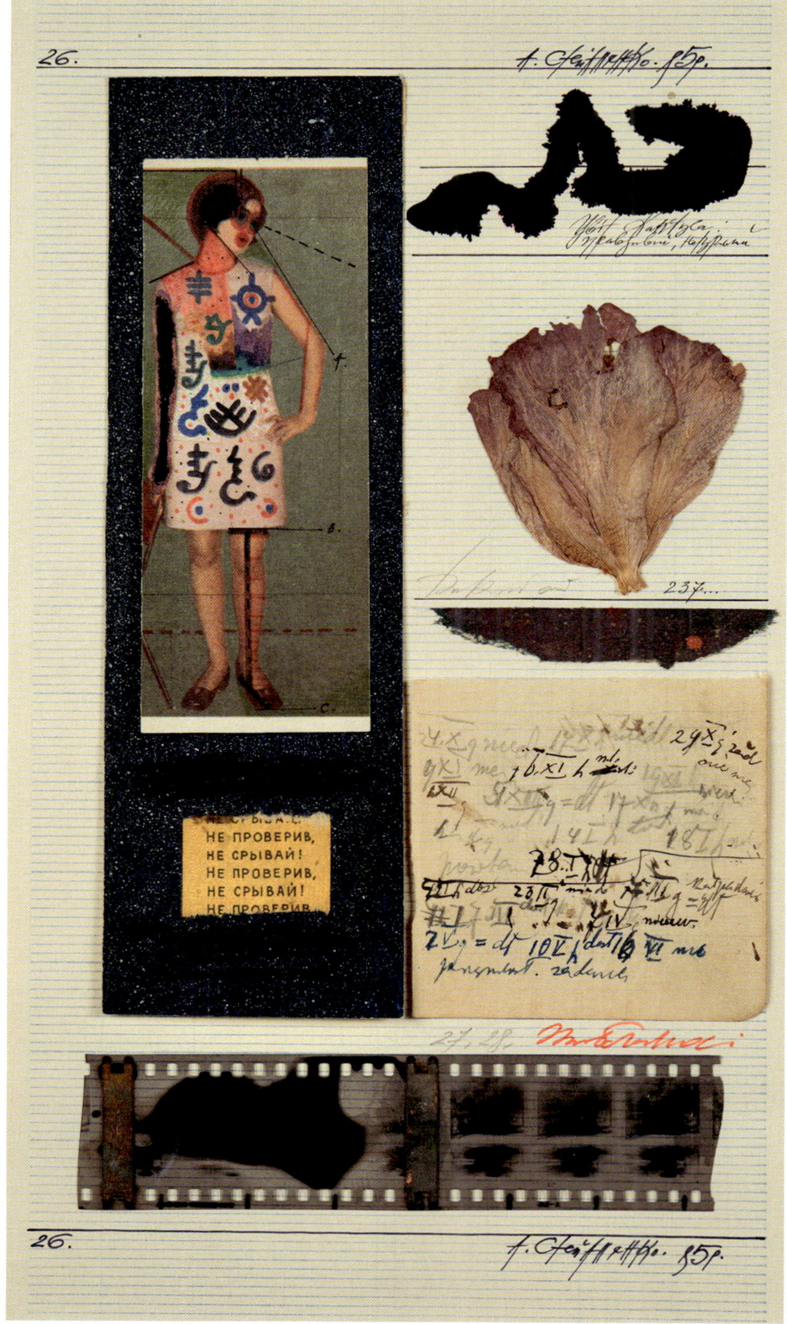

48 **Sergei Sviatchenko** (b. 1952)

Untitled from the series *Blue Country II*, 1991 | Mixed media on paper | 29½ × 21⅝ in. (75 × 55 cm)

ABRAMOVYCH FOUNDATION

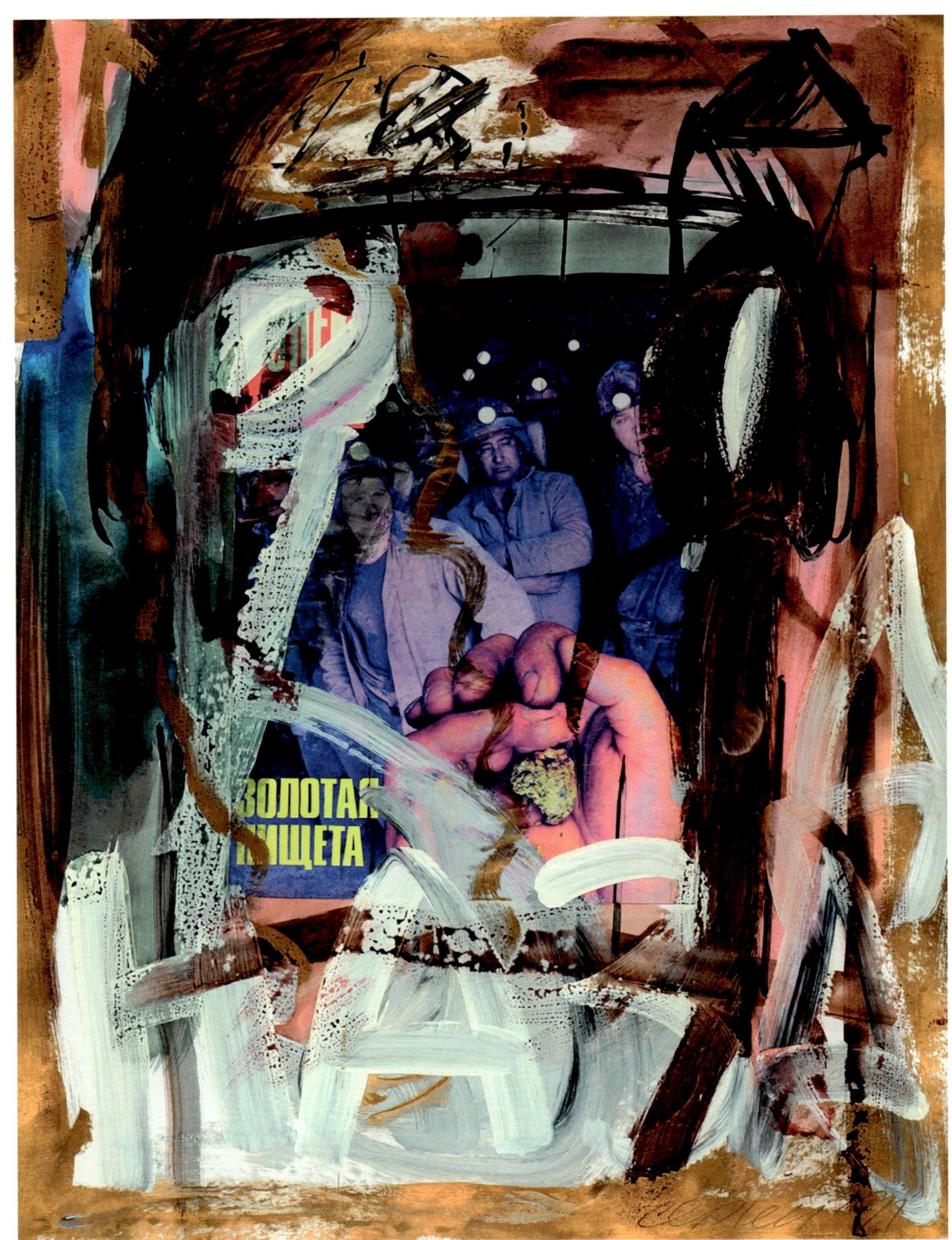

49 **Sergei Sviatchenko** (b. 1952)

Untitled from the series *Blue Country II*, 1991 | Mixed media on paper | 29½ × 21⅝ in. (75 × 55 cm)

ABRAMOVYCH FOUNDATION

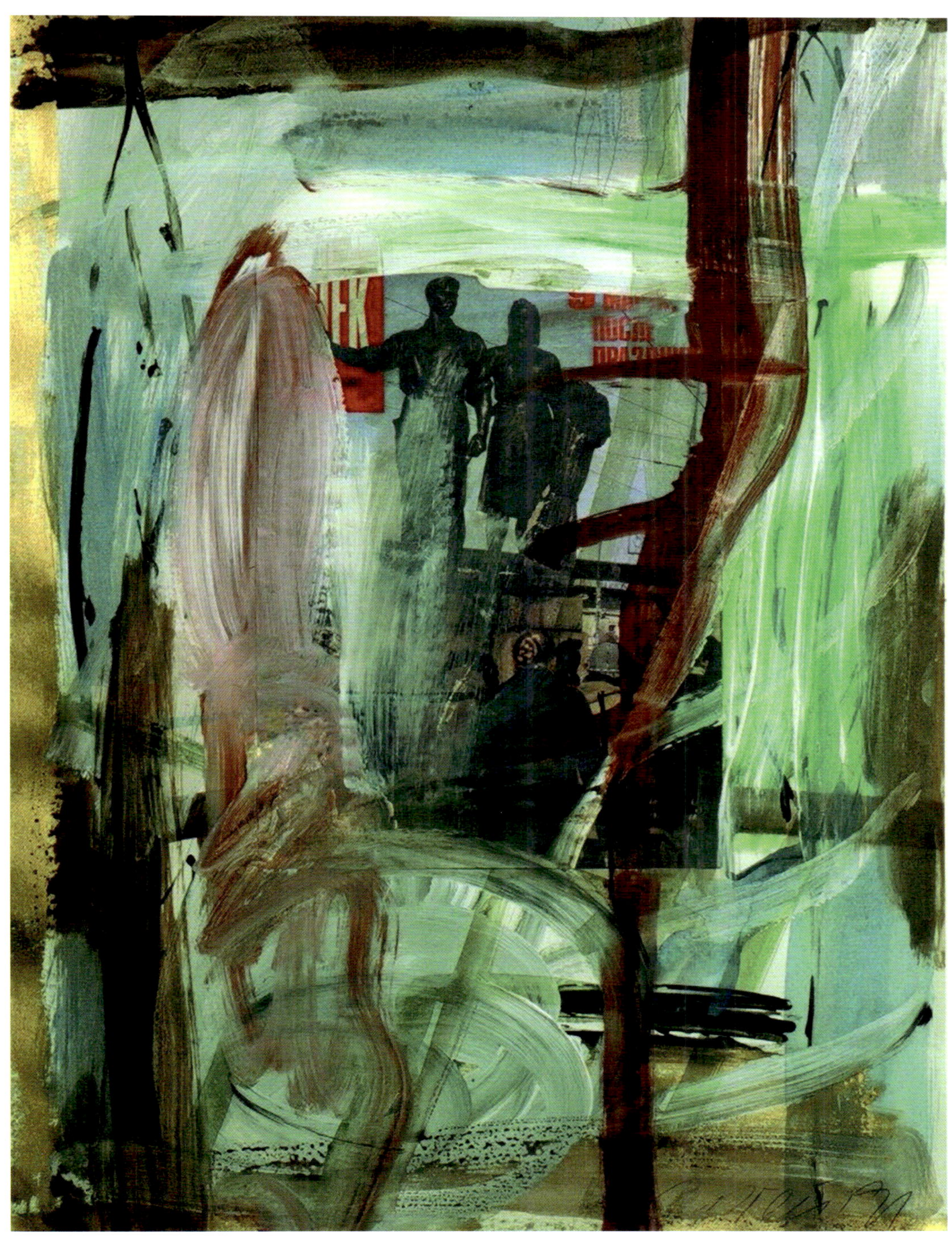

50 **Fedir Tetianych** (1942–2007)

UFO, 1970 | Tempera on paper | 5³⁄₁₆ × 7⁹⁄₁₆ in. (13.1 × 19.2 cm)

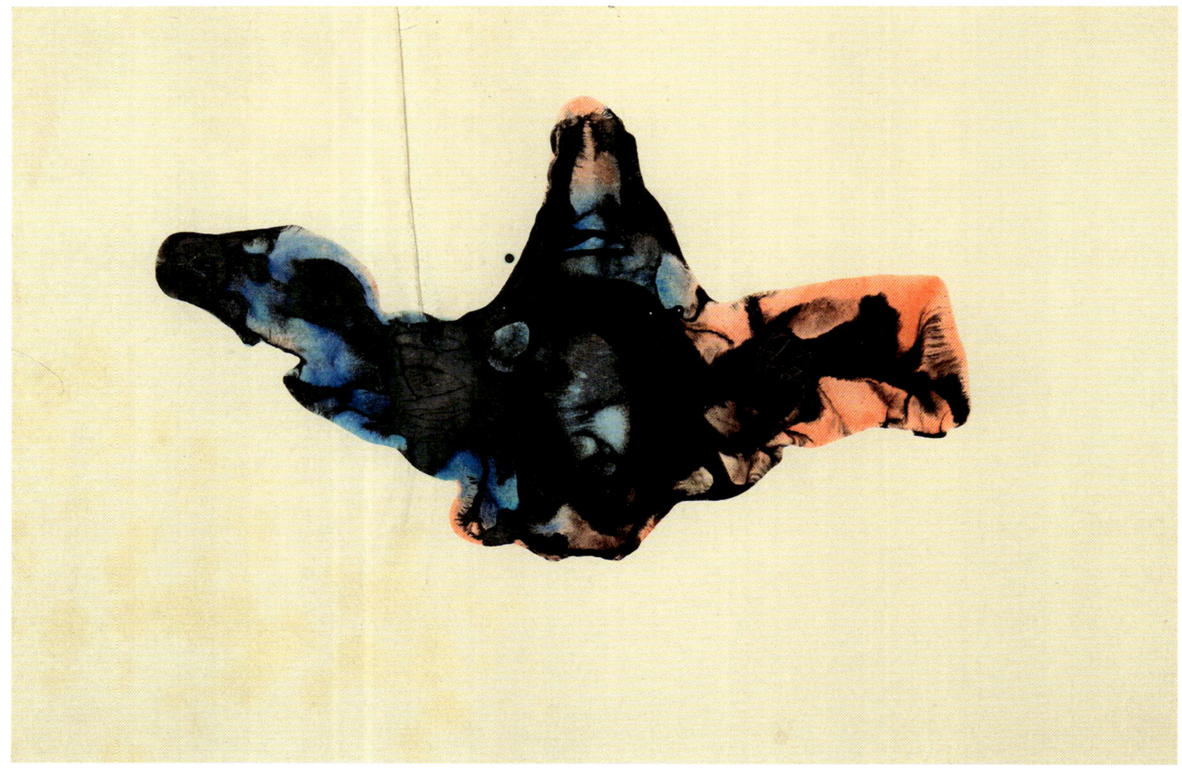

51 **Oleg Tistol** (b. 1960)

Self-Portrait with Ampules of Strychnine, 1981 | Oil on canvas | 19½ × 12⅜ in. (49.5 × 31.5 cm)

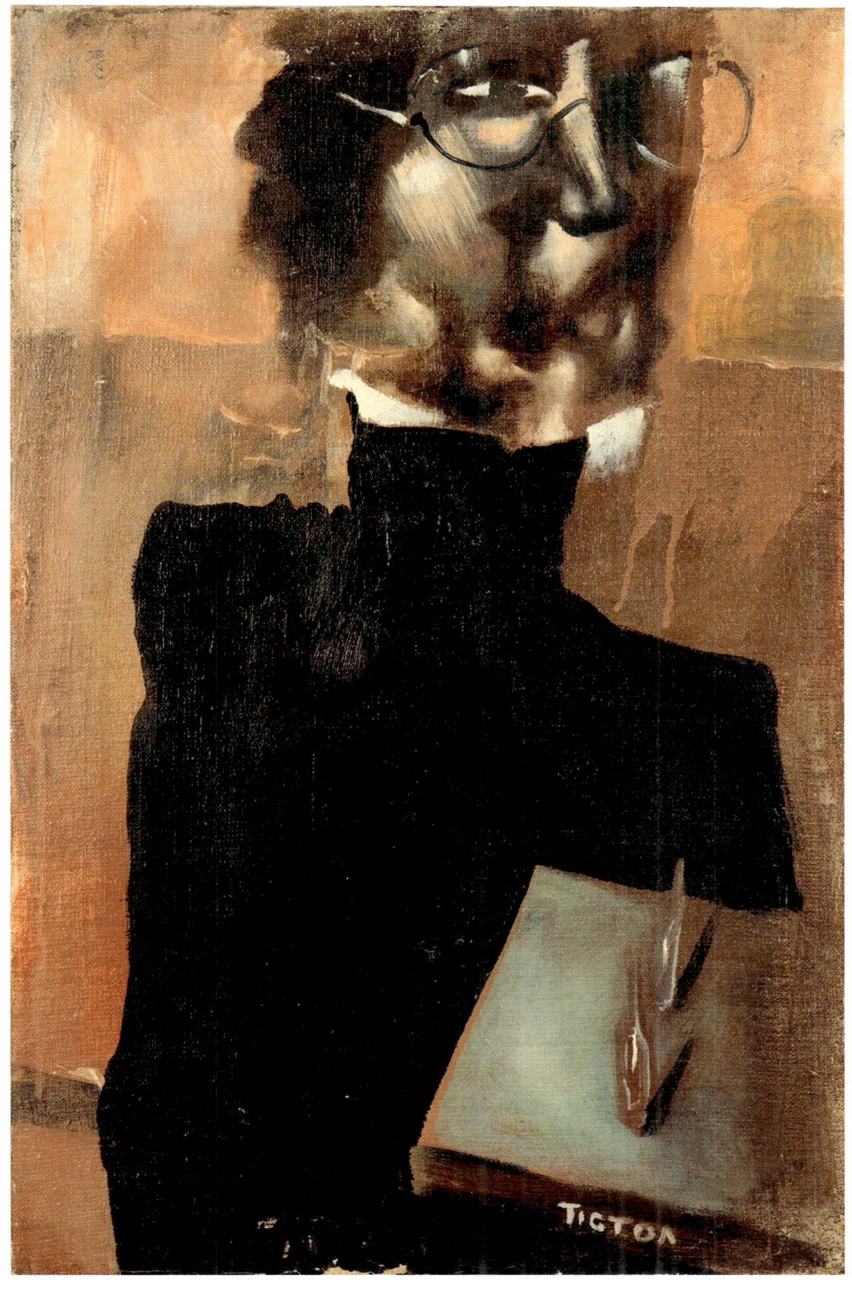

52 **Oleg Tistol** (b. 1960)

Buryat, 1985 | Gouache on paper | 12⁵⁄₁₆ × 7¹¹⁄₁₆ in. (31.3 × 19.6 cm)

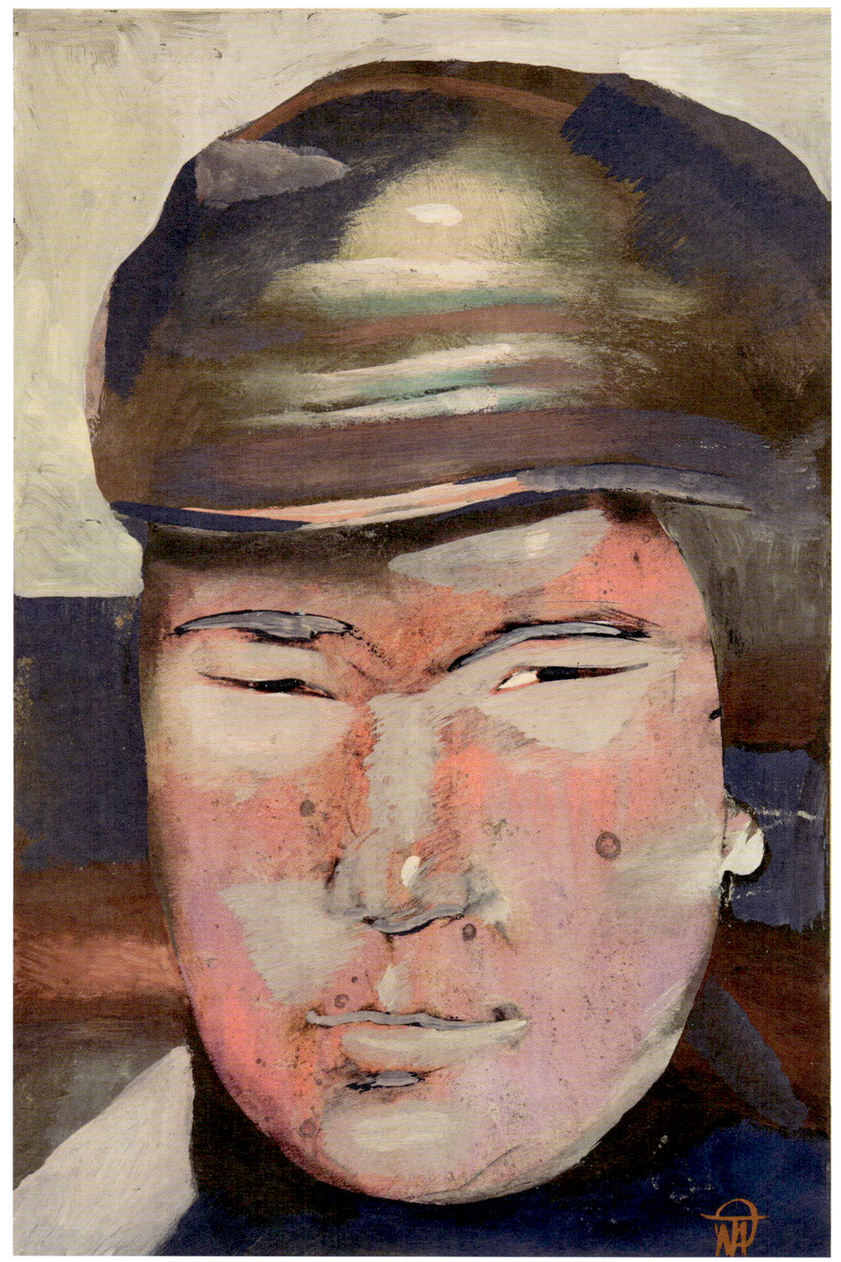

53 **Oleg Tistol** (b. 1960)

Buryat Kuznetsov, 1985 | Gouache on paper | 16⅞ × 13⁹⁄₁₆ in. (42.9 × 34.4 cm)

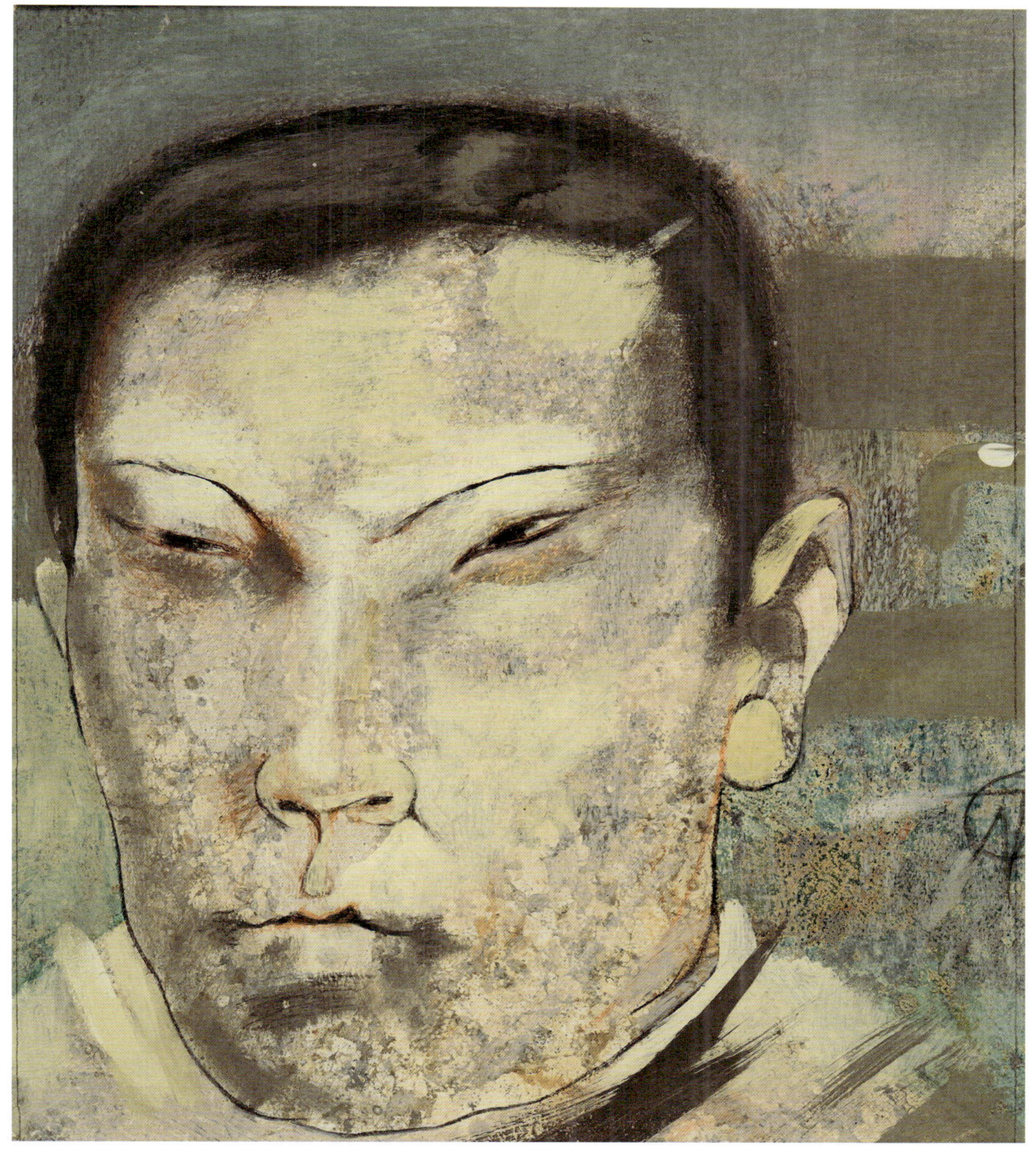

54 **Oleg Tistol** (b. 1960)

Four untitled works from the series *Ukrainian Money*, 1990 | Collage and ink on paper | 15¾ × 22⁷⁄₁₆ in. (40 × 57 cm) each

COLLECTION OF THE ARTIST

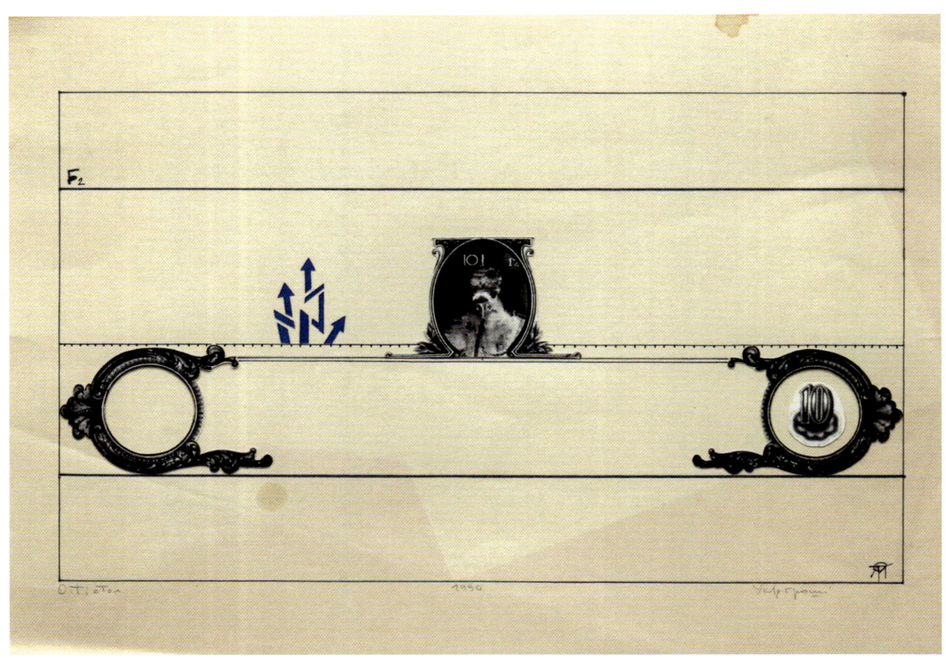

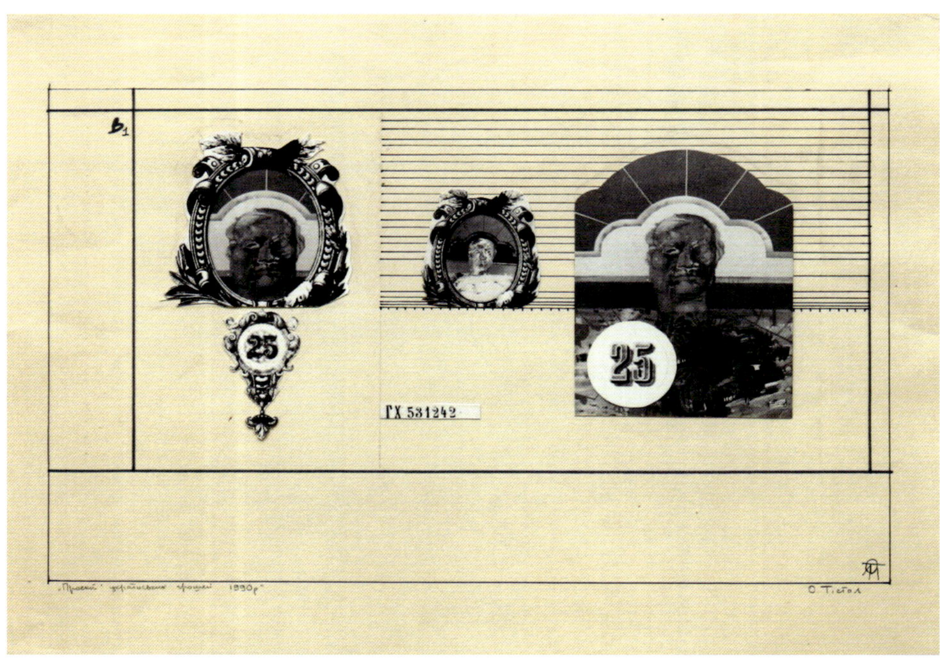

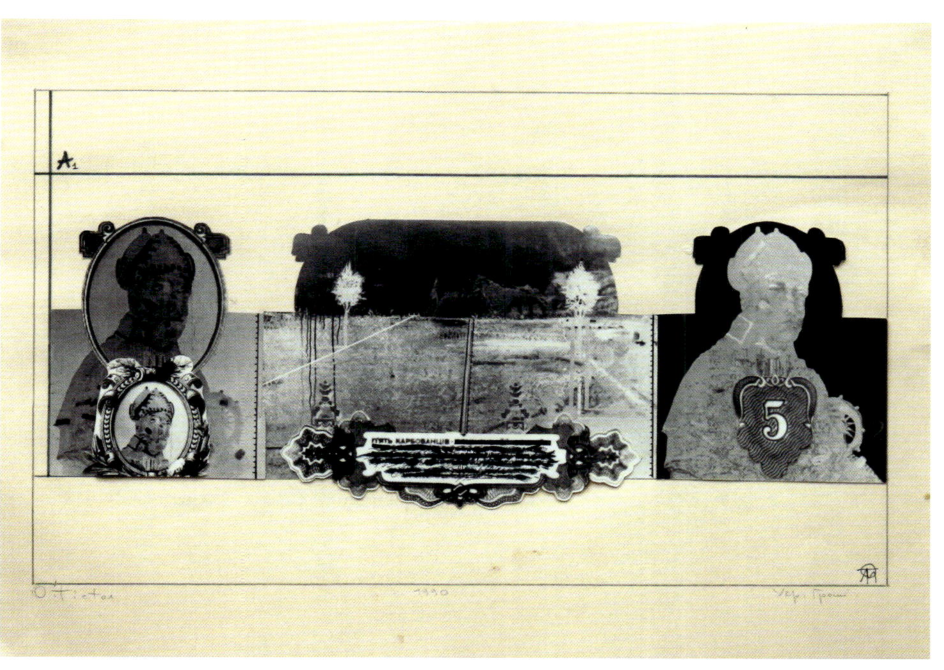
А1
ПЯТЬ КАРБОВАНЦІВ
5
1990

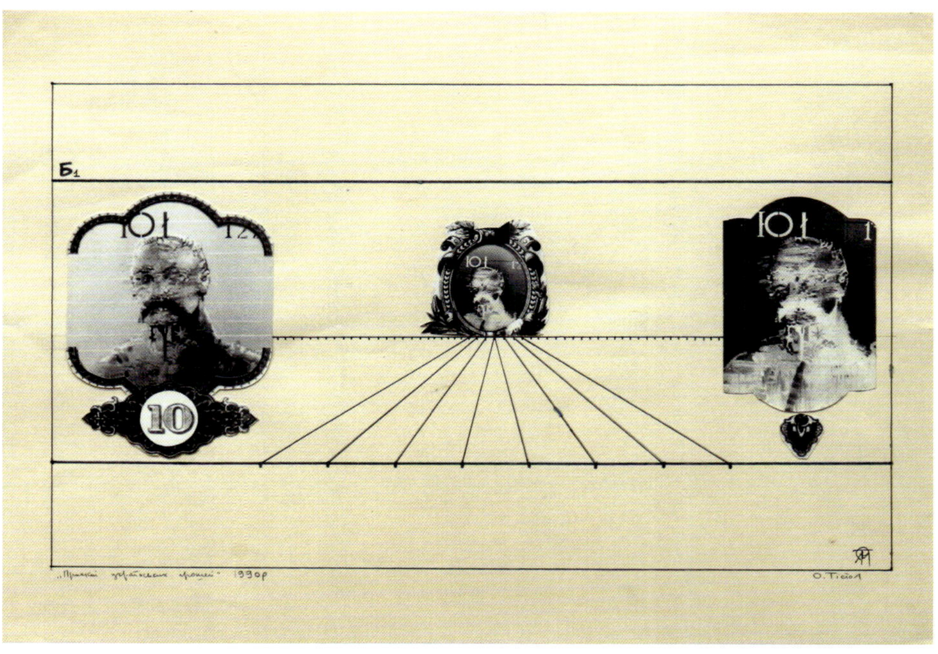
Б1
10
1990р
О. Тістол

55 **Valeria Troubina** (b. 1966)

Bowing, 1985 | Oil on canvas | 46$\frac{1}{16}$ × 30$\frac{11}{16}$ in. (117 × 78 cm)

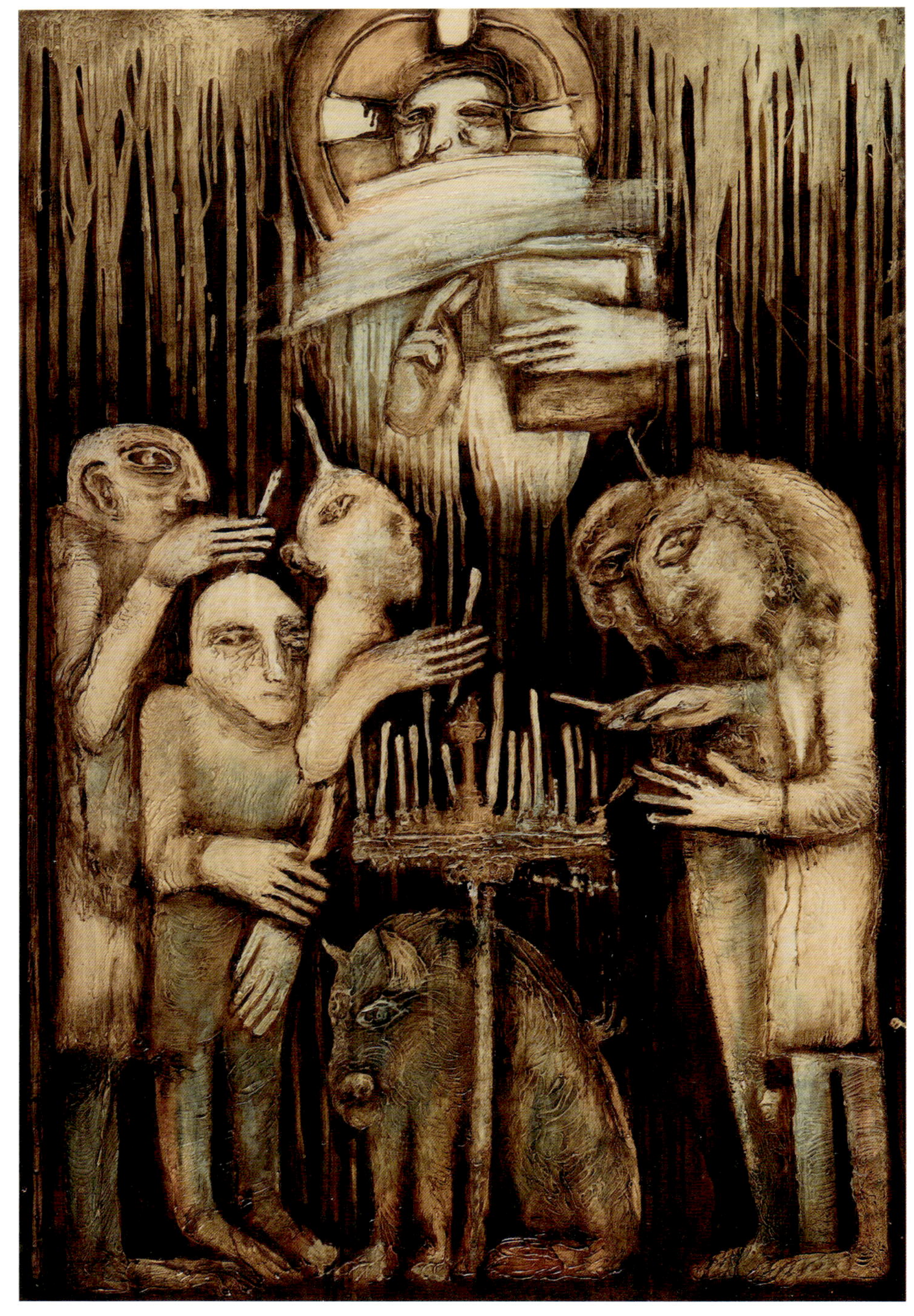

56 **Vasiliy Tsagolov** (b. 1957)

I Like My Job Very Much, 1992 | Color photograph on paper | 27 9/16 × 49 1/4 in. (70 × 125 cm)

ABRAMOVYCH FOUNDATION

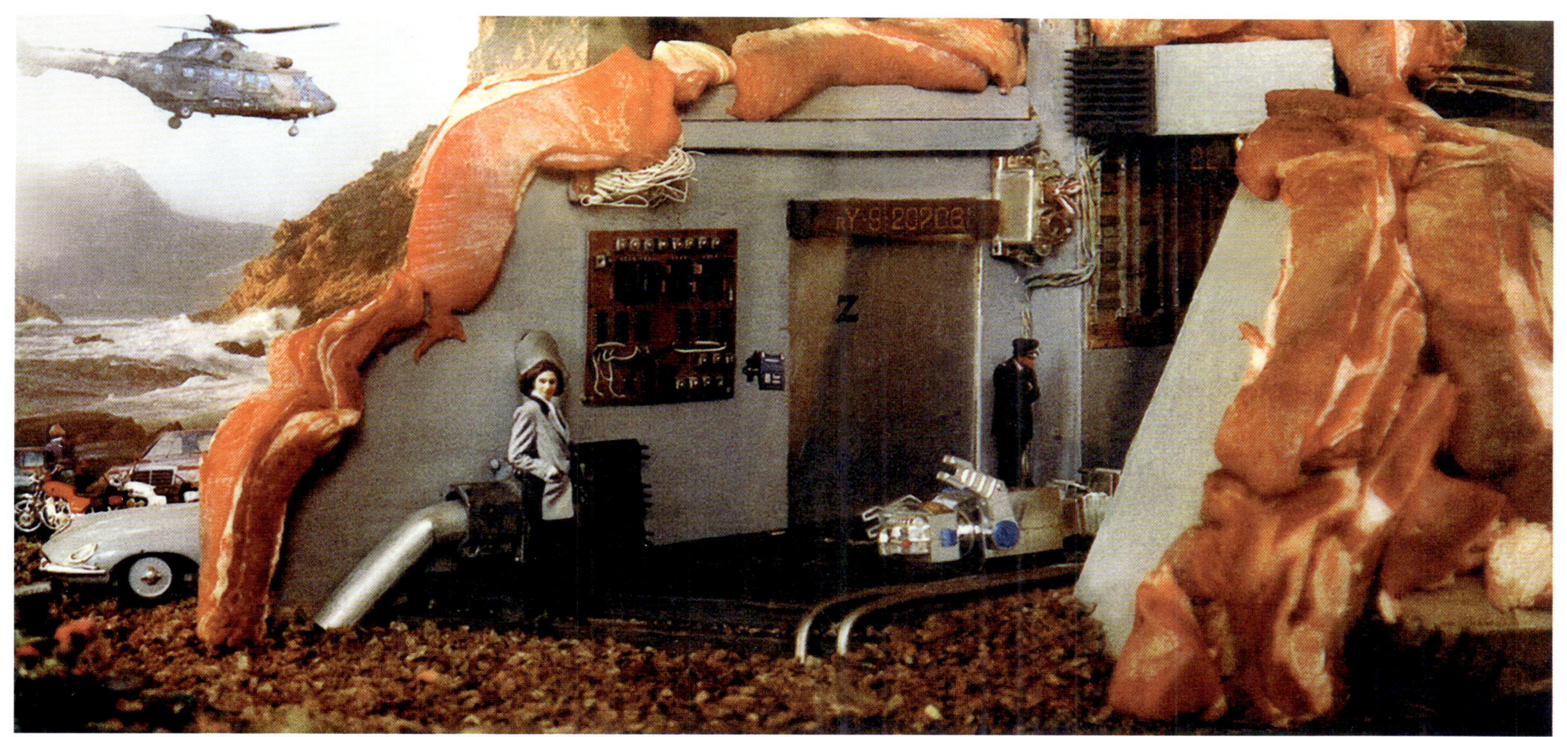

57 **Serhii Yakutovych** (1952–2017)

Untitled, 1981 | Hand-colored etching on paper | **9⁹⁄₁₆ × 25 in. (49.7 × 63.5 cm)**

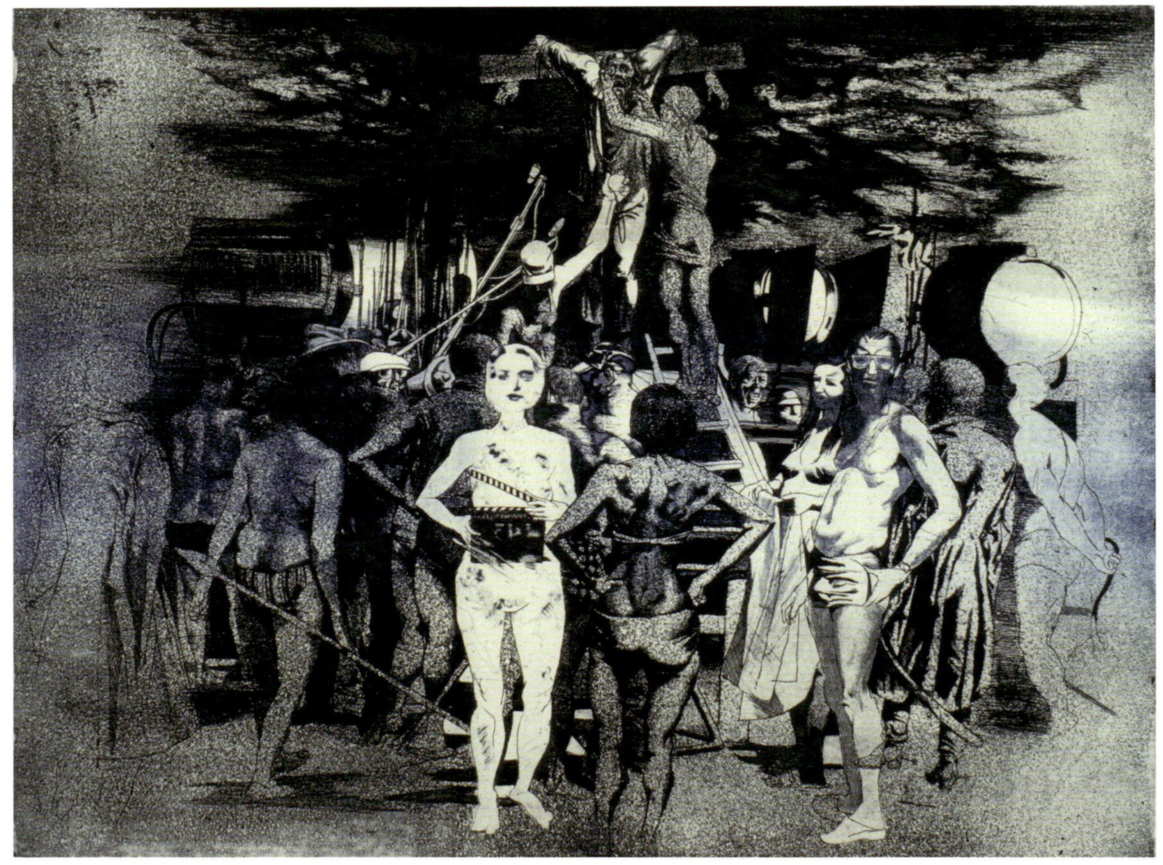

58 **Serhii Yakutovych** (1952–2017)

Untitled from the series *In Memoriam*, Dresden, 85, 1986 | Color etching on paper | 19⁵⁄₁₆ × 24¹¹⁄₁₆ in. (49.1 × 62.7 cm) (plate)

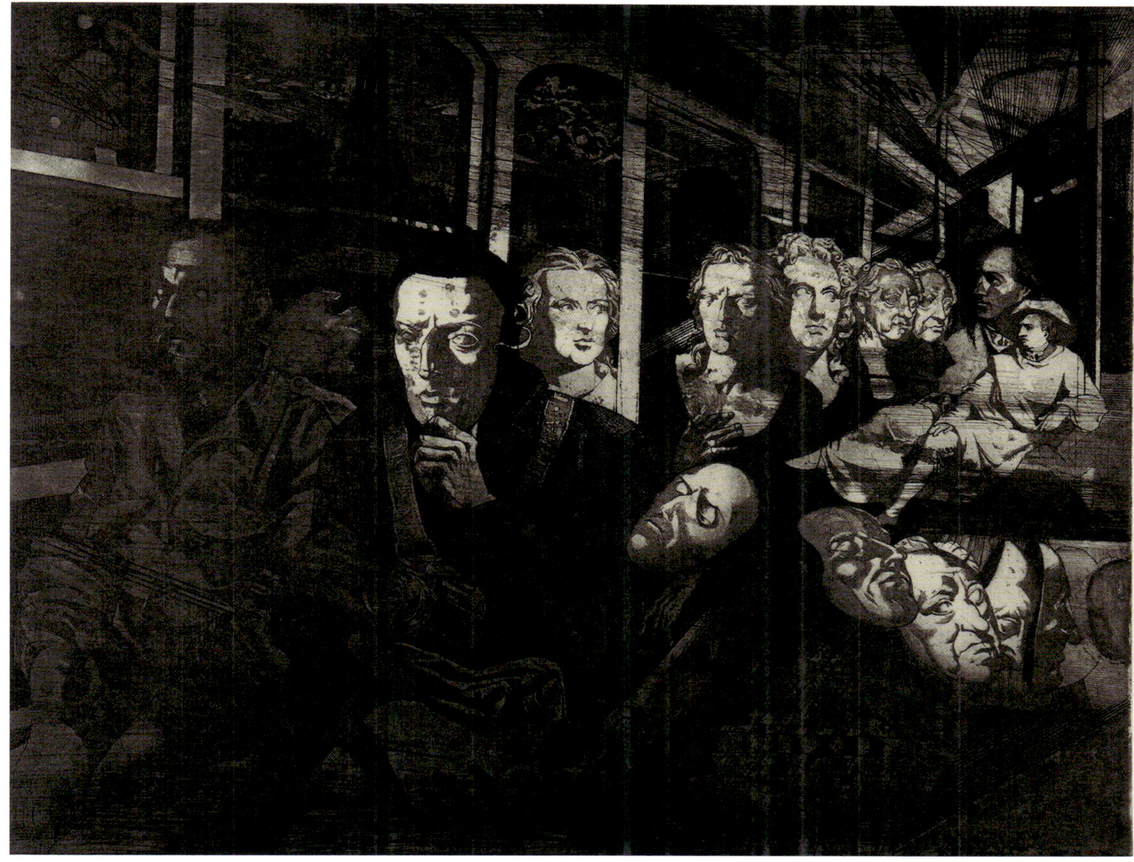

59 **Serhii Yakutovych** (1952–2017)

Peace Bicycle Race, 1986 | Etching on paper | 19$\frac{5}{8}$ × 24$\frac{1}{2}$ in. (49.9 × 62.2 cm) (plate)

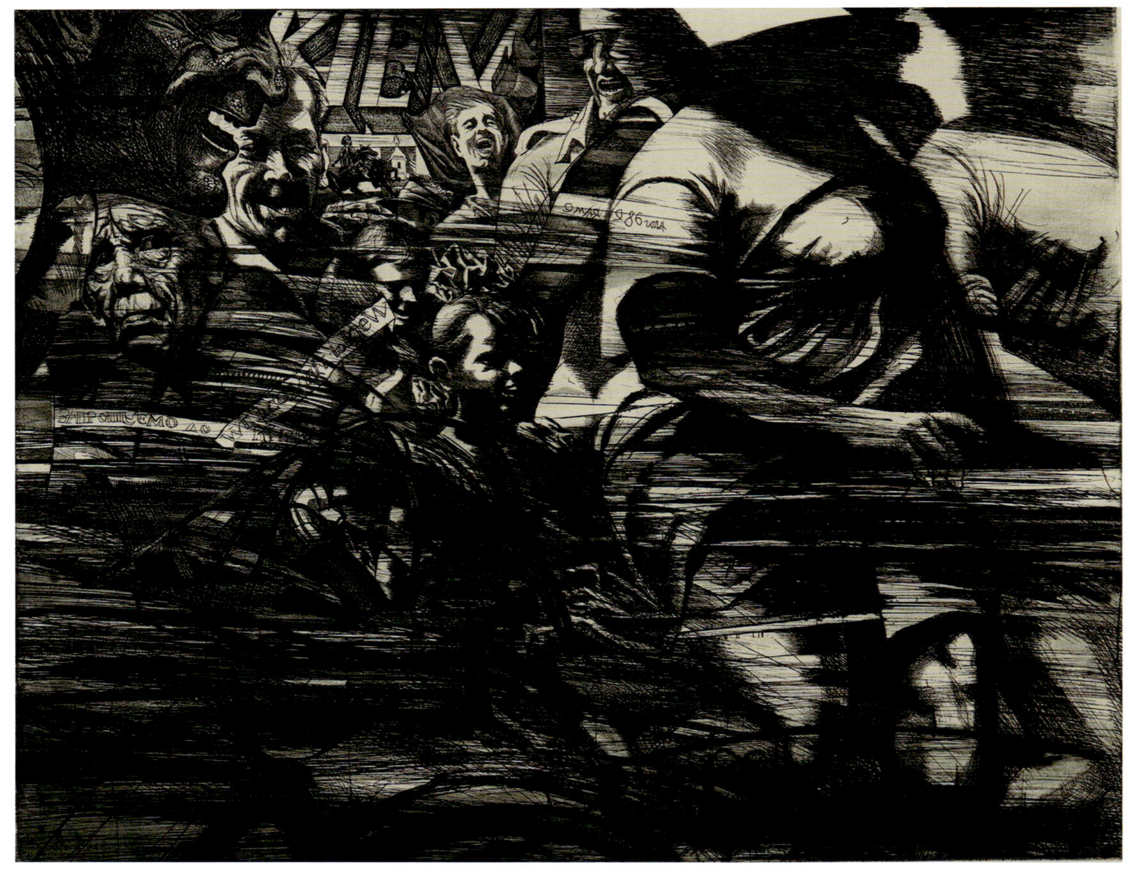

60 **Florian Yuriev** (1929–2021)

Siberian Snow, 1960 | Tempera on cardboard | 19½ × 14¹¹⁄₁₆ in. (49.5 × 37.3 cm)

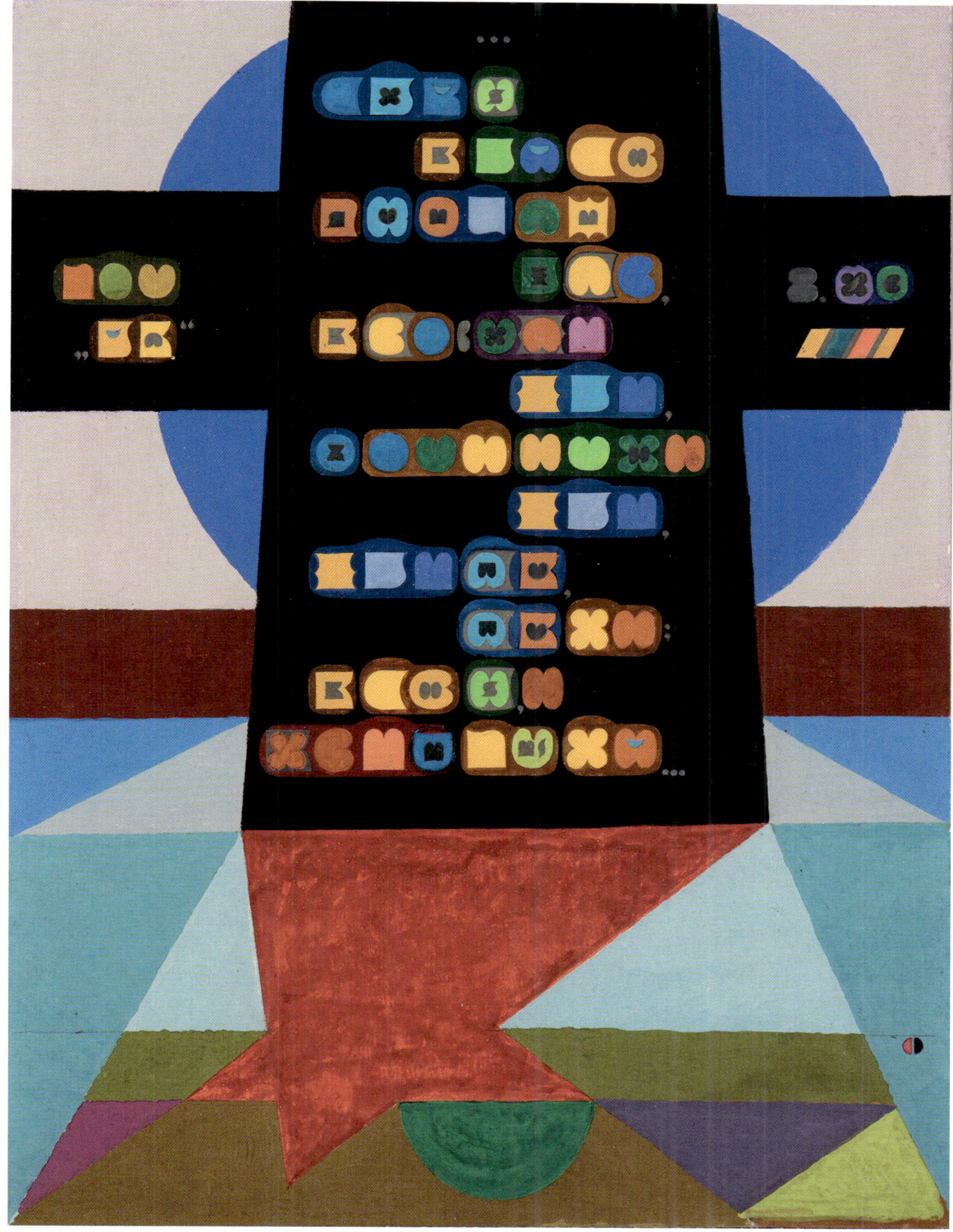

61 **Florian Yuriev** (1929–2021)

Crucifixion on E. Star, 1961 | Tempera on cardboard | 14⅞ × 12½ in. (37.8 × 31.8 cm)

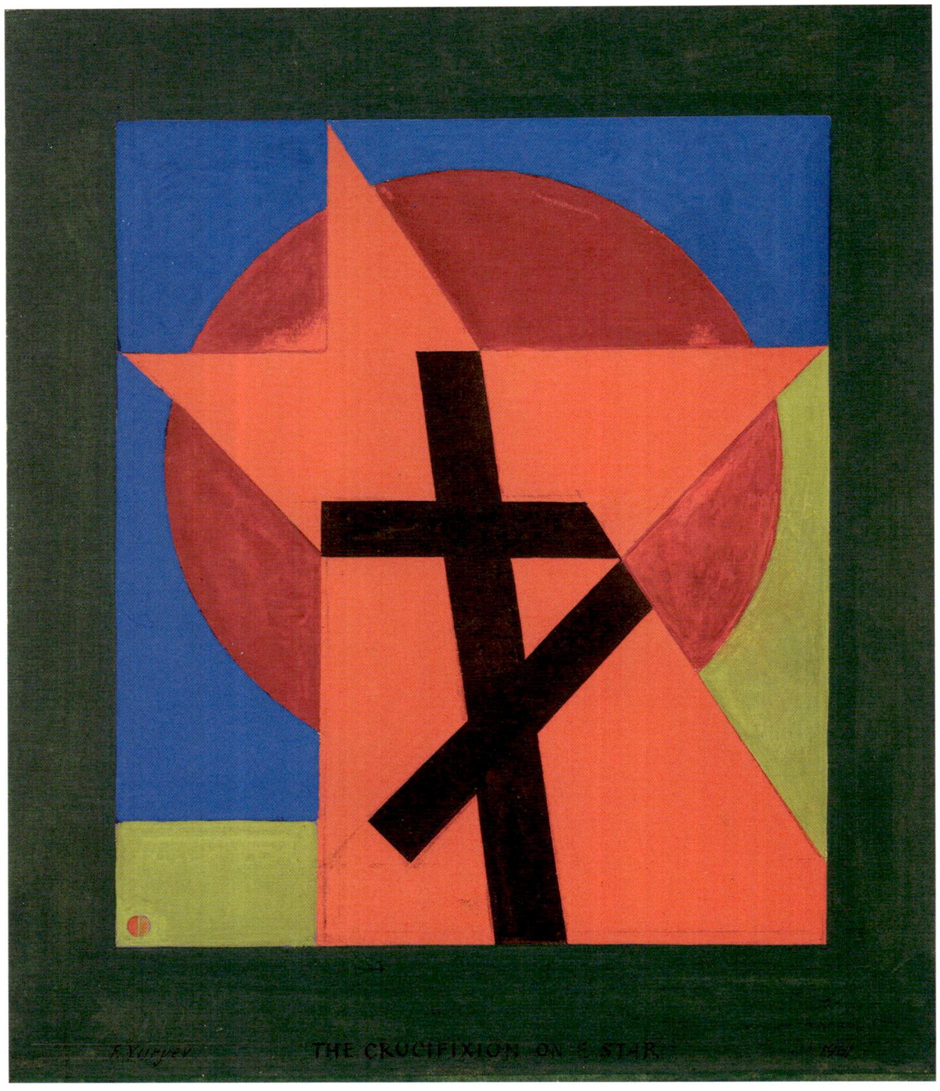

62 **Florian Yuriev** (1929–2021)

Modus: Cross of Malevich, 1967 | Tempera on cardboard | 15⅝ × 14 in. (39.7 × 35.5 cm)

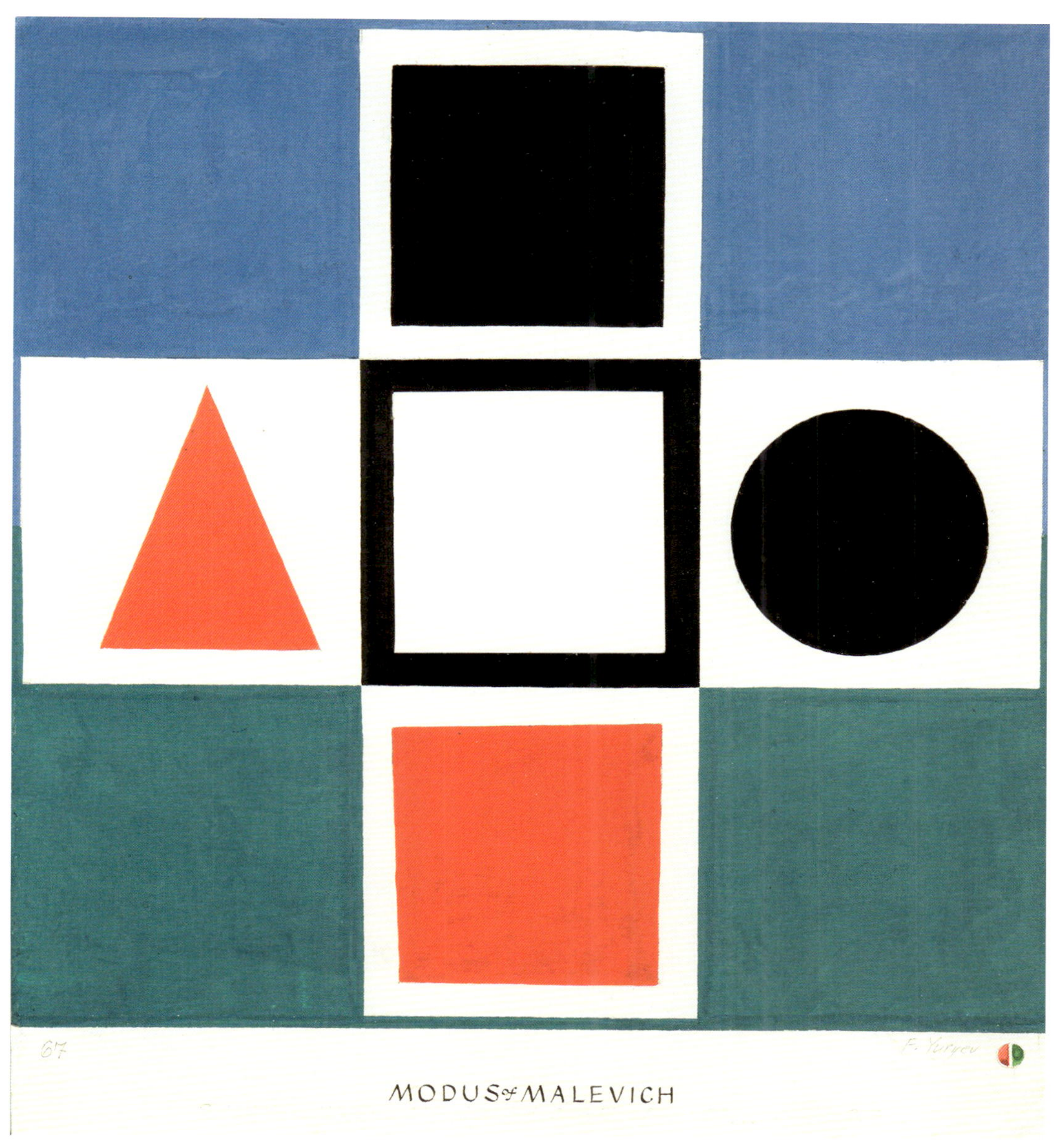

63 **Florian Yuriev** (1929–2021)

On Lena River, 1967 | Tempera on paper | 18 5/16 × 7 1/8 in. (46.5 × 18.1 cm)

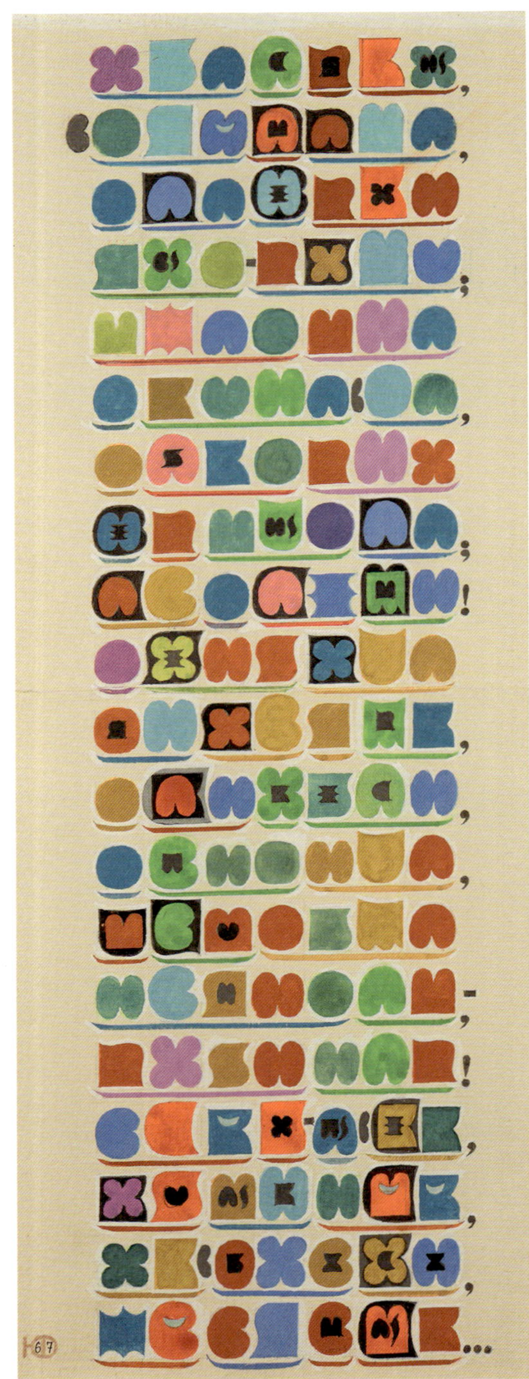

64 **Opanas Zalyvakha** (1925–2007)

Roll Call, 1970 | Etching on paper | 11¼ × 5³⁄₁₆ in. (28.5 × 13.2 cm)

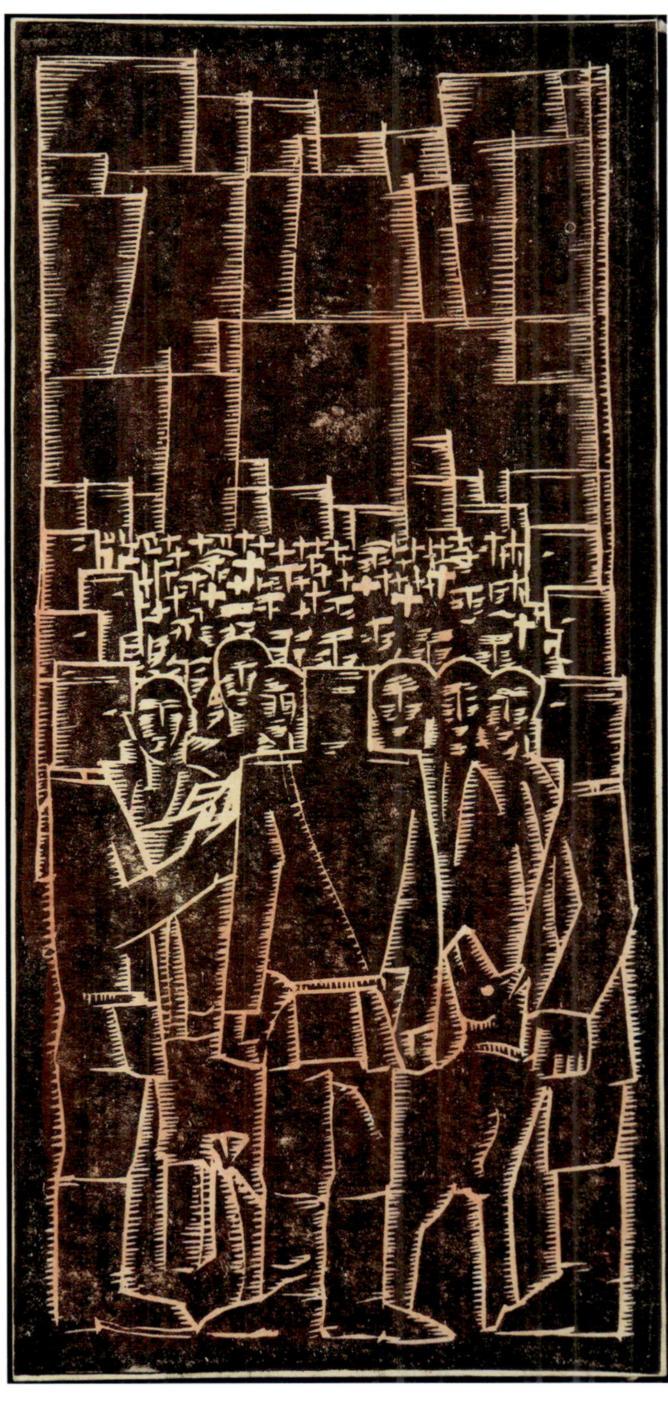

65 **Victor Zaretsky** (1925–1990)

Leda, 1980 | Tempera on canvas | 39 9/16 × 39 3/8 in. (100.5 × 100 cm)

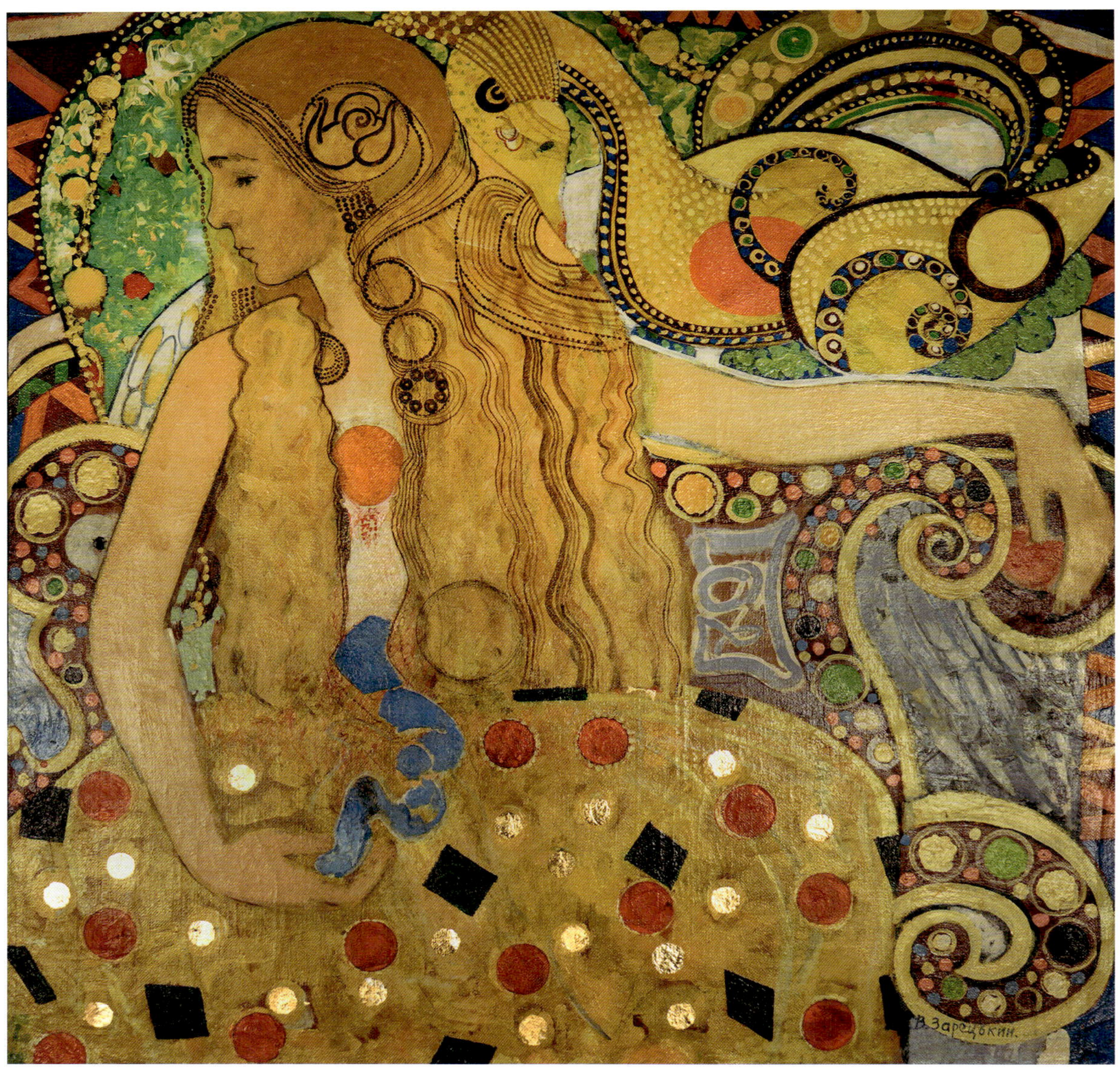

66 **Alexander Zhyvotkov** (b. 1964)

Annunciation, 1991 | Oil on canvas | 59 1/16 × 59 1/16 in. (150 × 150 cm)

STEDLEY ART FOUNDATION COLLECTION

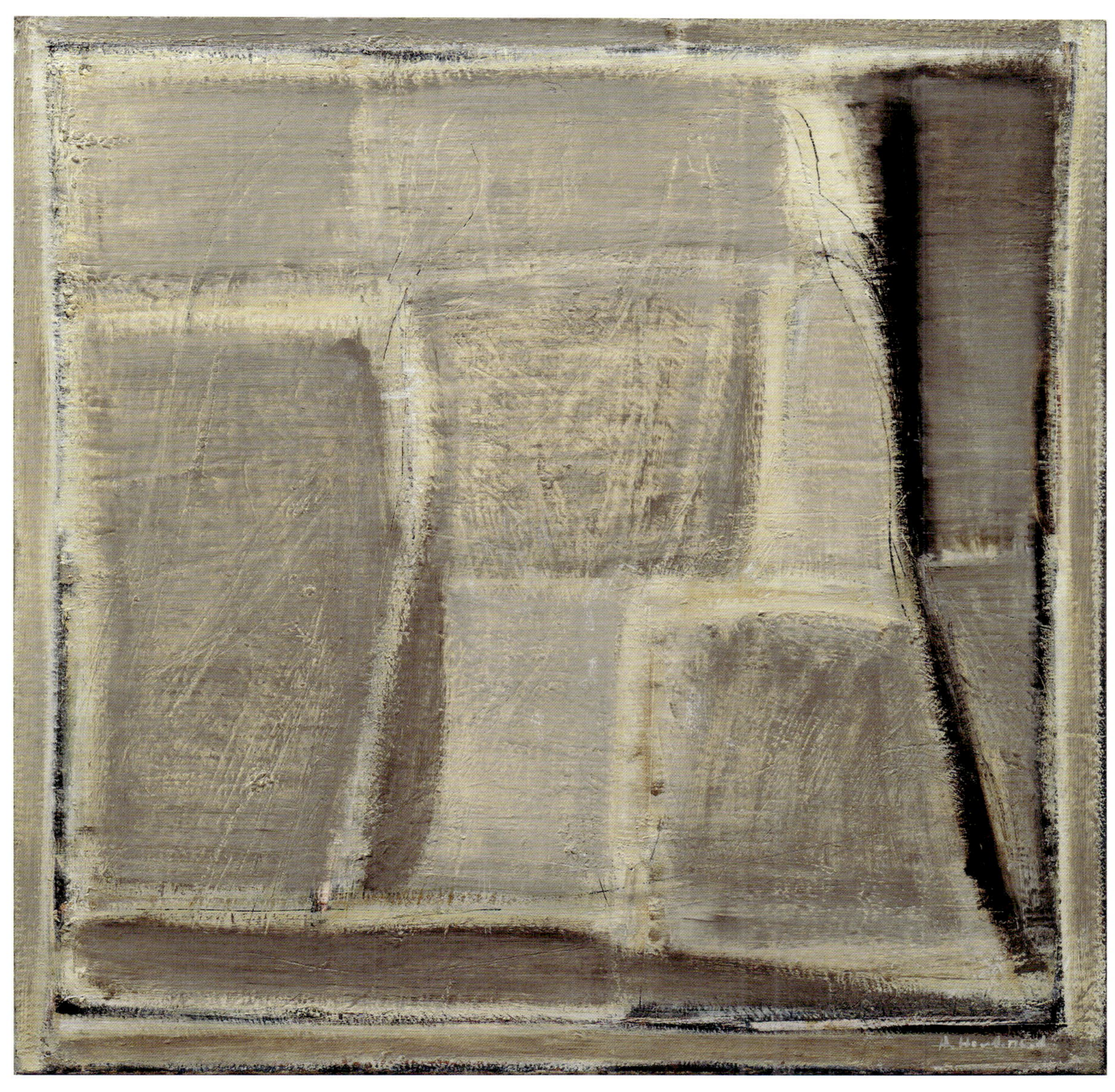

SELECTED **BIBLIOGRAPHY**

Angels Over Ukraine: Contemporary Ukrainian Painting. Exh. cat., Catholic Apostolic Church, Mansfield Place, Edinburgh, 1993.

Balashova, Olga, and Lizaveta German, eds. *Iskusstvo ukrainskikh shestidesiatnikov* [Art of the Ukrainian 1960s generation]. Kyiv: Osnovy, 2015.

Barshynova, Oksana. *New Ukrainian Wave*. Exh. cat., Kyiv: National Museum of Ukraine, 2009.

Barshynova, Oksana, and Halyna Skliarenko. *Mif "Ukraiinske Baroko"* [Myth "Ukrainian baroque"]. Kyiv: Natsionalny Khudozhniy Muzei Ukraiiny, 2012.

Bryzgel, Amy. "Cultivating Meaning: Arsen Savadov and Georgii Senchenko's Gardens Old and New." *Zimmerli Art Journal*, no. 2 (Fall 2004), edited by Phillip Dennis Cate and Alla Rosenfeld.

Burlaka, Viktoria. *Postmedia Optics: The Ukrainian Version*. Kyiv: ArtHuss, 2019.

Chernetsky, Vitaly. *Mapping Postcommunist Cultures: Russia and Ukraine in the Context of Globalization*. Montreal: McGill-Queen's University Press, 2007.

Guelman, Marat, ed. *Babylon*. Exh. cat., Moscow: Moscow Youth Center, 1990.

Hudimov, Pavlo, ed. *Real'nist'. Tiberii Sil'vashi* [Reality: Tiberiy Silvashi]. Kyiv: Artbuk, 2017.

———, ed. *Yakutovychi: Dovil'nyi konspekt* [The Yakutovyches: informal summary]. Kyiv: Artbuk, 2018.

Kaszuk, Larisa. *Furmanny Zaulek. Furmanny Lane. Furmanny Pereulok*. Warsaw: Dom Slowa Polskiego, 1989.

Kochubynska, Tetiana, ed. *Parkomuna. Mistse. Spilnota. Yavyshche* [Parkomuna. Place. Community. Phenomenon]. Kyiv: PinchukArtCentre, 2018.

Limina, Polina. *Profesiia: Khudozhnyk. Knyha pro Serhiia Yakutovycha* [Profession: Artist. The book about Serhii Yakutovych]. Kyiv: Artbuk, 2018.

Limina, Polina, and Pavlo Hudimov, eds. *Iak u Tini: Heorhii Yakutovych iak ilustrator knyhy «Tini zabutykh predkiv»* [As in shadows: Heorhii Yakutovych as the illustrator of the book *Shadow of Forgotten Ancestors*]. Kyiv: Artbuk, 2017.

Lopukhova, Olga, ed. *Iskusstvo Protiv Geografii* [Art against geography]. Exh. cat., Saint Petersburg: Gosudarstvenny Russkii Muzei, 2000.

Lozhkina, Alisa. *Permanent Revolution: Art in Ukraine, the 20th to the Early 21st Century*. Kyiv: ArtHuss, 2020.

Malyshko, Mykola. *Liniia* [Line]. Kyiv: Artbuk, 2018.

Michailovskaya, E., A. Roitburd, and M. Rashkovetskiy. *Portfolio: Art of Odessa in 1990s. A Collection of Texts*. Odessa, Ukraine: Soros Center for Contemporary Art, 1999.

Oleg Holosiy. Exh. cat., Moscow: Ridzhina Art Gallery, 1991.

Raievsky, Valentyn, ed. *Intervaly: Kosmizm v Ukraïnskomu Mystettsvi XX Stolittia* [Intervals: Cosmism in 20th-century Ukrainian art]. Kyiv: Fund New Creative Association, 2000.

Skliarenko, Halyna. *Ukrainski hhudozhnyky: Z vidlyhy do nezalezhnosti. Knyha persha.* [Ukrainian artists from the thaw to independence. Vol 1.] Kyiv: ArtHuss, 2018.

Skliarenko, Halyna. *Ukrainski hhudozhnyky: Z vidlyhy do nezalezhnosti. Knyha druha.* [Ukrainian artists from the thaw to independence. Vol. 2]. Kyiv: ArtHuss, 2020.

Solomon, Andrew. *The Irony Tower: Soviet Artists in a Time of Glasnost*. New York: Knopf, 1991.

CATALOGUE OF THE EXHIBITION

Unless otherwise noted, all works are from the collection of the Zimmerli Art Museum at Rutgers University, Norton and Nancy Dodge Collection of Soviet Nonconformist Art.

1.
Oleksandr Babak (b. 1957)
Untitled, undated
Oil on canvas
$74\frac{1}{2} \times 37\frac{3}{8}$ in. (189.3×95 cm)
D10643

2.
Oleksandr Babak (b. 1957)
Untitled, undated
Oil on canvas
$74\frac{1}{2} \times 37\frac{3}{8}$ in. (189.3×95 cm)
D10644

3.
Volodymyr Budnikov (b. 1947)
The Game, 1985
Oil on canvas
$39\frac{1}{16} \times 35\frac{7}{16}$ in. (99.2×90 cm)
D10532

 4.
Yana Bystrova (b. 1966)
The Deity of Chill During Her Crimean Stay, 1989
Oil on canvas
$47\frac{1}{4} \times 78\frac{3}{4}$ in. (120×200 cm)
Private Collection

5.
Oleksandr Dubovyk (b. 1931)
Black Square, 1980
Oil on canvas
$51\frac{3}{16} \times 51\frac{3}{16}$ in. (130×130 cm)
D23055

6.
Hryhorii Havrylenko (1927–1984)
Composition VIII-II, 1962
Tempera on paper
$23\frac{13}{16} \times 16\frac{3}{4}$ in. (60.5×42.6 cm)
D15618

7.
Hryhorii Havrylenko (1927–1984)
Composition, 1963
Gouache on cardboard
$14\frac{3}{4} \times 10$ in. (37.4×25.4 cm)
D15982

8.
Oleksander Hnylytskyj (1961–2009)
Yearning, 1988
Oil on canvas
$77\frac{15}{16} \times 66\frac{15}{16}$ in. (198×170 cm)
From the collection of Liudmyla and Andriy Pyshnyy

9.
Oleksander Hnylytskyj (1961–2009)
Untitled, undated
Marker on paper
$9\frac{13}{16} \times 14\frac{9}{16}$ in. (25×37 cm)
Abramovych Foundation

10.
Oleksander Hnylytskyj (1961–2009)
Untitled, undated
Marker on paper
$9\frac{13}{16} \times 14\frac{9}{16}$ in. (25×37 cm)
Abramovych Foundation

11.
Oleg Holosiy (1965–1993)
The Angel Has Come, 1992
Oil on canvas
$76\frac{3}{4} \times 39$ in. (195×99 cm)
Voronov Art Foundation

12.
Alla Horska (1929–1970)
Untitled (Silence), 1964
Gouache and graphite on paper
$20\frac{3}{8} \times 6\frac{5}{8}$ in. (51.8×16.9 cm)
D00622

13.

Dmytro Kavsan (b. 1964)
Who Comes Last Gets the Bones, 1986
Oil on canvas
$36\frac{5}{8} \times 35\frac{1}{16}$ in. (93 × 89 cm)
D10536

14.

Anatoly Kryvolap (b. 1946)
Four Substances, 1992
Oil on canvas
$25\frac{9}{16} \times 33\frac{1}{16}$ in. (65 × 84 cm)
Collection of the Artist

15.

Valery Lamakh (1925–1978)
Composition No. 8, 1959
Tempera on panel
$27\frac{1}{4} \times 19\frac{5}{16}$ in. (69.2 × 49 cm)
D21190

16.

Valery Lamakh (1925–1978)
Composition No. 10, 1962
Tempera on fiberboard
$27\frac{7}{16} \times 19\frac{3}{8}$ in. (69.7 × 49.2 cm)
D14217

17.

Yuri Lutskevych (1934–2001)
Madrigal, 1972
Oil on canvas
$35\frac{7}{16} \times 39\frac{3}{8}$ in. (90 × 100 cm)
D10539

18.

Mykola Matsenko (b. 1960) and
Oleg Tistol (b. 1960) (NATSPROM)
Piłsudski, 1993
Oil on paper
$97\frac{5}{8} \times 226\frac{3}{4}$ in. (248 × 576 cm)
Abramovych Foundation

19.

Halyna Neledva (b. 1938)
Untitled, undated
Oil on canvas
$35\frac{5}{16} \times 31\frac{3}{8}$ in. (89.7 × 79.7 cm)
D10538

20.

Yevhen Petrenko (1946–2016)
Landscape, 1980
Oil and tempera on canvas
$35\frac{1}{16} \times 35\frac{1}{16}$ in. (89 × 89 cm)
D10550

21.

Kostiantyn (Vinny) Reunov (b. 1963)
Only There, 1990
Oil on canvas
$76\frac{3}{4} \times 76\frac{3}{4}$ in. (195 × 195 cm)
Voronov Art Foundation

22.

Oleksandr Roitburd (1961–2021)
Untitled, undated
Collage and ink on paperboard
$18\frac{3}{4} \times 14\frac{3}{16}$ in. (47.7 × 36 cm)
D20034

23.

Oleksandr Roitburd (1961–2021)
Untitled, 1985
Oil on panel
$44\frac{1}{8} \times 32\frac{5}{16}$ in. (112 × 82 cm)
D24270

24.

Viktor Ryzhykh (b. 1933)
Untitled, undated
Oil on canvas
$35\frac{7}{16} \times 39\frac{3}{8}$ in. (90 × 100 cm)
D24257

25.
Arsen Savadov (b. 1962) and
Georgii Senchenko (b. 1962)
Gardens Old and New, 1986–87
Oil on canvas
36 13/16 × 57½ in. (93.5 × 146 cm)
D21728

26.
Arsen Savadov (b. 1962) and
Georgii Senchenko (b. 1962)
Gardens Old and New, 1986–87
Oil on canvas
37 × 57½ in. (94 × 146 cm)
D21729

27.
Arsen Savadov (b. 1962)
Untitled, 1986
Graphite, ink, red felt-tip pen on paper
11⅛ × 14 9/16 in. (28.2 × 37 cm)
1996.0743

28.
Arsen Savadov (b. 1962)
Untitled, 1986
Graphite, red felt-tip pen on paper
10 5/16 × 16 5/16 in. (26.2 × 41.5 cm)
1996.0744

29.
Arsen Savadov (b. 1962)
Untitled (Horse), 1987
Oil on canvas
79¼ × 120 × ⅞ in. (201.3 × 304.8 × 2.2 cm)
D10952

30.
Arsen Savadov (b. 1962)
Snake Charmer, 1989–90
Oil on canvas
121 × 85½ in. (307.3 × 217.2 cm)
Gift of Robert L. and Ann R. Fromer
1993.0592

31.
Arsen Savadov (b. 1962)
Untitled, undated
Pencil, ink on paper
8¾ × 11 9/16 in. (22.3 × 29.4 cm)
D15468

32.
Arsen Savadov (b. 1962)
Untitled, undated
Graphite, felt-tip pen on paper
7 5/16 × 16⅝ in. (18.5 × 42.3 cm)
D15469

33.
Georgii Senchenko (b. 1962)
Sacred Landscape of Pieter Bruegel, 1988
Oil on canvas
110 × 166 in. (279.4 × 421.6 cm)
Gift of Robert L. and Ann R. Fromer
1993.059

34.
Tiberiy Silvashi (b. 1947)
Midnight, 1981
Oil on canvas
39⅜ × 47¼ in. (100 × 120 cm)
D23121

35.
Tiberiy Silvashi (b. 1947)
Guest, 1982
Oil on canvas
39 3/16 × 59 13/16 in. (99.5 × 152 cm)
D23052

36.
Marina Skugareva (b. 1962)
Portrait of Anatoly Stepanenko, 1988
Tapestry
47¼ × 59 1/16 in. (120 × 150 cm)
Collection of the Artist

37.
Marina Skugareva (b. 1962)
Sevastopol Waltz, 1994
Oil and embroidery on canvas
47¼ × 70⅞ in. (120 × 180 cm)
From the collection of
Natalia and Volodymyr Spielvogel

38.
Anatoly Stepanenko (b. 1948)
Actuality, 1985
Collage, ink, and felt-tip pen on paper
12⅝ × 6 11/16 in. (32 × 17 cm)
D10436

39.
Anatoly Stepanenko (b. 1948)
Consequences Are Unknown
(Shadow of the Albatross), 1985
Collage, ink, graphite, felt-tip pen on paper
11 13/16 × 6¾ in. (30 × 17.1 cm)
D10443

40.
Anatoly Stepanenko (b. 1948)
The End of the Day of Jeans, 1985
Ink, felt-tip pen, collage on paper
11 13/16 × 6 11/16 in. (30 × 17 cm)
D10438

41.
Anatoly Stepanenko (b. 1948)
Etude 19, 1985
Ink, collage, and felt-tip pen on paper
11 13/16 × 6 11/16 in. (30 × 17 cm)
D10435

42.
Anatoly Stepanenko (b. 1948)
The Life as a Playing Machine, 1985
Mixed-media collage on paper
12⅝ × 6¾ in (32 × 17.1 cm)
D10437

43.
Anatoly Stepanenko (b. 1948)
Metaphoric Shot, 1985
Paper collage on paper
11 × 6 11/16 in (28 × 17 cm)
D10439

44.
Anatoly Stepanenko (b. 1948)
Metaphysics of Night Symbols, 1985
Foil, paper, and mixed media on paper
12⅝ × 6¾ in. (32 × 17.1 cm)
D10444

45.
Anatoly Stepanenko (b. 1948)
Remembrance of Concrete Objects, 1985
Mixed-media collage on paper
13 7/16 × 6 11/16 in (34.1 × 17 cm)
D10440

46.
Anatoly Stepanenko (b. 1948)
Sentimental Herbal Collection, 1985
Mixed-media collage on paper
12½ × 6¾ in. (31.1 × 17.1 cm)
D10441

47.
Anatoly Stepanenko (b. 1948)
Sleep, Uncle, Sleep, 1985
Collage, ink, graphite, felt-tip pen on paper
11 13/16 × 6 11/16 in. (30 × 17 cm)
D10442

48.
Sergei Sviatchenko (b. 1952)
Untitled from the series *Blue Country II*, 1991
Mixed media on paper
29½ × 21⅝ in. (75 × 55 cm)
Abramovych Foundation

49.
Sergei Sviatchenko (b. 1952)
Untitled from the series *Blue Country II*, 1991
Mixed media on paper
29½ × 21⅝ in. (75 × 55 cm)
Abramovych Foundation

50.
Fedir Tetianych (1942–2007)
UFO, 1970
Tempera on paper
5 3/16 × 7 9/16 in. (13.1 × 19.2 cm)
D18573

51.
Oleg Tistol (b. 1960)
Self-Portrait with Ampules of Strychnine, 1981
Oil on canvas
19½ × 12⅜ in. (49.5 × 31.5 cm)
D24273

52.
Oleg Tistol (b. 1960)
Buryat, 1985
Gouache on paper
12 5/16 × 7 11/16 in. (31.3 × 19.6 cm)
D18092

53.
Oleg Tistol (b. 1960)
Buryat Kuznetsov, 1985
Gouache on paper
16⅞ × 13 9/16 in. (42.9 × 34.4 cm)
D18091

54.
Oleg Tistol (b. 1960)
Four untitled works from the series
Ukrainian Money, 1990
Collage and ink on paper
15¾ × 22 7/16 in. (40 × 57 cm) each
Collection of the Artist

55.
Valeria Troubina (b. 1966)
Bowing, 1985
Oil on canvas
46 1/16 × 30 11/16 in. (117 × 78 cm)
D23109

56.
Vasiliy Tsagolov (b. 1957)
I Like My Job Very Much, 1992
Color photograph on paper
27 9/16 × 49¼ in. (70 × 125 cm)
Abramovych Foundation

57.
Serhii Yakutovych (1952–2017)
Untitled, 1981
Handcolored etching on paper
19 9/16 × 25 in. (49.7 × 63.5 cm)
D14073

58.
Serhii Yakutovych (1952–2017)
Untitled from the series *In Memoriam*, Dresden, 85, 1986
Color etching on paper
19 5/16 × 24 11/16 in. (49.1 × 62.7 cm) (plate)
D14076

59.
Serhii Yakutovych (1952–2017)
Peace Bicycle Race, 1986
Etching on paper
19⅝ × 24½ in. (49.9 × 62.2 cm) (plate)
D18699

60.
Florian Yuriev (1929–2021)
Siberian Snow, 1960
Tempera on cardboard
19½ × 14 11/16 in. (49.5 × 37.3 cm)
D21075

61.
Florian Yuriev (1929–2021)
Crucifixion on E. Star, 1961
Tempera on cardboard
14⅞ × 12½ in. (37.8 × 31.8 cm)
D21077

62.
Florian Yuriev (1929–2021)
Modus: Cross of Malevich, 1967
Tempera on cardboard
15⅝ × 14 in. (39.7 × 35.5 cm)
D21076

63.
Florian Yuriev (1929–2021)
On Lena River, 1967
Tempera on paper
18 5/16 × 7⅛ in. (46.5 × 18.1 cm)
D21080

64.
Opanas Zalyvakha (1925–2007)
Roll Call, 1970
Etching on paper
11¼ × 5 3/16 in. (28.5 × 13.2 cm)
D10451

65.
Victor Zaretsky (1925–1990)
Leda, 1980
Tempera on canvas
39 9/16 × 39⅜ in. (100.5 × 100 cm)
D11287

66.
Alexander Zhyvotkov (b. 1964)
Annunciation, 1991
Oil on canvas
59 1/16 × 59 1/16 in. (150 × 150 cm)
Stedley Art Foundation Collection

INDEX OF ARTISTS IN THE EXHIBITION

Page references in *italics* refer to illustrations.

CONTRIBUTORS

Asia Bazdyrieva

is an art historian whose practice revolves around writing, research, and education both independently and within cultural institutions in Ukraine and internationally. Her main expertise is the project of Soviet modernity and its ideological implications in public spaces, architecture, and art. Bazdyrieva holds master's degrees in art history from the City University of New York and in analytical chemistry from the Kyiv National University. She was a Fulbright scholar in 2015–17, an Edmund S. Muskie fellow in 2017, and the Digital Earth fellow in 2018–19. In 2018, she was a postgraduate in the New Normal program at Strelka Institute for Media, Architecture and Design in Moscow.

Alisa Lozhkina

is an independent Ukrainian curator, art historian, and critic currently based in the San Francisco Bay Area. From 2010 to 2016 she was the editor in chief of the major Ukrainian art magazine *Art Ukraine*. From 2013 to 2016 she served as a deputy director of Mystetskyi Arsenal in Kyiv. Alisa Lozhkina has organized seven large-scale international exhibitions of contemporary art, including *Permanent Revolution: Ukrainian Art Now* at the Ludwig Museum, Budapest, which was nominated for Global Fine Art Awards (New York) as one of the best museum exhibitions of postwar and contemporary art in 2018. Additionally, Lozhkina is the author of *Point Zero: The Newest History of Ukrainian Contemporary Art* (co-authored with Oleksandr Soloviov, 2010) and *Permanent Revolution: Art in Ukraine, the 20th to the Early 21st Century,* which was published in Ukrainian, French, and, most recently, in English. Alisa is currently an ABD in comparative history at Central European University (Vienna-Budapest), where she is writing her dissertation on the interconnection of art and revolutions in recent Ukrainian history.

Olena Martynyuk

is an art historian with an interest in art theory and philosophy. Her research focuses on Ukrainian and Russian art from the late twentieth century to the present. She received her PhD in art history from Rutgers University in January 2018. Currently, she is a Petro Jacyk Postdoctoral Research Fellow in Ukrainian Studies in the Harriman Institute of Columbia University, where she is doing research and teaching classes on Ukrainian and Russian art history from the Russian Empire period through the avant-garde and up to the present day. She was a recipient of the Louise Bevier Dissertation Fellowship and Andrew Mellon Summer Fellowship, taught art history classes at Rutgers University and CUNY College of Staten Island, and organized exhibitions at the Zimmerli Art Museum, the Ukrainian Museum, and the Ukrainian Institute of America in New York City.

Oleksandr Soloviov

is a prominent Ukrainian art critic born in Volgograd and based in Kyiv, a participant and a chronicler of the events of Ukrainian contemporary art since its origins in the late 1980s. He was a curator at the PinchukArtCentre in Kyiv (2006–13) and oversaw such major exhibition projects as *First Collection* (2003), *Farewell Arms!* (2004) and *Reality Check* (2005), based on Viktor Pinchuk's collection before the center was established. Currently Soloviov works as a curator (since 2010) and a deputy director (since 2013) of Mystetsky Arsenal in Kyiv. Among his curatorial projects there are *Independent: New Art of the New Country, 1991–2011* (2011), *Oleksander Hnylytskyj: Reality of the Illusion* (2017), *Flashback: Ukrainian Media-art of the 1990s* (2018), and *Oleg Holosiy: Non-Stop Painting* (2019). He served as a curator of the Ukrainian Pavilion at the Venice Biennale in 2003, 2007, and 2013.